TEACHING CULTURE:
PERSPECTIVES IN PRACTICE

Patrick R. Moran
School for International Training

A TeacherSource Book

Donald Freeman
Series Editor

HEINLE & HEINLE
— ✦ — ™
THOMSON LEARNING

Australia • Canada • Mexico • Singapore • Spain • United Kingdom • United States

HEINLE & HEINLE

THOMSON LEARNING ™

Teaching Culture: Perspectives in Practice
Patrick R. Moran

Vice President, Editorial Director ESL: Nancy Leonhardt
Acquisitions Editor: Sherrise Roehr
Associate Developmental Editor: Sarah Barnicle
Marketing Manager: Charlotte Sturdy
Production Editor: Jeffrey M. Freeland

Sr. Manufacturing Coordinator: Mary Beth Hennebury
Compositor: Ethos Marketing and Design
Cover Designer: Ha Nguyen
Printer: Webcom

For permission to use material from this text or product contact us:
Tel   1-800-730-2214
Fax   1-800-730-2215
Web   www.thomsonrights.com

Library of Congress Cataloging-in-Publication Data

Moran, Patrick R.
    Teaching Culture: perspectives in practice/
Patrick R. Moran.
        p. cm—(A TeacherSource book)
    Includes bibliographical references.
    ISBN- 13: 978-0-8384-6676-6
    ISBN- 10: 0-8384-6676-1
    1. Language and languages—Study and teaching.
    2. Multicultural education.
    I. Title. II. TeacherSource.

    P53.45 .M66 2001
    418'.0071—dc21

                                         2001024949

ASIA (excluding India)
Thomson Learning
60 Albert Street #15-01
Albert Complex
Singapore 189969

AUSTRALIA/NEW ZEALAND
Nelson/Thomson Learning
102 Dodds Street
South Melbourne
Victoria 3205 Australia

CANADA
Nelson/Thomson Learning
1120 Birchmount Road
Scarborough, Ontario
Canada M1K 5G4

LATIN AMERICA
Thomson Learning
Seneca, 53
Colonia Polanco
11560 México D.F. México

SPAIN
Thomson Learning
Calle Magallanes, 25
28015-Madrid
España

UK/EUROPE/MIDDLE EAST
Thomson Learning
Berkshire House
168–173 High Holborn
London, WC1V 7AA, United Kingdom

*To language teachers,
the bridges between worlds,
the vanguard of intercultural
understanding*

Thank You

The series editor, authors, and publisher would like to thank the following individuals who offered many helpful insights throughout the development of the **TeacherSource** series.

David Barker	Maine Township High School, Illinois
Linda Lonon Blanton	University of New Orleans
Tommie Brasel	New Mexico School for the Deaf
Jill Burton	University of South Australia
Margaret B. Cassidy	Brattleboro Union High School, Vermont
Louise Damen	Independent Consultant
Florence Decker	University of Texas at El Paso
Silvia G. Diaz	Dade County Public Schools, Florida
Margo Downey	Boston University
Alvino Fantini	School for International Training
Sandra Fradd	University of Miami
Jerry Gebhard	Indiana University of Pennsylvania
Fred Genesee	McGill University
Stacy Gildenston	Colorado State University
Jeannette Gordon	Illinois Resource Center
Else Hamayan	Illinois Resource Center
Sarah Hudelson	Arizona State University
Joan Jamieson	Northern Arizona University
Elliot L. Judd	University of Illinois at Chicago
Donald N. Larson	Bethel College, Minnesota (Emeritus)
Patsy Lightbaum	Concordia University, Canada
Numa Markee	University of Illinois at Urbana Champaign
Michael McCarthy	University of Nottingham
Denise E. Murray	NCELTR Macquarie University
Gayle Nelson	Georgia State University
Meredith Pike-Baky	University of California at Berkeley
Sara L. Sanders	Coastal Carolina University
Lilia Savova	Indiana University of Pennsylvania
Donna Sievers	Garden Grove Unified School District, California
Ruth Spack	Tufts University
Leo van Lier	Monterey Institute of International Studies

TABLE OF CONTENTS

ACKNOWLEDGMENTS

Chance led me to the Experiment in International Living and School for International Training in Brattleboro, Vermont. Here I met compassionate, expert educators who showed me how to unite theory and practice through a process they called experiential learning. This was a revelation to me. Not only did it help me begin to make sense of my immediate intercultural experiences, it eventually transformed my approach to teaching language and culture. In this book, I have adopted and adapted the lessons I learned long ago from these mentors and friends. Since then, I have had the good fortune to work with like-minded, committed colleagues and students at the School for International Training (SIT) and to apply these and other concepts to language teaching and intercultural education.

All of the teachers whose voices appear in this book worked with me through an SIT connection. It was a privilege to hear their stories: Roberta Kucer, Gary Allen, Ivanna Thrower, Julie McConville, Julie Versluys, Maureen McCarthy, Wendy Wen, Friederike Weiss, Jaimie Scanlon, Bridget Adams, Tom Kuehn, Val Hansford, Tae Kudo, Joe Barrett, Parfait Awono, Ani Hawkinson, Minhee Kang, and Yasuko Ohmi.

Thank-you to Kathleen Graves, Leslie Turpin, and Diane Larsen-Freeman, who discussed the manuscript with me at various points along the way, and to Donald Freeman, who offered me the opportunity to write this book and helped me put it together. I would also like to thank Alvino Fantini for the many stimulating discussions on culture, language, intercultural communication, and language teaching that we have had over the years. I am particularly grateful to the many students in the MAT Program at SIT who were so receptive to my ideas on learning and teaching culture.

A special word of thanks to my three families: one in the Oise valley in France, one on the prairie in Nebraska, and my immediate family here in the hills of Vermont—halfway between the other two, in more ways than one. All of them have granted me the time and space to write, and have supported me with patience and good humor. I especially thank my wife and partner, Annie Suquet, and our son, Jean-Christophe, for their companionship on this odyssey.

Finally, thank-you to my father, who saw nothing odd in a young Nebraskan setting out to become a Frenchman. There began the first steps of the long journey that led me to this book.

SERIES EDITOR'S PREFACE

As I was driving just south of White River Junction, the snow had started falling in earnest. The light was flat, although it was midmorning, making it almost impossible to distinguish the highway in the gray-white swirling snow. I turned on the radio, partly as a distraction and partly to help me concentrate on the road ahead; the announcer was talking about the snow. "The state highway department advises motorists to use extreme caution and to drive with their headlights on to ensure maximum visibility." He went on, his tone shifting slightly, "Ray Burke, the state highway supervisor, just called to say that one of the plows almost hit a car just south of Exit 6 because the person driving hadn't turned on his lights. He really wants people to put their headlights on because it is very tough to see in this stuff." I checked, almost reflexively, to be sure that my headlights were on, as I drove into the churning snow.

How can information serve those who hear or read it in making sense of their own worlds? How can it enable them to reason about what they do and to take appropriate actions based on that reasoning? My experience with the radio in the snowstorm illustrates two different ways of providing the same message: the need to use your headlights when you drive in heavy snow. The first offers dispassionate information; the second tells the same content in a personal, compelling story. The first disguises its point of view; the second explicitly grounds the general information in a particular time and place. Each means of giving information has its role, but I believe the second is ultimately more useful in helping people make sense of what they are doing. When I heard Ray Burke's story about the plow, I made sure my headlights were on.

In what is written about teaching, it is rare to find accounts in which the author's experience and point of view are central. A point of view is not simply an opinion; neither is it a whimsical or impressionistic claim. Rather, a point of view lays out what the author thinks and why; to borrow the phrase from writing teacher Natalie Goldberg, "it sets down the bones." The problem is that much of what is available in professional development in language-teacher education concentrates on telling rather than on point of view. The telling is prescriptive, like the radio announcer's first statement. It emphasizes what is important to know and do, what is current in theory and research, and therefore what you—as a practicing teacher—should do. But this telling disguises the teller; it hides the point of view that can enable you to make sense of what is told.

The **TeacherSource** series offers you a point of view on second/foreign language teaching. Each author in this series has had to lay out what she or he believes is central to the topic, and how she or he has come to this understanding. So as a reader, you will find this book has a personality; it is not anonymous. It comes as a story, not as a directive, and it is meant to create a relationship with you rather than assume your attention. As a practitioner, its point of view can help you in your own work by providing a sounding board for your ideas and a metric for your own thinking. It can suggest courses of action and explain why these make sense to the author. You in turn can take from it what you will, and do with it what you can. This book will not tell you what to think; it is meant to help you make sense of what you do.

The point of view in **TeacherSource** is built out of three strands: **Teachers' Voices**, **Frameworks**, and **Investigations**. Each author draws together these strands uniquely, as suits his or her topic and—more crucially—his or her point of view. All materials in **TeacherSource** have these three strands. The **Teachers' Voices** are practicing language teachers from various settings who tell about their experience of the topic. The **Frameworks** lay out what the author

believes is important to know about his or her topic and its key concepts and issues. These fundamentals define the area of language teaching and learning about which she or he is writing. The **Investigations** are meant to engage you, the reader, in relating the topic to your own teaching, students, and classroom. They are activities which you can do alone or with colleagues, to reflect on teaching and learning and/or try out ideas in practice.

Each strand offers a point of view on the book's topic. The **Teachers' Voices** relate the points of view of various practitioners; the **Frameworks** establish the point of view of the professional community; and the **Investigations** invite you to develop your own point of view, through experience with reference to your setting. Together these strands should serve in making sense of the topic.

It is now widely accepted that to teach a second language, the teacher and learners must work with the culture or cultures associated with that language and its communities. This position has evolved over the last century from a claim, rooted in the traditions of the liberal arts, that a principal aim of studying foreign (usually European) languages was intimately linked to reading their associated literatures and appreciating their fine arts. More recently arguments about the interrelation of language and culture as systems of meaning-making have come from anthropology and ethnography; these arguments hold that in order to master a language, learners need to understand and become functional within its culture. Current assertions drawn from critical theory and postmodernism see language and culture serving as lenses of identity and mechanisms for social participation.

In this book, *Teaching Culture: Perspectives in Practice,* Patrick Moran examines the threads of these evolving perspectives as they relate to the work of the teacher in the classroom: How can these powerful ideas serve language teachers both in organizing and reflecting on their work with learners in various settings? What exactly does it mean to teach and to learn a second language/culture? Moran introduces a series of useful frames, grounding them in direct experience, both his own and those of language teachers and learners with whom he has worked as a teacher educator. He points out quite rightly that rethinking language and culture in relation to one another is a process that engages the identities, values, and expectations of teacher and learners alike to reframe both subject matter and classroom pedagogy. This book is not a simple tour of techniques; it is a reexamination of the central work and content of the language classroom. The result is invaluable in supporting teachers in this complex process of expanding their ideas about how language and culture work as subject matter and how as teachers they can carry this vision into their classrooms to serve their learners.

—Donald Freeman, Series Editor

1

INTRODUCTION TO TEACHING CULTURE

"So what's your son studying at the university?"

"French," my father answered.

"French," his colleague repeated. He paused, then added, "What's he going to do with that?"

My father thought for a moment and replied, "Well, I guess he wants to be a Frenchman."

Neither realized that I was within earshot, taking it all in. My first inclination was to laugh, knowing my father's deadpan humor, and thinking that he was simply cracking a joke. The moment passed. I continued to think about it when I returned for my final year of school. I asked myself, "Why am I studying French? Where will I end up with this language?" I enjoyed French, but I had never been to France or to any other French-speaking region. In fact, I had only a few travel experiences outside Nebraska, none of these outside the country. My courses at the university all pointed toward literature and history, which, I confess, held little appeal. I didn't see any other career possibilities at the time. What other outcomes were possible? Becoming a Frenchman seemed as good as any. And indeed, I naively set out to become a native speaker of French, not knowing what this really meant, other than trying to sound just like the Parisians on the audiotapes in the language laboratory.

Judging from the range of courses offered during those years, and from the amount of reading and responding to reading that I did, I would say that the professors and the department intended that I graduate with an understanding of French civilization and an appreciation of French writers, although no one ever explicitly voiced this as an intended outcome. If I looked to my teachers as models of culture learners, I saw university professors who essentially occupied themselves with literature. My own goals were directed toward using French to communicate. Whenever I had the chance, I chose courses in conversation and composition over literature, history, and translation. I wanted to converse with French-speaking people and I wanted to talk the way they did; that's as much as I was able to articulate at the time.

Upon graduation, I decided to enter the Peace Corps, applied to serve in one of several French-speaking West African countries, and was accepted as a teacher of English as a Foreign Language (EFL) in Côte d'Ivoire. After a brief orientation in Philadelphia, my fellow Peace Corps trainees and I traveled to a small town in rural Quebec, where the first six weeks of our training were held in a parish school. Suddenly, all my studies of France, French history, and French civilization were turned upside down. The French I heard in Ste Anne de la Pocatière was new to me, as was the history of Quebec. Neither French Canada nor the French colonization of Africa had been topics in my undergraduate curriculum, and I knew next to nothing about these, and nothing at all about the culture of these former colonies of France. In our training sessions in classrooms in Quebec and Côte d'Ivoire, francophone African culture was not presented historically or through literature but as a concrete reality we were about to encounter, a way of life that we needed to learn how to navigate if we were to succeed in our jobs as teachers in local schools. The second part of our training took place in Bouaké, Côte d'Ivoire. Our classroom work there was expanded to include tasks that we carried out with Ivorians in their culture, including shopping, bargaining for goods in the market, eating in restaurants, and even spending a weekend as a guest in an Ivorian family.

When I reached my new home in Bondoukou, Côte d'Ivoire, now on my own, a whole new set of language and culture learning priorities rose up to meet me. For the first time, I had to use French to communicate with all sorts of people in many different situations: Ivorian and French teachers and supervisors at the school where I taught English, students, local merchants, town officials, and many others I met in the town where I lived and worked for two years. Eventually, my French improved to the point where I could handle virtually all the communicative situations I encountered. Beyond communicating, however, I also had to adapt to the Ivorian way of life, a process that took time, effort, and attention, and was alternatively exhilarating and maddening. My daily participation in life and work presented one challenge after another that I had to somehow handle appropriately without making a fool of myself or offending anyone. Looking back over my journal entries and unsent letters from that time, I see how confused I often was, how strong my emotions were, how categorical my judgments were, how much I wrote about my own culture, how many questions I asked, how much I wondered about myself.

The process I was going through was unlike anything I had ever experienced. I had no frame of reference for these experiences. Models of cultural entry, adjustment, adaptation, culture shock were not widely available at that time; consequently, I had to figure things out as best I could, observing others. My fellow Peace Corps volunteers and I all seemed to be in the same boat. All of us were trying to determine how to adjust to Ivorian culture and establish ourselves somewhere along a continuum, with membership in an insular expatriate American community on one end and, on the other, full assimilation into the Ivorian culture, leaving our own culture and language behind, what we termed "going native." Uneasy with these two extremes, I tried to fit somewhere in between, but I never knew exactly where to stand.

When I left Côte d'Ivoire, I traveled overland, crossing the Sahara Desert into Algeria, Morocco, Spain, and France. As I slowly moved from one country to the next, from one language and culture to another, I realized that my experiences in Ivorian culture had given me insights into the nature of culture and cultural adaptation in general. I was able to see with a greater sense of cultural relativity and to respond to cultural differences with greater equanimity, even though I did not speak Arabic or Spanish and knew little about these cultures.

I eventually made my way back to Nebraska, bewildered to find myself in the throes of adjusting to my own culture. I had changed, but somehow everyone that I knew seemed the same, and I could not find the words to express what I had undergone. I had no explanations. Ironically, only my friends returning from the war in Vietnam seemed to understand.

My original, naive intention of becoming a native speaker of French had led me into completely unexpected territories of language, culture, and identity. Becalmed on the prairie, I had no inkling of how much this experience would affect me, that I would go on to learn and teach Spanish, to teach French, to teach language teachers, and to integrate French and francophone culture into my life and work in ways I could never have imagined.

I begin this book on teaching culture with a story of my own experiences as a language and culture learner for a number of reasons. Above all, I want to underscore the centrality of culture learning to teaching culture. I want to emphasize that culture learning, whether it occurs in a foreign language or second language context, inside or outside the classroom, with or without teachers, through books or through people, is best seen as a lived experience, as a personal encounter with another way of life. This encounter, when all is said and done, is unique to every learner. Every learner has a distinct story to tell, and teaching culture is about constructing and hearing these stories. Finally, I want to stress that, as language teachers, we too have stories of learning language and culture. The way we teach culture springs from our histories as language and culture learners and our understanding of ourselves. Bringing our own stories to light can help us see how to foster culture learning in the students in our language classes.

This book is addressed to practicing and prospective language teachers, both nonnative teachers and teachers of their native language. Although the primary audience is foreign and second language teachers in North America, the approach to teaching culture that I present in this book is applicable to language teachers in other countries as well.

Because this is a book on culture, I use cultural examples to illustrate various points. To the greatest extent possible, I have tried to offer examples that can be applied to many cultures, consistent with a culture-general approach. However, there are also culture-specific examples, drawn from my personal experiences with French-speaking cultures, from North American culture, and from the voices of other teachers that appear in the book.

INVESTIGATIONS

There are two types of Investigations in this book: **learning culture** and **teaching culture**. The Investigations that feature learning culture invite readers to concentrate on analysis of a particular cultural topic and to reflect upon the strategies they employ as learners. My intention here is to provide opportunities for teachers to bring their culture learning experiences to awareness, as a form of cultural autobiography, and to offer opportunities for teachers to practice culture learning strategies. These Investigations are also designed to help readers focus on culture of origin as well as second culture. The teaching culture Investigations invite teachers to try out culture learning activities with language learners in their classes and to study the results. Both sets of Investigations are culture-general, not specific to any single culture, so that teachers of any language can apply them to their particular situations, both with their culture of origin and with their second culture.

TEACHERS' VOICES

A variety of teachers' voices appear in this book, both native and nonnative teachers of different languages: French, Spanish, ESOL, Japanese, and Swahili. Excerpts of my own story as a learner and teacher of French and of my work with language teachers are also included at the beginning of every chapter.

In the pages that follow, I provide a bird's-eye view of the place of culture within the field of language teaching, situate my approach within the field, and describe the content, organization, and purposes of this book.

CULTURE IN LANGUAGE TEACHING

As a metaphor for views of culture in language teaching, Ray Clark (in Gaston, 1984) cites John Godfrey Saxe's poem "The Blind Men and the Elephant," which evokes an image of six blind men attempting to describe an elephant. In the poem, each blind man touches a different part of the beast, from tusk to tail, and, based on this narrow encounter, draws his conclusion about the identity of this strange animal. Six men thus proclaim six different descriptions, none of which is an elephant. There is certainly some truth to each of their views, but the parts do not define the whole animal. This metaphor still holds for culture in language teaching. Instead of six blind men describing an elephant, we have numerous theorists and practitioners from many disciplines, each bringing different viewpoints on culture, culture learning, and teaching culture. Using the frame of multiple views, let me briefly describe the situation.

Many Views of Culture

Culture is viewed as **civilization**, the great achievements of a people as reflected in their history, social institutions, works of art, architecture, music, and literature—commonly referred to as "big C" culture. Culture is also viewed as the customs, traditions, or practices that people carry out as part of their everyday lives—"small c" culture (Halverson, 1985). Both views are culture-specific and, broadly speaking, use the nation as the frame of reference for culture. Thus, there are references to French culture, Moroccan culture, Mexican culture, Brazilian culture, or the culture of any nation in the world.

Culture is viewed as **communication** (Hall, 1959) and all that people of a particular culture use to communicate, namely language, verbal and nonverbal, including a variety of forms: body movements, eye contact, time, space, smells, touching, and the use of the social situation. Language teaching interprets these under the concepts of "sociolinguistics" (Chaika, 1994), "proficiency" (Omaggio-Hadley, 1993), and "communicative competence" (Canale and Swain, 1980)—knowing how to communicate accurately and appropriately in a specific culture and language.

Culture is viewed as a **general concept**, without reference to any specific culture (Kohls, 1994). This view is prevalent in intercultural education and training and consists of culture-general components that apply to any and all cultures.

These components include generalized conceptions such as intercultural aware-ness, value orientations, attitudes, and behaviors. The contrasts between cul-tures are emphasized, particularly those that produce cross-cultural conflicts or misunderstandings. These are presented through case studies, critical incidents, and simulated cultural experiences.

Culture is viewed in terms of **intercultural communication** (Lustig and Koester, 1999), the capacity and ability to enter other cultures and communicate effectively and appropriately, establish and maintain relationships, and carry out tasks with people of these cultures. This ability is not specific to any one culture but is applicable to all cultures. Here, culture is viewed as a process, what peo-ple go through as they think, do, and feel in order to successfully communicate across cultures. Concepts such as "intercultural competence" (Fantini, 1999) and "intercultural communicative competence" (Byram, 1997) reflect this view.

Culture is viewed as an arena where **groups or communities interact**, vying for power, influence, authority, or dominance. The insiders and the outsiders, the haves and the have-nots, the privileged and the underprivileged, or the oppressors and the oppressed are seen as participants in an ongoing struggle to achieve their ends—either to change or to maintain the cultural status quo. This view originates from critical pedagogy (Freire, 1973; Giroux, 1988) and from multicultural education (Banks, 1991), where the focus is often social justice.

Culture is viewed as a **dynamic construction between and among people**, con-sisting of the values, meanings, or beliefs that they create in their unique social cir-cumstances (Geertz, 1973). Culture is thus not a static, fixed body of knowledge but is constantly evolving, being actively constructed through interpersonal rela-tionships, always in the process of becoming. Seen in this way, culture exists as a mental phenomenon, and is relative, a function of a particular social situation.

Culture is viewed in terms of biology or **evolutionary psychology** (Brown, 1991), where many aspects are seen as universal to all members of humankind, derived from the nature and functions of the human brain. These universals, as in language, music, or in the universal facial expressions associated with emo-tions are the shared basis of communication across cultures. Culture is thus seen not as relative or variable but in terms of innate biological commonalities.

Saxe wrote his poem about the blind men to satirize the "disputants" in "the-ologic wars" of the nineteenth century. Ironically, in the field of language teach-ing today, the nature of culture is also a matter of dispute (Atkinson, 1999).

Many Disciplines and Fields of Study

Culture lies at the crossroads of a number of fields of study and academic dis-ciplines, each of which views culture through a different lens. Stern (1983) cites anthropology, sociology, and sociolinguistics as key disciplines. Also relevant are communication theory, intercultural communication, the study of a specific language, multicultural education, critical pedagogy, cultural studies, ethnic studies, history, and semiotics. In addition, there are hybrid fields of study such as anthropological linguistics, cultural linguistics (Palmer, 1996), and the ethnography of communication (Saville-Troike, 1982). Because of their respec-tive views of their subject matter, these fields of study all offer a distinct perspective on culture.

One Language, Many Cultures

Some languages are used in more than one country, including French, Spanish, Arabic, English, Portuguese, Chinese, Swahili, and German. Consequently, there are many cultures for such languages. Can we assume that there is a culture of each language that transcends or underlies all? Is there, in effect, a francophone or anglophone culture? Or are all the cultures of a language different, with little in common? Beyond this, is there a form of these languages that constitutes a separate kind of culture, such as "international English" or "*le Français standard*"? The multiple cultures/countries of languages pose a dilemma for teachers of these languages. Which culture(s) to teach?

To further complicate this quandary, within a single national culture, multiple communities (subcultures, cocultures, microcultures) use the national language. Consider, for example, the various ethnic, racial, socioeconomic, regional, or religious communities that use English in the United States, or Spanish in Mexico, or German in Germany. Many of these communities exist alongside the dominant or mainstream culture and do not necessarily share the same practices, beliefs, or values. Yet these groups do share the same language, generally speaking. Which communities/culture(s) to teach?

Many Contexts of Culture Learning

The many situations or circumstances where languages are taught affect the nature of the culture to be learned. Perhaps the most influential factor is whether the culture learning takes place in a foreign language context or a second language context. In other words, are students learning the culture from afar, in a foreign language context, such as learning English in Japan, or French in the United States? Or are students learning the culture directly, in a second language context, such as learning Spanish in Argentina, or Swahili in Kenya?

Other contextual variables relate to the schools, curricula, materials, learners, and learning objectives for language and culture learning. Curricula can emphasize different conceptions of culture.

Many Outcomes for Culture Learning

There are many potential outcomes for culture learning, depending on the view of culture that is presented. These include, among others, cultural understanding, cultural awareness, cultural adaptation, assimilation, integration, social change, communicative competence, identity transformation, and language proficiency.

Many Models of Culture Learning

The process of culture learning is seen alternatively as one of shifts in awareness, attitudes, behaviors, feelings, identity, or cognition.

Many Approaches to Teaching Culture

There is no shortage of useful materials and valid techniques for teaching culture. Teachers can employ critical incidents, cultural assimilators, culturgrams, role-plays, cultural simulations, field experiences, ethnography, experiential activities, crosscultural training techniques, values clarification, film, video, literature, realia, authentic materials, and many more.

In writing this book, my challenge has been to attempt to synthesize these multiple views of culture, culture learning, and culture teaching. For better or worse, like the blind men, I have tried to describe the whole elephant. I do not propose to resolve the multiple views outlined above, only to acknowledge that they exist and that they are the subject of much discussion among academics and theorists. Although I am interested in this discussion, at heart I am a practitioner, looking for classroom solutions. I have attempted a broader view that integrates these multiple perspectives in very practical ways. Hence the book's title: perspectives in practice.

In a conversation with Roberta Kucer, a high school teacher of Spanish and English, I asked her why she taught Spanish. She answered this way:

> I somehow see being a Spanish teacher the same way I see being an English teacher. I feel that one of the central things about teaching —about being a teacher—is to help people make connections. To feel connected and rooted. Spanish is a different material from English, but in this sense, the language is not simply a set of techniques to use to say this and that. It's really a way for people to get a sense of the humanity of other people who use that language. And when you have a sense of the humanity of other people, it's very hard to hurt them.

Roberta Kucer

Milton Bennett (1993) makes the point that ethnocentrism is the natural state for peoples of the world. Our instinctive reaction is to assume that our culture, our way of life, is the right one, and that all others are not. Whether we simply tolerate these other ways of life or treat them as enemies, our attitude toward them is essentially the same—ethnocentric. Bennett suggests that we have only to look at the number of wars and other forms of aggression between cultures to conclude that ethnocentrism is the norm in the history of human events. Acceptance of cultural differences is the exception. Overcoming these ingrained cultural perspectives, according to Bennett, has to be consciously learned. Developing sensitivity to cultural differences, in other words, does not come naturally. I would agree.

Culture is often referred to as if it were a subject matter like any other— geography, mathematics, science, or linguistics. Describing it this way engenders a strong inclination to view culture only as a body of knowledge, a compendium of facts, data, or other information. There is much truth to this viewpoint, especially when culture is seen as civilization or history. However, this view is only part of the picture. I take the broader view that culture is a dynamic, living phenomenon practiced daily by real people, together or alone, as they go about their shared way of life, living and creating their history or civilization. When you cross the border from your way of life into theirs, your challenges become communicating, building relationships, and accomplishing tasks in their language using their set of rules. To achieve these ends you have to manage your language, actions, emotions, beliefs, and values through trial and error—through experience.

In this book, I advocate an experiential approach to teaching and learning culture. Many language educators (Archer, 1986; Damen, 1987), interculturalists (Hess, 1994; McCaffrey, 1993; Weaver, 1993; Ting-Toomey, 1994), critical pedagogues (Freire, 1973; Wallerstein, 1983; Auerbach, 1992) have proposed similar approaches, whereby learners engage in participatory culture learning activities (planned or unplanned) and subsequently undertake a methodical description and analysis of their experience of these activities. This purposeful reflection leads to greater cultural understanding and more informed action and interaction.

In my case, I adapt the experiential learning cycle proposed by Kurt Lewin (in Kolb, 1984) to what I call the **cultural experience**. The cultural experience consists of any encounter between learners and another way of life, be it first-hand through direct involvement with people of the other culture or indirectly through learning materials in the language classroom. These encounters elicit four kinds of culture learning, or cultural knowings: **knowing about**, **knowing how**, **knowing why**, and **knowing oneself**. In other words, learners go through an iterative cycle of acquiring cultural information, developing cultural behaviors, discovering cultural explanations, and articulating personal responses to what they are learning. Teaching culture, in turn, involves orchestrating and implementing these cultural knowings in a purposeful manner, consistent with the stages of the experiential cycle. Each stage, each cultural knowing, calls for specific teaching roles and learning strategies.

By advocating an experiential approach to teaching culture, I am also proposing that it can be applied to language learners in any context, studying any language or culture. Whatever the circumstances, at the heart of the culture learning experience is the encounter with difference. Learners tend to view this difference through the lens of their own cultures. As a result, they react to the "different" using what they already know—their own culture, their own view of the world. Learners describe, explain, act, and interact using their own culture and language as the frame of reference. Such actions are frequently inaccurate or inappropriate, since they do not take into consideration how people of the other culture describe, explain, or conduct their way of life. To break through this deep-seated, often unconscious tendency, learners need conscious learning strategies to help them understand and enter other ways of life and, in the process, recognize the role of their own cultural conditioning. The stages of the experiential cycle and the accompanying cultural knowings provide strategies to this end.

In going through these stages, learners not only learn a particular culture and language, they also develop their overall abilities as learners of culture, a personal competence (Stevick, 1986) that they can apply to other culture learning situations or, for that matter, to any encounter with "difference." With practice and awareness, they learn to distinguish observation from interpretation, insider viewpoints from outsider viewpoints, their own culture from the new culture, and they are in a better position to accept, even empathize with, people from other cultures. Or, as Roberta Kucer says, "to get a sense of the humanity of other people."

ORGANIZATION OF THIS BOOK

The book is organized into three parts: cultural content, culture learning, culture teaching.

Cultural Content

The second chapter, The Cultural Experience, outlines my approach to teaching culture. As mentioned above, this approach is based on three frameworks: culture as both content and process, the experiential learning cycle, and the four cultural knowings that accompany each stage of this cycle. To join content and process, culture needs to be seen from the perspective of the learner and learning. Whatever the cultural content may be—history, behaviors, traditions, beliefs—teachers need to link this content to the way that learners are to engage in it. Linking cultural content to the learners' engagement leads to knowing about, knowing how, knowing why, knowing oneself. The cultural knowings are best integrated through the four stages of the experiential learning cycle as a sequence for the four cultural knowings. Teachers thus guide learners through a repetitive cycle of participation in cultural experiences, description and interpretation of these experiences, and articulation of personal responses.

In the third chapter, Defining Culture, I present a conception of cultural content, drawn primarily from the field of anthropology. Following in the footsteps of cultural anthropologists, I define culture as an evolving way of life consisting of shared products, practices, and perspectives of persons within specific social settings and communities. This conception assumes that culture exists in the material world, that it can be described, analyzed, and explained. It also assumes that the overall purpose of culture learning is to enter another way of life, to form relationships with the people of this culture, using their language, and to participate with them in the activities of their daily lives, on their terms.

Language-and-Culture, the fourth chapter, addresses the relationship between language and culture. Here, I draw two key distinctions: language to participate in the culture, and language to learn culture. In the first case, I show how language is reflected in the five dimensions of culture, as language-and-culture (Byram, 1997). In the second, I discuss the language of the classroom, the language to learn culture, particularly how this language derives from the four cultural knowings and the accompanying stages of the experiential learning cycle.

The next five chapters examine each of the five dimensions of culture in greater detail. In Cultural Products, I organize the material aspect of culture through artifacts, places, institutions, and art forms. In Cultural Practices, I show how cultural and linguistic behaviors can be grouped as operations, acts, scenarios, and lives. In Cultural Perspectives, I present perceptions, beliefs, values, and attitudes, as well as etic (outsider) and emic (insider) views of the meanings that govern culture. In Cultural Communities, I present three aspects: the national community, coexisting communities, and relationships. In Cultural Persons, I discuss concepts of identity and life histories. Although each of these five dimensions can be examined in relative isolation, it is the connections with the other dimensions that reveal the culture. By going into detail in describing these dimensions of culture, I hope to provide language teachers with an approach to the content of culture.

Culture Learning

The following two chapters examine culture learning. In Culture Learning Outcomes, I address the variety of purposes that teachers and learners bring to

culture learning. I present six goals for culture learners: culture-specific understanding, culture-general understanding, competence, adaptation, social change,
and identity. The choice of outcomes depends on a number of factors: the context in which the learning takes place, the curriculum, the teacher, the learner's
intentions and opportunities, and the people of the target culture—their receptivity to the learner. To transcend these variables, I propose an overarching culture learning outcome: personal competence (Stevick, 1986), the capacity and
ability of the learner to learn from experience and to manage differences.

The next chapter, The Culture Learning Process, examines the development
of culture learning, how culture is acquired. I advocate that this process needs
to be made explicit in the language-and-culture curriculum. At the core, learning culture is a matter of navigating successive encounters with difference, leading to one of many potential outcomes.

Culture Teaching

The last chapter, Teaching Culture, revisits the cultural knowings and the experiential learning cycle from the perspective of teaching. A summary
of teaching emphases and options is presented, along with a discussion of the
particular roles required of the teacher for each of the knowings.

In Appendix A, I provide additional information on etic cultural perceptions, and in Appendix B, brief summaries and illustrations of models of
culture learning.

As mentioned above, the range of culture learning circumstances is vast, from
foreign language to second language contexts. Consequently, the challenges of
teaching culture vary considerably. Compare the following accounts.

Gary Allen teaches French at a high school in the United States where language study is a required subject. He describes the reality of language study for
these students and how he has responded:

Gary Allen

> The Advanced Placement students do develop a certain degree of
> proficiency. They can basically get around in France, and they can
> ask questions, and all that. But many of these students will never
> be language majors or ever do much with French. If anything, I can
> at least help them to develop some kind of interest in traveling, or
> to feel confident about getting out of this area and going up to
> Quebec. Or maybe some time in their life going to Europe, or sim-
> ply feeling comfortable in getting along with other people. They
> might not remember any French at all, but we do a ton of group
> activities, team activities, and working with pairs, which, frankly, I
> don't see a lot of in today's high school.
>
> I have other students in my other French classes who don't like
> school and whose experience in education in this country of ours
> has been negative. They're just constantly beat upon. They don't do
> their homework, they're getting 60s and 70s; they just can't wait to
> get out of school. Fortunately there are sports programs.
> Fortunately they have friends. And fortunately there are a lot of
> other things that kind of offset this. If I do have to give grades, and
> if French isn't their thing, if they're just not going to learn to speak
> French quite as fluently as somebody else, maybe out of my class,

they can make a new friend. I believe that there's something everybody can take out of it. If it looks like, "Hey, I met Mary in French class, and we're friends," then great! Sometimes it doesn't look like French at all. And if that's what it is, then that's dandy with me.

I believe there's a lot of possibility for growth. Growth can look like linguistic growth, but it can also look like personal growth. I think that it's possible for students at senior year in high school to talk a lot more about themselves, and that they're more willing to talk about themselves with a linguistic and cultural context. I've found that when we can relate, and when I can talk to them on a personal level, what's going on in my life, they can see value in it beyond it just being French.

In contrast, Ivanna Thrower teaches in a second language context, teaching ESL in the United States, where the challenges of culture learning are quite different.

Ivanna Thrower

I teach a listening-speaking class in an intensive ESL program in the United States. My students are mostly high-intermediate college-bound students: speakers of Japanese, Korean, Chinese, Spanish, German, Thai, and Arabic. The class is based mostly on non-textbook materials such as movies, realia, community activities, and some TOEFL preparation.

My challenge is to get students to be open-minded when exploring the cultures of their classmates, in or out of the classroom. Students are very open to the cultural activities done in class, but conflicts periodically arise when one culture strongly contrasts with another in a sensitive area, such as religion. Instead of learning about the differences, students become argumentative and judgmental. Because this particular class has developed a strong sense of community, these incidents do not become too intense, but I need to be prepared to address this issue in future classes.

How can I promote open-minded students' exploration of the cultures of their classmates and the host country, the United States? In other words, different is not wrong, only different.

Here in these two accounts we have two extremes that are a fact of life for language teachers: students who are in our classes and will not likely use the language ever again, and students who have already entered another way of life and are struggling with cultural conflicts as they learn the language.

Despite the great differences, both teachers are attempting to help learners make a transition from one world, one way of life, into another. This, as I see it, is our shared calling as language teachers.

2

THE CULTURAL
EXPERIENCE

I often begin courses on teaching culture by asking teachers to jot down a brief list of the "culture" they have taught in their language classes. I do this before presenting any definitions of culture in order to allow teachers to respond openly, using whatever notions they have about culture. As they read from their lists, I write their words on the blackboard. Before long, the blackboard fills with a dizzying array of topics, all with some connection to culture in the minds of these teachers. The range of topics looks like this:

Figure 2.1: The Collage of Culture

accepting differences	films	making comparisons
acting differently	fitting in	making friends
adapting	fluency	male/female language
art	food	music
becoming bilingual/bicultural	good pronunciation	nonverbal language
changing your attitudes	greetings	overcoming stereotypes
communicating	history	politeness
conversational skills	holidays	politics
curiosity about the culture	humor	television
current events	idioms	thinking in the language
customs	keeping your own identity	understanding the values
daily life	knowing your own culture	using gestures
doing everyday tasks	literature	using slang
education		

Seen separately, each topic is recognizable, with an understandable connection to culture. There are also obvious connections between and among certain items, such as *communicating, using slang, idioms, conversational skills, using gestures*. Finding the links between and among other topics, however, is less obvious, more tenuous, even baffling. What, for instance, is the connection between *using gestures* and *literature*? Or *food* and *good pronunciation*? Imaginative teachers may see connections, but the rest of us are left scratching our heads. In a dramatic way, the words on the blackboard portray the complexity and breadth of culture—not unlike a collage where snippets of magazine pictures, photographs, and newspaper headlines fall alongside and across one another in no apparent logic or organization. Looking at the blackboard as a whole, culture looks like...well, a collage.

Even though the nature of this exercise tends to produce such juxtapositions, I believe nonetheless that the "collage" notion of culture is a dominant conception among language teachers. As teachers, we have little difficulty listing cultural topics, but organizing them is another matter entirely. For good reasons. Culture is multifaceted and complex, and there is no consensus on what culture is.

As language teachers, our challenge is to bring some order to the apparent randomness of culture, both for ourselves and for the students in our classes, as a first step in making culture accessible. One approach to this challenge is to sort through the perspectives that the various definitions of culture describe. Such an approach makes a lot of sense, for if you can find a good definition, it will provide order and organization to the cultural collage. In the next chapter, I do present such a definition. At this point, however, let us postpone defining culture and instead examine another approach to ordering the randomness of culture, based on students' engagement in learning culture.

In this chapter, I present and discuss the three frameworks that define and organize culture in terms of this learning engagement: the cultural experience, cultural knowings, and the experiential learning cycle.

THE CULTURAL EXPERIENCE

Culture has many definitions, because it is multifaceted, and also because theorists and practitioners bring their own perspectives to their definitions. For the most part, these definitions present culture as an abstract entity that can be separated from the experience of participating in it. While they do help us understand the nature of culture, these definitions remain abstract, disconnected from the people who live in that culture and, more importantly, from the experience of participating in that culture. This disconnection is not unlike the distinction between a book and reading a book, between a restaurant and eating in a restaurant, between a song and singing a song, or between language and using the language. Simply put, it is the distinction between culture as a way of life and participating in that way of life. Therefore, instead of using "culture" as the focal point of definitions, I will use "cultural experience"—the encounter with another way of life.

As language teachers, we all provide our students with cultural experiences of one kind or another, all with the intention of helping them learn culture: food, clothing, literature, music, films, realia, personal anecdotes, native speakers, and more. We do need to define the culture that they are to learn, without question. But it is the nature of these cultural experiences that we need to define, not just culture alone. The cultural experience, therefore, consists of the cultural content, the activities in which students engage this content, the outcomes that are intended or achieved, the learning context, and the nature of the relationship the teacher develops with students.

Figure 2.2: The Cultural Experience

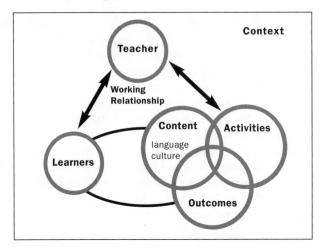

Another way of putting this is that the cultural experience consists of content and process (Crawford-Lange and Lange, 1987). Learners encounter another way of life. The way of life is the content, and the learners' encounters are the process, the kinds of activities they undertake and the outcomes they achieve. The teacher, through a working relationship with the learners, is an integral part of this experience. This experience, in turn, is very much a function of the particular context or learning circumstances where the culture learning takes place.

Consider the student encounters with the way of life in the United States that Julie McConville, an ESL teacher in Massachusetts, describes below.

Julie McConville

I am a full-time teacher in a refugee resettlement program for recent arrival adults from Vietnam, Ethiopia, Somalia, and Haiti. The curriculum emphasizes U.S. life skills and employment skills. Students can take a maximum of three cycles (33 weeks). I work very closely with my department's five job developers. Most students are under severe pressure to find jobs before their welfare is terminated.

I am challenged with the question of how to teach students to be aware of certain American-valued character qualities that they need to exhibit in order to find success in their new lives, surroundings, and at work. Attitudes such as assertiveness, self-reliance, healthy skepticism, forthrightness—to name a few. Each one of these qualities calls to mind an incident where a student, because he or she did not exhibit one or more of these qualities, either got into trouble or missed out on an opportunity.

The real difficulty in teaching these American-valued qualities lies in the fact that my students are new and seem to be holding tight to identities from cultures that do not value the same character qualities.

- How can I teach students about these American-valued character qualities and not threaten their cultural identity?

- How can I tackle such a challenge, making it relevant to all of my students, and complete it, when I have students from vastly different cultures and limited time?

Julie describes the features of the U.S. way of life that students encounter and, as language teachers do, she poses this as a learning/teaching challenge. She gives names to the culture students need to learn (content), seeks ways they might be able to learn it (activities), and specifies what they need to achieve (outcomes).

2.1 *Teaching Culture: Defining Cultural Content*

Review Julie's description of her students' encounters. Describe the culture that you think her students need to learn. Explain your answers.

As teachers of culture, we are engaged in working with learners' cultural experiences. There are two frameworks that illuminate this teaching task: the cultural knowings framework and Kolb's model of experiential learning. In later chapters, these frameworks are explained in greater detail, but I will provide a brief introduction to them below.

Cultural Knowings Framework

The cultural knowings framework offers a means for describing culture in terms of what students need to do in order to learn it—their encounters with another way of life.

Once these interactions are specified, the learning objectives follow, as do the choice of teaching and learning activities and the appropriate means of evaluation. Also, each interaction calls for a distinct teacher role. For the moment, however, we will concentrate on the learning interactions, and apply these to Julie's students.

The cultural experience consists of four interconnected learning interactions:

- Knowing About
- Knowing How
- Knowing Why
- Knowing Oneself

Knowing About

This interaction includes all activities that consist of gathering and demonstrating acquisition of **cultural information**—facts, data, or knowledge about products, practices, and perspectives of the culture. This is information about the specific culture and language, as well as about the nature of culture and the processes of learning and entering other cultures in general, or information about students' own culture(s). Learners need to master information about the culture.

What kinds of information do Julie's students need? What do they need to know? Generally speaking, Julie's students appear to need information about the American workplace. In particular, they need to know about how the work is accomplished at specific worksites, the kinds of jobs that are done there, the rules and regulations, the roles and responsibilities of the people who work there, and other relevant information. Also, as Julie emphasizes, they need information about the values that underlie the practices at the workplace, such as assertiveness and self-reliance.

Knowing How

This interaction involves acquiring **cultural practices**—behaviors, actions, skills, saying, touching, looking, standing, or other forms of "doing." This calls for direct or simulated participation in the everyday life of the people of the target culture, according to their customs and traditions, using their tools or technology—and their language—to establish bona fide relationships with them. Learners need to be able to adapt and/or integrate into the culture—to say and do things in the manner of the people of the culture. This means changing behaviors to develop others that are appropriate for the culture.

What kinds of behaviors do Julie's students need to carry out? What do they need to know how to do? In broad terms, they need to be able to get and keep a job. There are multiple practices involved in jobs. Students need to perform them in an appropriate manner, ranging from being forthright and assertive (presumably in interactions with coworkers and superiors) to carrying out all that is involved in being self-reliant. These practices involve using language, to be sure, but they also involve other actions such as body posture, eye contact, facial expressions, and other nonverbal elements. Other practices might include actions related to time, such as punctuality; still others might involve displaying behaviors that job interviewers or supervisors perceive as dependable.

Knowing Why

This interaction deals with developing an understanding of fundamental **cultural perspectives**—the perceptions, beliefs, values, and attitudes that underlie or permeate all aspects of the culture. This is a process of learners' structured inquiry into observations, information, and experiences with the culture. Knowing why requires skills in probing, analyzing, and explaining the cultural phenomena learners encounter, which necessarily involves a comparison with their own culture and themselves. Learners need to understand insider and outsider perspectives: the emic and the etic. Learners need to understand the culture on its own terms by using their own powers of cultural analysis and comparison. The basic values of a culture are an important point of comparison with the values of the culture of the learners.

What do Julie's students need to find out about the culture? What cultural understandings do they need to discover? Clearly, Julie has identified values as a primary content area, believing that this is what students need to learn. In this case, students need to observe, describe, and offer explanations of the cultural phenomena they encounter outside the classroom, including the workplace. They also need to surface and give voice to the perspectives that underlie their own cultures, in particular the values, attitudes, and beliefs surrounding work and workplaces. They need, in other words, to develop the ability to interpret their experiences in cultural terms.

Knowing Oneself

This interaction concerns the individual learners—their values, opinions, feelings, questions, reactions, thoughts, ideas, and their own cultural values as a central part of the cultural experience. It deals with **self-awareness**. The cultural experience is highly personal, and therefore idiosyncratic. Individual learners need to understand themselves and their own culture as a means to comprehending, adapting to, or integrating into the culture. They need to recognize and manage the emotional highs and lows involved in the culture learning process. Ultimately, it is the learners who decide the extent to which they engage in, accept, explore, or become part of the culture and develop expertise as culture learners.

What do Julie's students need to articulate about themselves and their experiences? Julie sees her students as undergoing an internal conflict, an identity crisis of sorts. They are faced with a choice between "keeping" or "giving up" their cultural identities. Perhaps this is indeed how they see it, but students themselves need to articulate their own experiences and their responses to them. They are faced with the task of adapting to life in the United States and are apparently finding it a challenging undertaking. They need to give voice to their responses to determine if the challenge is indeed a matter of identity loss, or if it is something else.

Again, in the end, individual learners set the limits of knowing about, how, and why. They decide. For this reason, knowing oneself is the organizing dimension of the cultural knowings.

Figure 2.3: Knowing Oneself: The Organizing Dimension

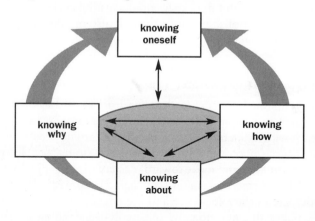

Learners' abilities to make such decisions depend on their awareness of themselves, their situation, and their intentions. The more aware they are, the more focused their work becomes in the acquisition of cultural information, skills, and understanding. Lacking this awareness, learners tend not to see the point of culture learning or even to see themselves in such a process, as appears to be the case for the students in Julie's class.

These four knowings, as the examination of Julie's students shows, overlap and interconnect. Nonetheless, they do represent distinct learning transactions with distinct learning strategies and ends. As the following chart portrays, each of the cultural knowings addresses a distinct composite of content, activities, and outcomes.

Table 2.1: Cultural Knowings: Content, Activities, Outcomes

	Content	Activities	Outcomes
Knowing About	cultural information	gathering information	cultural knowledge
Knowing How	cultural practices	developing skills	cultural behaviors
Knowing Why	cultural perspectives	discovering explanations	cultural understanding
Knowing Oneself	self	reflection	self-awareness

2.2 *TEACHING CULTURE: CATEGORIZING CULTURAL CONTENT*

Deciding on the cultural content for language classes is a critical skill. Look again at Figure 2.1, the collage of culture. Categorize each of the cultural topics on this list as content in terms of the four cultural knowings. Choose one of the topics and go into greater detail, listing specific cultural information, cultural practices, cultural perspectives, and self-awarenesses. What challenges do you encounter?

The cultural knowings can be addressed separately and effectively as a means of joining content and process in teaching culture. Students can be invited to engage in any one of the dimensions. However, I have found it useful to situate the cultural knowings within the experiential learning cycle. This not only suggests an order and a relationship among them, it also organizes them all in terms of learning from experience.

THE EXPERIENTIAL LEARNING CYCLE

Kolb (1984) published a model for learning from experience (derived from the work of Kurt Lewin, John Dewey, and Piaget) that proposes a cycle of four distinct stages, each with a different learning purpose. Learning occurs through experiences. Through a cycle of observation, theorizing, and strategizing, learners go from one experience to another and move toward mastery of the subject matter at hand.

In this model, the stages occur in sequence: (1) **concrete experience**, where learners participate in the experience and are engaged on a number of levels—intellectually, physically, emotionally, spiritually—depending on the nature of the content and the form of the experience itself; (2) **reflective observation**, where, subsequent to the experience, the learner pauses to reflect on what happened in order to describe what happened, staying with the facts of the experience; (3) **abstract conceptualization**, where the learner assigns meaning to the experience by developing explanations or theories—either the learner's own or drawn from other sources; (4) **active experimentation**, the point at which the learner prepares to reenter experience by devising strategies consistent with personal learning goals, the nature of the content, and the form of the experience.

I have adapted the stages of this model to more directly incorporate the cultural knowings and the cultural experience. The cultural experience, students' encounters with another way of life, parallels Kolb's notion that all learning is experience. Content and process are joined, whether in a direct engagement in the culture itself or in a vicarious, indirect one, such as reading cultural notes in a language textbook, watching a film, or listening to a teacher's stories about a trip to Italy. The nature of this encounter is played out in each of the four stages.

In terms of the stages of the cycle, *concrete experience* becomes *participation*, where the task is direct or indirect engagement in the culture, with an emphasis on knowing how. *Reflective observation* becomes *description*, with a focus on knowing about. *Abstract conceptualization* becomes *interpretation*, where learners concentrate on knowing why. *Active experimentation* becomes *response*, with an emphasis on self-awareness, knowing oneself.

The following diagram illustrates the experiential cycle. Note that the learner appears at the center. In the participation, description, and interpretation stages, the learner's attention is on the culture, whereas in the response stage, the learner's focus shifts to self.

Figure 2.4: The Experiential Learning Cycle

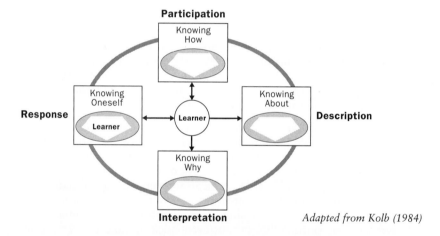

Adapted from Kolb (1984)

Each of the stages provides a clear pedagogical focus. Content, activities, and outcomes merge in a distinct way for each stage. Together, they present an overall procedure that teachers and learners can use to work on the cultural experience.

How are students in Julie's classroom responding to their experiences in the U.S. workplace? Julie suggests that they are acting or interacting inappropriately and that they are suffering the consequences by "missing opportunities" or "getting into trouble." While Julie is understandably anxious to move to solutions (strategies for reentering the workplace), it is not clear that students have fully described what happened in these workplace experiences, nor that they have fully interpreted those experiences so as to understand the cultural implications.

Imagine that Julie McConville comes to you to discuss how to apply the experiential model to her language class. What would you suggest that she do for each stage of the cycle?

Organizing culture learning through the stages of the experiential learning cycle requires that learners and teachers consciously apply themselves at each stage. Julie Versluys, a Spanish teacher, describes how she was asked to employ a variation of the experiential learning cycle in learning the culture of the Dominican Republic.

Julie Versluys

As the *guagua* (a public van, typically dilapidated and crammed full of passengers) barreled by, the words hit me like bricks: "*Grande, grande.*" I had been in the Dominican Republic for six months and I was already fed up with the comments that men would utter in passing: *rubia* (blondie), *americana*, *mamasota* (big mama). I was especially tired of the comments about my size and height. So I started to vent to my expatriate friend. "I'm so tired of hearing how tall or big I am. Do they have to point out the obvious? Do they think I don't know? Why can't they just drive by without saying anything—like normal people?" My friend, being the kind and patient person that she is, merely waited for me to stop ranting and said, "Julie, I think the driver was calling out '*Playa Grande, Playa Grande*'. You know, saying where they're headed."

Chagrined best describes how I felt at that moment of realization. Once again, I'd gone jumping to conclusions. It was in thinking about this experience that I started to unravel the mystery of why Dominican women had fixed expressions on their faces in the streets. I had noticed that Dominican women would walk around town wearing a mask of non-emotion. After a few weeks of seeing this behavior, I started forming the assumption that Dominican women were unfriendly, perhaps even stuck up (and I was starting to think it was especially with Americans). But upon further observation, I realized that their tendency to look down at the sidewalk or straight ahead and to rarely respond was not just in response to me, but also to the same men who were making comments to me as I passed by.

I decided to ask my Dominican coworkers their opinion. I wanted to see if they know why Dominican women tended to be so unresponsive and reserved in the street. At first, they didn't understand what I was trying to ask them since they had never consciously realized it was occurring. But once I explained what I was observing and how I was used to women in the United States behaving in the street, they were able to explain. They said that they, and many other women, looked so detached in the streets so that such men wouldn't think they were interested in them or see them as a certain type of woman.

When I first moved to the Dominican Republic, I was required to attend a cultural orientation seminar that made an impact on me. Some of the best advice I received had to do with analysis. We were all assigned the task of choosing a feature of Dominican society that we wanted to investigate further. Our orientation leader suggested that if we did our research on something that was especially troubling or bothersome to us, it might be more meaningful. We were first to identify the event or area, do observations and describe what was happening, and then analyze why it was happening. The hitch was that we were not allowed to consult any guidebooks or expatriates. We were to consult the experts of Dominican culture, Dominicans themselves. In doing our analysis, we were to go right to the source.

I chose the behavior of the Dominican women that I had observed in the street. However, this was no easy task. I had only been in the country for a couple of months and I hadn't built up the kind of *confianza* with someone to be able to ask them the questions I wanted. I didn't take the step of consulting a Dominican friend about the puzzling cultural behavior that I observed until I knew her quite well. And even then, when I brought the subject up, I first asked her if it was something that she noticed and that bothered her. Once she said that she had noticed it and that it bothered her as well, I felt much freer to ask her if she knew why this behavior existed. The time that I waited to ask my friend these questions also gave me time to improve my spoken Dominican Spanish. Now that I've been reflecting on my experiences with making assumptions, observing different cultures, and analyzing events and customs that I didn't understand, I'm coming to see how large a role language and friendship play.

2.4 *LEARNING CULTURE: ANALYZING CONTENT AND PROCESS*

What do you notice about Julie Versluys' culture learning? How does she join content and process? How does she carry out stages of the experiential learning cycle? How do the cultural knowings appear in her account?

Investigations

As illustrated at the beginning of this chapter, many topics fall under the umbrella of culture. Definitions of culture can help teachers organize topics, but defining culture from the perspective of learning is also critical to teaching culture. Seen this way, culture and learning culture are joined through the cultural experience, cultural knowings, and the experiential learning cycle.

The cultural experience varies, due to differences in context, curricula, students, teachers, and many other factors. The nature of the cultural information, the specific cultural behaviors, the particular cultural perspectives will vary, as will the individual responses of students. However, the nature of the cultural learning transactions and the experiential process of learning culture, I contend, remain constant. Regardless of variables, language learners are engaged in an experiential cycle of gathering cultural information, developing cultural behaviors, discovering cultural explanations, and developing self-awareness. These are the keys to the cultural experience.

At the heart of cultural experience, at the same time, is a concept of culture. I have defined culture as "a way of life." In the next chapter, we will explore in greater detail what makes up a way of life.

Suggested Readings

Experiential approaches to education have a long history in language teaching and intercultural training. In *Beyond Experience* (Gochenour, 1993) there are many informative articles on the theory and practice of experiential learning. In her book *Culture Learning: The Fifth Dimension in the Language Classroom,* Louise Damen (1987) was among the first to bring to language teaching the many disciplines and fields of study that address culture. Her description of "pragmatic ethnography" is a wonderful application of the experiential learning cycle to teaching and learning culture. From the field of intercultural communication, the D.I.E. framework (describe, interpret, evaluate) is a tried-and-true teaching strategy for understanding cultural conflict situations as they occur, first published as "D.I.E.: A Way to Improve Communication," by J. Wendt in 1984. Michael Byram has written many useful books on culture in language, and in *Teaching and Assessing Intercultural Communicative Competence* (1997), he outlines an approach to teaching culture and language based on knowledge, skills, attitudes, and education which he interprets as: *savoirs, savoir comprendre, savoir apprendre/faire, savoir être,* and *savoir s'engager.* Intercultural educators also simplify the nature of culture learning, using knowledge, behavior, and attitudes as the core. Michael Paige, Helen Jorstad, Laura Siaya, Francine Klein, and Jeanette Colby have compiled an excellent overview of content and process in culture teaching and learning using this tripartite frame in "Culture Learning in Language Education: A Review of the Literature" (2000), available at CARLA, The Center for Advanced Research on Language Acquisition, at the University of Minnesota (http://carla.acad.umn.edu/).

3

DEFINING CULTURE

If culture lies at the heart of the cultural experience, what then is culture?

A few years ago, I decided to tackle this question through a study of cultural anthropology, the discipline dedicated to the study of culture. I delved into books and articles that dealt with definitions of culture from the anthropological perspective. The results were overwhelming. Anthropologists, I soon discovered, possessed no agreed-upon definition. Instead, they had multiple answers to the question, "What is culture?" Answers ranged from cultural materialism to a host of various anthropologies: interpretive, psychological, cognitive, social, feminist, symbolic, linguistic, and reflexive. Each school of thought had a different perspective on culture. To my eyes, they all seemed to make perfect sense. Yet when I held them up against one another, I found them contradictory, inconsistent, and, ultimately, confusing. In the end, I attempted to synthesize these various views, but I had a very hard time doing so. The task was very much one of struggling with complexities and avoiding the simplicities.

In large part, the complexities do come from the myriad definitions of culture that are in circulation. Each definition slices the cultural pie differently. Each does offer insights into the complex phenomenon of culture (not to mention insights into the minds of those who proposed the definitions). To be fair, the complexity comes not just from definers and definitions but from the nature of culture itself. If, as some definitions purport, culture is all that humankind creates, from mascara to myths, marriage vows to slang, then complexity comes as no surprise. In fact, we have to accept and embrace the complexity of culture. The challenge is finding a simple approach to its complexities.

In this chapter, I present a definition of culture based on the realities and potential of the language classroom. Above all, these realities call for a view of culture that integrates language and culture in an understandable and accessible manner, all the while allowing for the complexity and mysteries of culture.

THREE COMPONENTS OF CULTURE

The foreign language teaching profession in the United States published a comprehensive set of standards for foreign language education, including standards for culture (National Standards in Foreign Language Education Project, 1996). They based their definition of culture on three interrelated dimensions, the three poles of an equilateral triangle: products, practices, perspectives. Seen in these broad terms, culture consists of artifacts, actions, and meanings. The three components of culture—products, practices, perspectives—reflect a similar triangular concept, described in different words by other educators or scholars who have defined culture, language, or communication. They are called products, behaviors, ideas (Nemetz-Robinson, 1988; Tomalin and Stempleski, 1993); artifacts, behaviors, knowledge (Spradley, 1980); artifacts, sociofacts, mentifacts (Fantini and Fantini, 1997; Klopf, 1998); form, distribution, meaning (Lado, 1997); form, use, meaning (Larsen-Freeman, 1987). There is also a direct connection to semiotics, the study of signs (linguistic and cultural): syntax, semantics, pragmatics.

CULTURE AS PRODUCTS, PRACTICES, PERSPECTIVES, COMMUNITIES, PERSONS

This view of culture is understandable and relatively easy to apply, with two important exceptions. Cultural artifacts, actions, and meanings do not exist apart from the people of the culture. People—alone and with others—make and use artifacts, carry out actions, and hold meanings. To capture the active role of people in their culture, I have added two dimensions to this definition: communities and persons. The diagram below illustrates the interplay of these five dimensions.

Figure 3.1: The Five Dimensions of Culture

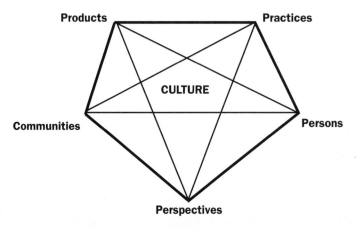

Drawing upon these five interrelated dimensions, I define culture as follows: *Culture is the evolving way of life of a group of persons, consisting of a shared set of practices associated with a shared set of products, based upon a shared set of perspectives on the world, and set within specific social contexts.*

- The **evolving way of life** reflects the dynamic nature of culture—that there is a history and tradition to the products, practices, perspectives, and the communities of the culture. It also stresses that the persons of the culture are in the process of actively creating and changing products, practices, perspectives, and communities.

- **Products** are all artifacts produced or adopted by the members of the culture, including those in the environment, such as plants and animals. Products range from tangible objects—such as tools, clothing, written documents, or buildings—to more elaborate yet still perceptible constructions such as written and spoken language, music, or complex institutions of family, education, economy, politics, and religion. Products, both tangible and intangible, are located and organized in physical places.

- **Practices** comprise the full range of actions and interactions that members of the culture carry out, individually or with others. These include language and other forms of communication and self-expression as well as actions associated with social groups and use of products. These practices are both verbal and nonverbal and include interpretations of time, space, and the context of communication in social situations. Practices also involve notions of appropriateness and inappropriateness, including taboos.

- **Perspectives** represent the perceptions, beliefs, values, and attitudes that underlie the products and that guide persons and communities in the practices of the culture. These perspectives can be explicit but often they are implicit, outside conscious awareness. Taken as a whole, perspectives provide meaning and constitute a unique outlook or orientation toward life—a worldview.

- **Communities** include the specific social contexts, circumstances, and groups in which members carry out cultural practices. These contexts range from broad, amorphous communities—such as national culture, language, gender, race, religion, socioeconomic class, or generation—to more narrowly defined groupings—a local political party, a social club, a sports team, a charity organization, coworkers, or family. These communities coexist within the national culture and are in particular relationships with one another: separation, cooperation, collaboration, or conflict.

- **Persons** constitute the individual members who embody the culture and its communities in unique ways. Each person is a distinct mix of communities and experiences, and all persons take on a particular cultural identity that both links them to and separates them from other members of the culture. Culture resides both in the individual members of the culture and in the various social groups or communities that these persons form to carry out their way of life. Culture is thus both individual and collective—psychological and social.

This definition holds that there are five dimensions to all cultural phenomena. I use the term *cultural phenomenon* broadly, simply as a way of defining a cultural topic. A cultural phenomenon involves tangible forms or structures (products) that individual members of the culture (persons) use in various interactions (practices) in specific social circumstances and groups (communities) in ways that reflect their values, attitudes, and beliefs (perspectives). Cultural phenomena can therefore be identified from any of these five dimensions. By looking for the connections from one to the other four, we can develop a more profound and informed picture of a culture.

For example, a cultural phenomenon such as law enforcement can be approached from the point of view of an individual police officer (person) including the officer's own unique experiences and outlook on work. It can be seen from any of the activities he or she (depending on the culture) undertakes as part of his or her work (practices) such as directing traffic, patrolling a beat, making arrests, gathering evidence, resolving disputes. It can be seen from the things the officer uses (products), such as handcuffs, tickets, badges, two-way radios, accident report forms, or from the institutional structures the officer works within, such as the local government, the judicial system, the police union, or community service organizations, and from the physical settings where he or she works, such as the police station or the neighborhood the officer patrols. It can be seen from explicit values or beliefs (perspectives) that underlie police work, such as views of law and order, civic duty. Finally, it can be seen from the social circumstances in which the police officer plays a role (communities), like the neighborhood, fellow officers, the police station, the professional organization of police officers.

To illustrate further, consider another cultural phenomenon and the interplay of these five dimensions.

Drive-Through Restaurants

A common sight in many, many towns, cities, and highways in the United States (and other countries) is the drive-through restaurant. Customers drive their cars through the restaurant parking area, place their orders, pay for and collect their meals at the window, and exit the restaurant area without ever leaving their automobiles.

The drive-through restaurant is a rather sophisticated cultural phenomenon. If we take the time to name all the products, practices, and perspectives involved, our list of items for each dimension would be quite long.

The number of **products** associated with drive-through restaurants is legion, including everything from straws and paper napkins, worker uniforms and signs, to the blueprints for the buildings, and the physical organization of the space the restaurant occupies. Beyond this, drive-through restaurants themselves are products of the economic institutions of the culture and operate within its legal and political systems.

As for **practices**, in order to get a meal, a person needs to know how to drive a car, obey traffic laws, manipulate currency, distinguish among an array of available food items, proceed through the drive-through sequence, order the desired meal, participate in any exchanges with the drive-through personnel, recognize an appropriate product (i.e., a properly prepared meal), and last but certainly not least, the person must know how to eat and drive at the same time! All these practices must be done appropriately, within the boundaries of acceptable behavior. Deviating from these practices would cause consequences: deviations might include not paying for one's meal, not moving one's car through the drive-through stations at the right tempo, or going through the drive-through on foot instead of by car.

Multiple **communities** are involved in the cultural practice of the drive-through restaurant. Patrons are confined to those who have automobiles. If the restaurant is local, members of that town or neighborhood are the likely participants. If the restaurant is a regional or national franchise, the groups that drive through its restaurants may represent a much larger range of social groups. If all the groups involved with drive-through restaurants are included, the list expands significantly to encompass employees, managers, owners, stockholders, as well as other groups that support or depend upon the restaurant, such as restaurant suppliers, food distributors, and so on. Also, other groups may choose not to participate in this practice, for various reasons, or actively organize against it, as in the slow eaters association (an organization I discovered on the Internet).

Innumerable **persons** participate in drive-through restaurants, each one with a distinct story and response to this cultural phenomenon. Factors such as age, gender, race, ethnicity, social class, religion, education, profession all play into individual differences, as do the life experiences and outlooks of persons. The manager of a drive-through restaurant, the owner, the stockholders, the employees, the patrons all bring different outlooks to this phenomenon. Some may be stockholders in the national franchise while others may simply pass through to get coffee on their way to work in the morning. Persons of the culture have a history with the phenomenon and incorporate it—or choose not to incorporate it—into their lives in their own ways.

The **perspectives** that underlie this cultural phenomenon are numerous. A few that stand out are attitudes toward meals and food, perceptions of time, mobility, and values associated with the automobile. The perception of time as a commodity that can be saved, wasted, or spent wisely, as well as the value placed on efficient use of time, are present in the products and practices of drive-through restaurants. The phrase *fast food* carries these and other meanings for members of U.S. culture. At the same time, other communities and individual members of the culture may hold perspectives that oppose fast-food practices and perspectives.

CULTURE AS ICEBERG

To a certain degree, we can articulate many of these perspectives through reflection, drawing on our knowledge of history or traditions. Many other perspectives, on the other hand, remain unspoken, outside our awareness. A common metaphor to illustrate these two dimensions of cultural perspectives is the iceberg (Levine et al., 1987; Weaver, 1993; Brake et al., 1995), where explicit culture represents the tip of the iceberg and tacit culture is all that lies beneath the surface of the sea, out of sight. Imagining the pentad of culture as an iceberg, tacit and explicit dimensions are portrayed in the following diagram:

Figure 3.2: The Iceberg of Culture

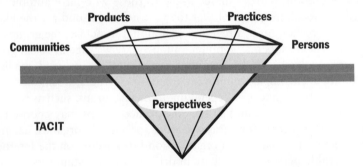

Thus, cultural products, practices, persons, communities, and some perspectives are explicit—visible or tangible—whereas many perspectives are tacit—invisible or intangible.

Language teachers deal with products, practices, perspectives, persons, and communities, particularly as they intersect with the use of language. Seen separately, each of these dimensions constitutes a clear, accessible content area. And when we add language, we provide the means for working with this content through participation, description, interpretation, or personal responses.

By answering the following questions, we can identify the content of the cultural experience we present to learners.

- •What are the key products?

    What are the physical settings, the artifacts, the social institutions, the art forms?

- •What are the essential practices?

    What do people say and do? How do they act and interact with one another?

- •What are the central perspectives?

    What are the underlying perceptions, values, beliefs, or attitudes?

- •Which specific communities are involved?

    What groups participate directly?

    What groups participate indirectly?

- •How do individual persons respond?

    Who are the people that participate?

    What is their personal relationship with this phenomenon?

3.1 *LEARNING CULTURE: ANALYZING CULTURAL PHENOMENA*

The purpose here is to examine the interconnectedness of the five dimensions of culture. Answer the model questions above. Make a list of products, practices, perspectives, persons, and communities for the cultural phenomenon below, using your native language and culture. After completing this, do the same for the culture of a second language that you speak.

- a restaurant
- a musical instrument
- a marriage ceremony
- a mode of transportation
- a game
- a harvest
- a food market
- a concert

What did you notice about your ability to compile lists and make connections?

3.2 *TEACHING CULTURE: GUIDING ANALYSIS OF CULTURAL PHENOMENA*

Present your students with (or elicit from them) a list of cultural phenomena. Have them brainstorm additional ones. Choose one together, and pose the five questions. On the blackboard, write their answers for each question. After all answers are listed, have the students make statements that connect each of the five dimensions. (As an option, have students do this in the culture of their native language first as a point of comparison.) Ask students to make observations about the nature of culture based on this exercise.

The five dimensions of culture present a relatively straightforward construct for defining cultural content. However, as you probably noticed while doing the Investigations, the connections are not always obvious. It can take some effort to identify products, practices, perspectives, and communities of cultural phenomena that we do not know firsthand. Even with phenomena that we do know directly, naming the underlying cultural perspectives can be quite challenging—and limited—if we rely solely on our own knowledge and experience. This kind of cultural description and analysis calls for research outside ourselves. To do this well, we language teachers need to acquire more information about the culture—its products, practices, perspectives, communities, and persons. Maureen McCarthy, a teacher in a class on learning and teaching culture, describes how this can be done.

> I remember the very first day of class. I faced the board where a fast-food hamburger was drawn, and people said what they associated with it. Their ideas were written in categories, some ideas under products, perspectives, and practices. I was amazed that they could so easily be broken up into groups. "Isn't culture some sort of phenomenon that can't be boxed into categories? It's massive, ever changing, and organic, isn't it?!" I thought to myself. As the semester progressed, I realized I was beginning a new awareness. I began to learn that culture is indeed complicated but is not

Maureen
McCarthy

impossible to handle. An ESL teacher and a biracial American woman, I was learning my greatest lesson of culture in a classroom from a hamburger. I have learned how culture is so pervasive yet so implicit that it is not easy to understand or detect.

I will go into my own process of revealing hidden values in a Taiwanese folktale, "The Dried Fish Award." The process involved looking at the obvious/explicit—the products and practices—and then shifting to what is not obvious/tacit—perspectives and values. It is my opinion that in order to really get inside the emic view, an outsider needs an informant who is aware of the values and is able to articulate them, but it is also possible to conduct research and draw from experience with the culture in order to make connections between products and practices, perspectives and values.

Here is the opening of the Taiwanese folktale "The Dried Fish Award." It is from this section that I will illustrate the process I went through to understand the explicit and tacit cultural perspectives.

> Once there was a fisherman named Wen-Cheng who became lost in a terrible storm off the west coast of Taiwan. For many hours Wen-Cheng swirled around and around in his little boat in the fierce winds of the storm. He prayed to Matsu, the goddess of fishermen in trouble, to carry him to a safe harbor.
>
> Matsu felt sorry for Wen-Cheng, and decided to help him. After all, he was a good man, he showed proper respect to his ancestors, and he was fair and generous with all his friends, relatives, and neighbors. As he prayed, the waters suddenly became calm. He found that he had landed in a large and strange port on mainland China!
>
> Wen-Cheng beat his chest in self-punishment because he had forgotten to beg Matsu to carry him home safely, to his own safe harbor. Now he was surely lost. But Wen-Cheng was not in the habit of being unhappy, so he said to himself that he had better go and see the king's palace while he had the chance.

Cynthia Dresser, *The Rainmaker's Dog: International Folktales to Build Communicative Skills.* New York: St. Martin's Press, 1994.

The first and second paragraphs talk about Matsu, the goddess of fishermen. The main character, Wen-Cheng, prays to her to bring him to safety. She responds to him because he is a good man. The reader can visualize a man lost at sea, alone amid a storm, who then prays to a woman god. This is the obvious piece, this is what is explicitly said and done. What I see beneath this is the idea that when one is lost one must not rely on oneself or one's own wits; rather one must pray to another being, another source of power outside oneself. In fact, a superior power exists and is waiting to help those who are in helpless situations. We can go deeper and possibly say that whatever will happen is meant to happen because the fisherman is not in charge of his fate; rather, an outside power determines success or defeat. He can, however, control his situation insofar as he prays. He must also pray to the correct god or goddess, so as a fisherman, he must pray to Matsu.

So what the reader sees is a man lost at sea amid a storm. Beneath the surface are the values and perspectives, which are: relying on your own expertise will not necessarily help you out of a bad situation, you must rely on a supreme power that undoubtedly exists in some form and this supreme power will control your fate; you can ask for help if you pray to her when you are in trouble. Can we go deeper? Yes, we can begin to ask why one masters a certain discipline or trade, like fishing or sailing; are there certain things a person can control? What are they? On the flip side, what things can a person not control? What is beyond the individual's power? What would happen if Wen-Cheng didn't pray? Would he definitely be doomed, or would he have any chance of surviving?

As a teacher it might be interesting to give students this scenario and ask them what they would do in order to help the situation. In an ESL classroom, students may reveal certain values and perspectives about survival, control, and fate when they come up with their own strategies for surviving.

But for Wen-Cheng it is not his past experiences or expertise but Matsu, the goddess of the fishermen, that will save him. Who is Matsu, and why Matsu? Does this reflect a hidden value that religion and faith are more important than the realities of life? What does this reveal? Matsu was a woman who lived between C.E. 900 and 1000 who, when she died, became a deity and is revered for a dream she had where she saved her drowning brother in the sea. She is now one of the most popular gods in Taiwanese temples, but she is only one of many gods who are prayed to. In Taiwan there are three main religions: Taoism, Buddhism, Confucianism. Matsu is one of the deities of the Taoist religion. She is usually portrayed seated, with a red face, eyes looking downward, and wearing a crown. She is not depicted as a fighter or swordsman like some of the other deities found in Taoist temples. She sits solemnly, looking downward.

My relatives in Taiwan are committed to their religion, Taoism, but the elders are the most active participants. My aunts and uncles with their community of Taoists built a mammoth temple on top of a mountain in southern Taiwan. They donated thousands of dollars, cooked and donated bags of food for the workers, and attended classes, meditation, or retreats every Saturday or Sunday.

Religion is an enormous part of my aunts' and uncles' lives. The top floor of my aunt's house is dedicated to remembering ancestors by leaving food and burning incense and ghost money. My aunt, whose knees are swollen from arthritis, climbs the two flights of stairs around sunrise, after lunch, and after dinner to pray at the altar. She stands and then bends her knees on a padded stool and lowers her head to the ground, then repeats this several times. She scuffs her small feet around throughout the day and rubs Tiger balm on her knees but nothing seems to stop her from praying to the gods and remembering her ancestors.

What I'm trying to illustrate is the pervasiveness of faith and praying. It is a part of the home where praying and remembering happens. It does not occur outside the home under the leadership of well-dressed men. My aunt can pray by herself with her own spirituality and faith in her own home. My aunt lays out apples, mangoes, and oranges daily, and burns incense to her deceased husband and other relatives. She burns ghost money, a special paper that is burned and that is believed will go to the deceased so that they have a prosperous afterlife.

On the surface we can see explicit products and practices: praying, altars with gods and pictures of ancestors, fruit, burning incense, bowing to gods in one's own home, burning ghost money, an older woman who has trouble walking yet who kneels on the ground. Beneath the surface are the perspectives and values, which are: Gods have an effect on daily life; people can connect or reach gods and ancestors by performing certain acts; what a living person does can affect a dead person and the living should always remember the deceased (e.g., burning ghost money); people can and should take charge of their own spirituality despite any hindrances (e.g., my aunt's arthritic knees); tangible items have an effect on gods and ancestors; praying now will help in the future.

What I've hoped to capture with my details of the "Dried Fish Tale" from Taiwan is that a great deal of cultural information is embedded within a folktale. I was able to draw from my own experiences in Taiwan, my learning in class, and my mother the informant to make connections between what is practiced and what is hidden. I only looked at the first few paragraphs of the folktale, yet an abundance of related perspectives came out of it. Clearly there are many more that I haven't been able to reveal.

This unraveling of the hidden perspectives is a process involving careful reading. The more times I read the tale, the more I've been able to make connections and reveal what is underneath. Many of these ideas didn't come to me until I went into further depth through discussion with peers. With careful examination and conscious awareness of the etic/emic perspectives, it is possible to reveal that which is hidden.

3.3 *Learning Culture: Analyzing a Folk Tale*

Maureen refers explicitly to products, practices, and perspectives. Less directly, her account also refers to communities and persons. Which communities and persons does Maureen describe?

In the chapters that follow, we will explore each of the five dimensions in greater detail, beginning with an examination of language and its relationship to culture.

Suggested Readings

In *Standards for Foreign Language Learning: Preparing for the 21st Century* (National Standards in Foreign Education Project, 1999), the foreign language teaching profession in the United States charts the course for foreign language education in the United States. In addition to their triangular model for culture, four other areas with strong cultural dimensions are delineated: communication, comparisons, communities, and connections. The Center for Advanced Research on Language Acquisition, (CARLA), at the University of Minnesota has a number of useful resources on culture for language teachers, including an interesting list of various definitions of culture (http://carla.acad.umn.edu/). Another very useful on-line resource for definitions of culture is the web site hosted by Richard Wilk, a professor in the Department of Anthropology at Indiana University; on this site, you can find concise summaries of the many schools of anthropology, prepared by students (http://www.indiana.edu/~wanthro/theory.htm). Roger Keesing (1974) wrote a thoughtful examination of the many anthropological definitions of culture, "Theories of Culture," which helped me begin to sort all this out. More recently, in "TESOL and Culture," Dwight Atkinson (1999) provided a very informative overview of the various conceptions of culture prevalent in the field of TESOL.

4

LANGUAGE-AND-CULTURE

I had crossed the line, and René let me know immediately.
"Attention!" he cautioned, wagging his finger playfully at me, but
seriously, I could tell. We were in the courtyard behind the house, in
the middle of a game of boules. *I had just congratulated him on a*
fine play he had made, knocking my boule *away from* le cochonnet.
My mistake? In my words of praise to him, Tu as bien joué, *I had*
used the tu *form instead of* vous *(the informal "you" instead of the*
formal "you"). Even though I had known René for well over 15
years at that time, he insisted that I use the vous *form with him,*
while he used the tu *form with me. After all, he explained, I was the*
son-in-law, he was the father-in-law. It was the right thing to say.

This lesson on the use of *tu* and *vous* in French is one among many that I've learned over the years. Like all French students, I learned the linguistic forms early on, with all the appropriate verb endings for *tu* and for *vous*, but the lessons on appropriate use, or culture, started with my first encounters with French speakers and have continued to this day. Some may say that this is a relatively obvious example of the intersection of language and culture, but in my experience with French and French speakers, learning the appropriate use of *tu/vous* has been an ongoing challenge of figuring out social relationships in the culture and my place within them. The formulas of formality/informality, politeness/intimacy that I first learned, although useful, have proved too simplistic.

Once, at a dinner party in France with a gathering that included a few French high school teachers, I told them of the difficulty I had in teaching the "rules" of *tu/vous* to students in the United States, since there is no equivalent in English. I asked them all the question, "How do you use *tu/vous* with the students in your classes?" Naively, I expected them to answer with one voice, providing a simple formula that I could pass on to my students. In fact, there was great variation. One said, "I use *vous* with the students, and they use *vous* with me." Another said, "I use *tu* with them, and they use *vous* with me." A third said, "I use *tu* with the students, and they use *tu* with me." All three teachers worked in the same school. When I asked them to explain their answers, all talked about how they wanted to present themselves to students and how they wanted the students to perceive them and their role in the classroom. Each had a different view of these roles and relationships. "So much for the teacher-student formality theory," I thought to myself.

Ironically, during the course of this very dinner party, we had been using *vous* with one another, those of us who had met for the first time. As time passed and as we talked, the ambiance became warmer and more relaxed among us. At some point, I don't remember exactly when, I noticed that everyone had begun using *tu* with one another and with me. I joined in, assuming that we had all now reached the kind of friendlier relationship that called for *tu*. We continued this way right through to the late hour when we all said our goodbyes. By chance, the next morning on my way to buy a newspaper in town, I met one of these people in the street. I greeted her, using the *tu* form. Coolly, she responded with *vous*. The color rushed to my face; I had made another mistake. Obviously, the "now-we-know-each-other-so-we-can-use-*tu* theory" did not apply here.

In this chapter, I examine two dimensions of language and culture: language in the culture, and language in the classroom. I present language from two viewpoints: (1) language as an integral part of the five dimensions of culture; and (2) language to learn culture. In the first, I will show how language cannot be separated from the products, practices, perspectives, communities, and persons of the culture. In the second, I propose that language must be separated from culture in order to learn culture, using the stages of the experiential learning cycle and the cultural knowings as a pedagogical guide.

LANGUAGE-AND-CULTURE

In the culture, the language is literally everywhere. Anyone immersed in the culture sees and hears the language all around. In this context, language and culture are clearly fused; one reflects the other. Recently, language educators have attempted to coin new words to reflect this fusion: linguaculture (Kramsch, 1989; Fantini, 1995), languaculture (Agar 1994), or language-and-culture (Byram and Morgan, 1993). The latter is the term I will use. Language-and-culture conveys both unification and separation. It acknowledges that we can deal with each separately and with both together.

To state the obvious, language embodies the products, practices, perspectives, communities, and persons of a culture. To fully reveal the culture, we must examine the language. Language is a product of the culture, as any other, but it also plays a distinct role. Members of the culture have created the language to carry out all their cultural practices, to identify and organize all their cultural products, and to name the underlying cultural perspectives in all the various communities that comprise their culture. The words of the language, its expressions, structures, sounds, and scripts reflect the culture, just as the cultural products and practices reflect the language. Language, therefore, is a window to the culture. The fact that *tu* and *vous* exist in French, for example, tells us that French speakers need this distinction in their culture. They need it in order to establish roles and maintain relationships with other French speakers, which is crucial to enacting their cultural practices.

To practice the culture, we also need language. We need to be able to express ourselves and to communicate with members of the culture as we engage with them in the myriad practices and products that make up their way of life. Moreover, we need to do this appropriately, using the right language in the right way, according to the expectations of the members of the culture. This is the language of self-expression, communication, and social interaction. It is based on direct experience in the culture and interactions with members of the culture, in all the complexity this entails. For instance, the use of *tu* and *vous*, in terms of practicing a French-speaking culture, quickly becomes more than an interesting fact about French language and culture. Meeting and interacting with French speakers immediately calls for using either *tu* or *vous*, namely, establishing an interpersonal relationship with them. Nothing could be more daunting, especially if there is ambiguity about this relationship.

The following table summarizes how language-and-culture appears in the five dimensions of culture.

Table 4.1: **Language-and-Culture**

Cultural Dimension	The Nature of Language-and-Culture
Products	The language used to describe and manipulate cultural products
Practices	The language used to participate in cultural practices
Perspectives	The language used to identify, explain, and justify cultural perspectives
Communities	The language used to participate appropriately in specific cultural communities
Persons	The language individuals use to express their unique identity within the culture

Language and Cultural Products

The products of a culture range from isolated objects, artifacts, or tools to places, complex social institutions, and other constructions, like art, literature, architecture, and music. To manipulate or use these varied products, members of the culture use language. As a matter of fact, many cultural products—literature, tax codes, telephone directories, operating instructions, passports—consist entirely of language (and the paper they are printed on).

Consider again the products of a drive-through restaurant, where operating a car or handling money do not necessarily require spoken language to enact. Language, nonetheless, plays a critical role. Even though people may drive a car or manipulate currency in silence, we can assume that they learned the use of these products through language. More important, if asked about these products, people are able to describe them and their use through language. They can also describe the history of these products, how they originated and changed over the years. They can make comparisons with other products, as well as relate any particularities of note, even explain their significance in the culture. Moreover, should something unexpected occur with the operation of the car or with the exchange of currency, people rely on language to resolve the matter. And if asked about the role of drive-through restaurants in their lives, people use language to express their experiences, opinions, feelings, concerns, or questions about this cultural phenomenon.

Remember, too, that language is a cultural product in and of itself. Words, expressions, and structures are continually added or discarded. When spoken and written, language takes on tangible and perceptible forms. We can see written language, and we hear language when spoken. These tangible forms, as with any cultural product, can be described through language. Linguists and grammarians have articulated a whole range of terminology to describe language and how it works. Linguistic terms such as noun, verb, complement, alphabet, phoneme, syllable, determiner, relative clause stand alongside linguistic processes such as question formation, subject-verb agreement, pluralization, inflections, and the like. As language teachers, describing language using such terms is our stock-in-trade. We constantly employ metalanguage—the language used to discuss language itself.

Language and Cultural Practices

Perhaps the most obvious use of language in culture occurs in cultural practices. When people come together and engage in cultural practices, they talk. Cultural practices almost always require language, the language of participation. The actions and interactions between and among members of the culture demand speaking and listening and, in literate cultures, reading or writing. The social circumstances, the people involved, the topic, and a number of other factors influence the nature of the language used. The language can be simple or quite complicated, depending on the nature of the practice in question. Say, for example, the social situation is a marriage ceremony, where numerous practices are required, from writing and sending invitations, through welcoming guests, giving and receiving gifts, participating in the ceremony, eating, making conversation, giving public speeches, to leave-takings—to name only a few. To participate appropriately, one needs to say the right words in the right way at the right time.

Language and Cultural Perspectives

Language also reflects and embodies perspectives. We use language to name and understand the perceptions, values, attitudes, and beliefs that govern our way of life. Through language, we make tacit perspectives explicit. We talk and write about perspectives. We read about them. We hear them in exchanges with members of the culture. Words, phrases, idioms, expressions—when we examine what they mean—reveal values, attitudes, and beliefs intrinsic to the culture. American English words (*liberty, competition, teamwork, blues*), if examined, lead to cultural perspectives, as do expressions (*the buck stops here, time is money, one-stop shopping*), and constructions (*S/he, Ms.*) or statements ("Call me by my first name," "I stole home and won the game").

In fact, through disciplines in the field of social science, there is an extensive vocabulary of cultural inquiry and explanation that explores the nature of cultural perspectives, resulting in terminology such as cultural patterns, kinship, proxemics, collectivism, and the like.

Wendy Wen, a Taiwanese ESOL teacher, did an in-depth study of a common U.S. cultural artifact that embodies perspectives: the bumper sticker.

> As an English teacher, when I first came across this cultural phenomenon, I was quite amazed at the efficiency with which bumper stickers convey their various messages in such minimal space and economy of language....Some bumper stickers are straightforward, thus they are easy to interpret. Others can be quite difficult to understand for those who are not familiar with the American cultural context. A few straightforward, easily understood ones read as follows: "Honor Teachers." One can assume that, unlike in

Teachers' Voices

Wendy Wen

some Asian countries, where teachers are highly regarded, in America the teacher's status is relatively low, so this encourages people to honor and respect them. The following is less obvious to the foreign observer: "I is a college student." There is a comically conspicuous grammatical error in the sentence: the verb form should be "am," not "is." But what has poor grammar to do with a college student? Does this suggest the poor quality of a college education or the falling standards of education generally?

The perspectives are indeed embodied in words, phrases, and sentences, but the perspectives are not always immediately obvious, especially to outsiders.

Language and Cultural Communities

When we situate language in specific communities or groups, we see variations in forms, meanings, and use according to these social settings and circumstances. Communities develop distinct language to describe and carry out the particular practices and products associated with their group and its activities. For example, consider all the specialized vocabulary and interactional language used in occupations or professions. Plumbers, veterinarians, carpenters, politicians, farmers, lawyers, and computer technicians all have specialized language that describes the work they do and fits the interactions they have with others in this work.

When combined with cultural practices, communities also define norms for language use. Within groups, roles, relationships, and other social factors influence who speaks, what they say, and how they say it. Appropriate use of language becomes essential. The language forms we use in one set of social circumstances with certain communities are not necessarily the ones we use in others, even though we may be conveying a similar message.

Language and Persons

Finally, language, like culture, is not only collective but also personal. We share it with others in our culture, yet each of us uses language in an idiosyncratic manner, based upon our background, experiences, social groups, our personal outlook, and our identity. Each of us has a unique manner of self-expression in the language—a tone of voice, a certain pitch, a way of pronouncing, an accent, a writing voice, a communicative style, a preference for certain words, expressions, and idioms. We use our own version of language to describe, understand, and respond to our experiences and ourselves.

To summarize at this point, in the culture itself, language-and-culture is embedded in cultural products, practices, perspectives, communities, and persons. One reflects the other, and they are best seen as joined. In the language classroom, however, the circumstances are different.

LANGUAGE TO LEARN CULTURE

Language is the central means of learning culture in the language classroom. In the language classroom, as in the culture at large, the language is also everywhere. You find it in textbooks, audiotapes, videos, books, newspapers, magazines, and in the words exchanged between and among students and teachers. The culture is also present in many of these same materials, especially if they are authentic language material, used by members of the culture.

In the classroom context, however, language and culture tend to be distinct and treated separately. While this perhaps has the disadvantage of providing a incomplete portrait of language-and-culture, the separation also has an undeniable advantage. Language and culture can be separated for pedagogical reasons. First of all, learners do benefit by concentrating only on mastery of linguistic forms; including the cultural dimension could add unnecessary complexity. Second, and most relevant to culture, we use language to learn culture, a separation that helps language learners. The language we use to learn culture is specialized. It is the language of the classroom, where culture is the topic and language the means to comprehend, analyze, and respond to it.

To achieve this, four language functions are needed: language to **participate in the culture**, language to **describe the culture**, language to **interpret the culture**, and language to **respond to the culture**. These four functions mirror the stages of the cultural experience cycle: participation, description, interpretation, response—knowing how, knowing about, knowing why, and knowing oneself. In order to learn culture through experience, therefore, we need to use certain kinds of language at each step along the way.

Table 4.2: Language to Learn Culture

Stage	The Nature of Language
Participation: Knowing how	The language used to participate in the cultural experience
Description: Knowing about	The language used to describe the cultural experience
Interpretation: Knowing why	The language used to identify, explain, and justify cultural perspectives and to compare and contrast these with perspectives from the individual's own culture and other cultures
Response: Knowing oneself	The language individuals use to express their thoughts, feelings, questions, decisions, strategies, and plans regarding the cultural experience

A FUNCTIONAL VIEW OF LANGUAGE

The language to learn culture is based on a functional view of language, that is, its communicative and expressive purposes. H.H. Stern (1983, p. 224) provides a clear and cogent summary of different categories of language functions proposed by five linguists. Carol Orwig (1999) offers useful lists of communicative functions in five topic areas: survival functions, social functions, self-expressive functions, cognitive functions, functions for managing conversations. Her lists are intended for self-directed learners of any language but they are also useful for language teachers looking for lists of functions. The foreign language profession in the United States (NSFLEP, 1999) proposes three central language functions, or communicative modes: interpersonal, presentational, and interpretive. Other useful sources for lists of basic English language-specific functions are Wilkins (1976) and Van Ek and Alexander (1975).

LANGUAGE TO PARTICIPATE IN THE CULTURAL EXPERIENCE

This language derives from the five dimensions of the culture and is represented in the classroom through the cultural experience. The cultural experience, you will recall, can consist of any representation of the culture in which learners engage through listening, speaking, reading, writing, observing, or doing. The culture presented can be products, practices, perspectives, communities, or persons. I will use the term *cultural text* to define any representation of the culture that is presented in the language classroom, be it a reading passage, watching a film, preparing or eating food, participating in a role-play, writing in a language journal, performing a folk dance, singing songs, or listening to a guest speaker or a teacher's anecdotes about the culture.

Consider practices as a cultural text. This features the language-and-culture needed to participate in cultural practices, where people need to express themselves, communicate, and carry out the affairs of their shared way of life. In the language classroom, the language of participation is removed from the cultural context in which it occurs. There are exceptions, of course, but for the most part the language to participate is modified to fit the classroom. It is tailored according to the curriculum, students' background and knowledge, their level of proficiency, and other factors. This language-and-culture is condensed, simplified, excerpted, or otherwise modified so that learners can manage it.

This modification is accomplished through activities that replicate social interactions in the culture—dialogues, role-plays, simulations, interviews, games, or other activities that feature communication in the manner of members of the culture. In addition, other kinds of classroom-based activities incorporate the language of participation. These include activities in which the language is used for self-expression or communication, such as asking questions, giving answers, or discussing what happened on the weekend. Regardless of the activity, in order to master the language of participation, learners need practice in manipulating linguistic forms. This is often best achieved by separating language from culture, especially at lower levels of proficiency.

Again, this aspect of language is commonly referred to as *functions*—language functions or communicative functions. Functions emphasize the purposes that language serves for people of the culture, such as greeting, complimenting, storytelling, or thanking. The specific language that we use to carry out functions depends, of course, on the social situation, the people involved, the topics at hand, and other factors. Knowing and choosing the appropriate language is essential to functions. Keep in mind that verbal language is just one of many means of communication that people use in these situations. Gestures, facial expressions, eye contact, touching, physical distance, silence, and other factors all play an important role in functions, but for the moment, let us concentrate on written and spoken language.

Practices, the social interactions and transactions of the culture, are simply too numerous to list. People are involved in all sorts of activities that require language functions to complete. And as culture changes, new practices are established and others discarded. Linguists have categorized functions using various classification systems, and those related to social interactions of one kind or another apply most to participating in the culture.

Carol Orwig (1999) has developed a list of "social functions" that is particularly useful in mapping the language to participate in the culture. The following chart illustrates her categories, along with some of the functions she lists for each one.

Table 4.3: **The Language of Participation**

Stage	Sample Language Functions
Participation: Knowing how	**Socializing**—greeting/addressing people; taking leave; introducing/meeting people; etc. **Establishing/Maintaining Relationships**—getting to know each other by sharing; etc. **Influencing People**—requesting that others perform actions; requesting/ giving permission; etc. **Giving and Responding to Feedback**—expressing and acknowledging compliments; etc. **Arguing**—agreeing/disagreeing/disputing; persuading/convincing; threatening; negotiating; etc. **Avoiding Trouble**—denying guilt or responsibility; explaining; making excuses; etc. *Orwig (1999)*

The above list is far from comprehensive, but it does suggest the range of communicative functions or acts involved in the language of participation in the culture.

4.1 *Teaching Culture: Identifying Language-and-Culture*

The purpose here is to explore and identify language-and-culture. Use the picture below as the focus for a language lesson. Using your native language, imagine yourself as one of the characters in this social situation. Identify one or more functions needed to carry out the communication called for in this situation. Write a brief dialogue with appropriate statements, questions, answers, or expressions.

Figure 4.1: **Congratulating**

Moran (2001)

Change the social circumstances of this interaction, the new baby scenario, and write new dialogues that are appropriate to these circumstances. For example:

- a husband and wife celebrating the adoption of their child, being congratulated by the grandfather
- a doctor and a nurse holding the baby they just delivered, being congratulated by a colleague
- three childhood friends holding the newborn sibling of one of them
- three family members, each outwardly expressing happiness, but also conveying messages of self-importance, envy, bitterness

Then set these same scenarios within different organized religions. Identify the exchanges that would occur.

What do you notice about the language of participation?

As mentioned earlier, I draw a distinction between language used to participate in the culture and language used to learn the culture. Strictly speaking, participating in the culture does involve using language to learn the culture. Simply by interacting with members of the culture, we learn language and culture. However, the distinction applies when we consider the use of language in the cultural experience and the experiential learning cycle. Participation in this case involves the experience of culture in the classroom, not in the culture itself. From participation in this classroom cultural experience, the subsequent steps of description, interpretation, and response involve an examination of that experience. Because of their differences, each of these steps emphasizes a particular use of language.

BLOOM'S TAXONOMY

Since this examination involves distinct cognitive activities, Bloom's taxonomy of educational objectives is a useful guide. Bloom et al. (1956) list six areas of cognitive learning: knowledge (recall of information), comprehension (interpretation of knowledge), application, analysis (breaking knowledge down into parts), synthesis (bringing together parts of knowledge into a whole), and evaluation (judgments based on a set of criteria). They proposed that these areas be sequenced in increasing levels of abstraction or complexity of thinking. To demonstrate learning in each of these areas, students carry out distinct learning behaviors, which are stated in the form of actions, or, in language teachers' terms, verbs. These verbs can be construed as language functions. Even though the stages of the experiential cycle do not explicitly match Bloom's sequence, the overall direction is similar.

LANGUAGE TO DESCRIBE CULTURAL PHENOMENA

Following the participation phase of the cultural experience cycle, the next stage is to reflect upon that experience and describe the cultural phenomenon. This calls for the language of description. The language of description involves functions that elicit or provide information about cultural phenomena. This can be information about products, practices, perspectives, communities, or people. The essential feature is describing what is observed, either witnessed directly or through texts. The functions range from formal reporting in speech or writing to answering factual questions about a cultural text.

It is important to distinguish the language of description from the language of interpretation. This discipline of separating description from interpretation is a fundamental competence in culture learning, and the language needs to reflect this separation. A useful schema for categorizing the language of description can be found in Bloom's categories of "knowledge" and "comprehension." Also, Orwig (1999) has a category called "cognitive functions" that features the language of description.

Table 4.4: The Language of Description

Stage	Sample Language Functions
Description: Knowing about	**Knowledge**—listing; defining; telling; identifying; shopping; labeling; quoting; etc.
	Comprehension—summarizing; distinguishing fact from opinion; paraphrasing; etc.
	Description—describing who, what, where, when, how, how much, and why (if the reasons are explicit in the event/text); correcting factual errors; etc.
	Cognitive Functions—identifying/seeking identification; defining/asking for definitions; etc.

4.2 *LEARNING CULTURE: DESCRIBING*

Study the picture of the new baby scenario on page 41. Describe this situation, both as portrayed in the drawing and from your own experiences and general cultural knowledge. As you go through this exercise, consciously avoid any tendency to interpret or explain the underlying cultural perspectives. Also resist any temptation to offer your personal opinions or feelings about this cultural practice. Stay with description.

- What's happening in this scenario?
- What happened beforehand?
- What will happen afterwards?
- Where might this scenario take place?

A: Describe this practice in general terms as it is carried out in your native culture. Expand your description to include reference to specific communities in your culture, along with specific products, perspectives, and also how individual persons whom you know respond to this practice.

B: Tell a story about a personal experience you have had with this scenario. Tell it as if it were a journalistic account—just the facts.

What do you notice about the language of description?

LANGUAGE TO INTERPRET CULTURAL PHENOMENA

Functions for this stage of the cultural experience cycle consist of the language used to develop and substantiate cultural interpretations. These interpretations are based on cultural information elicited or presented during the description stage. At this juncture, the topics shift from the concrete of description to the abstract of interpretation, from visible culture to invisible culture, from products and practices to perspectives. These functions thus involve inference, hypotheses, substantiation, justification, comparison and contrast, and other forms of language that link concrete to abstract.

Table 4.5: The Language of Interpretation

Stage	Sample Language Functions
Interpretation: Knowing Why	**Rational Inquiry and Exposition** (Wilkins, 1976) implying; deducing; supposing; conjecturing; assuming; proposing; hypothesizing; generalizing; etc. **Analysis** (Bloom, 1956) analyzing; categorizing; inferring; distinguishing; etc. **Cognitive Functions** (Orwig, 1999) comparing and contrasting; drawing conclusions; making predictions; discussing possibilities and probabilities; etc.

4.3 *LEARNING CULTURE: INTERPRETING*

Return to the picture of the new baby scenario (Fig. 4.1, p.41). Interpret this cultural practice, both as portrayed in the drawing and from your own experiences and general cultural knowledge. Begin with these questions, and add your own.

- What cultural attitudes, values, beliefs, or perceptions are explicitly portrayed in this scene?
- What cultural attitudes, values, beliefs, or perceptions are implicit or suggested in this scene?
- How might participants in this scene differ in their perceptions of this event?
- How do distinct communities within the culture differ in their perspectives on childbirth, birthing practices, birth rituals, or naming ceremonies?
- How do these attitudes, values, beliefs, or perceptions contrast with those of other cultures that you know? Provide information about these other cultures to substantiate your comparisons.

What do you notice about the language of interpretation?

Jaimie Scanlon, an ESOL teacher in Japan, describes how she approaches the language needed for this stage and the next.

Knowing why and knowing oneself are the most challenging stages to reach for several reasons. First, students' ability to communicate what they feel and to hypothesize in the language greatly depends on their proficiency level. My students were around ACTFL Intermediate–Low. They needed more language in the beginning to produce the kinds of statements necessary for a good discussion of the topics. My first couple of attempts at in-class discussions failed because of the students' inability to communicate their thoughts in English. Following that, I presented language for guessing, hypothesizing, and expressing opinions, such as, "It might be…", "Maybe it's because…" "I guess…", "I think/feel/believe/agree/disagree…". This helped a little. After one class, I decided to ask students to finish their thoughts in writing and gave them some guiding questions. The results prompted me to stick to that method of reaching these knowings. Students were much better able to express their thoughts in writing.

Jaimie Scanlon

LANGUAGE TO RESPOND TO CULTURAL PHENOMENA

The language functions involved at this stage all serve to help learners express their responses to the cultural phenomenon at hand. In keeping with the emphasis of this stage, the topic of discussion shifts from the culture to the learner. The learner's world becomes the subject matter. Learners' responses include feelings, opinions, values, beliefs, questions, concerns, or awarenesses, as well as intentions, strategies, decisions, or other plans the learners may formulate as they anticipate further involvement in the cultural phenomenon. Essentially, these functions entail learners' self-expression. The focus is knowing oneself, self-awareness.

Table 4.6: The Language of Response

Stage	Sample Language Functions
Response: Knowing oneself	**Evaluation** (Bloom, 1956) appraising; judging; criticizing; defending; valuing; evaluating; supporting; validating; attacking; etc. **Expressing Emotions** (Orwig, 1999) expressing likes or dislikes; pleasure or displeasure; satisfaction or dissatisfaction; disappointment; fear or worry; surprise; hope; gratitude; sympathy; want or desire; etc. **Expressing/Inquiring about:** intentions; plans; strategies; beliefs; opinions; questions; concerns; values; decisions; etc.

4.4 *LEARNING CULTURE: RESPONDING*

Study the picture of the baby scenario on p. 41 once again. Offer your personal views on this scenario, both as portrayed in the drawing and from your own experiences and general knowledge.

- What thoughts, feelings, or opinions do you have about this cultural phenomenon?
- Describe any personal experiences you have had with this cultural phenomenon.
- Do you share the cultural values, beliefs, attitudes, or perceptions of this cultural phenomenon?
- What more would you like to know or do in regard to this phenomenon?

What do you notice about the language of response?

The language of response also involves the language used to illuminate the process of crossing cultures, whether this be naming and managing cultural stereotypes, contrasting cultural values, or examining the applicability of models of cultural adaptation to learners' experiences. This can be an academic intellectual exercise or, if learners' beliefs and values are engaged, an exploration of emotions.

In an ESOL course that she taught in the United States, Friederike Weiss included the acculturation process (Brown, 1994) as a specific component of her curriculum, which meant teaching the necessary language.

Teachers' Voices

Friederike Weiss

Language skills are part of the culture learning process, so we need to aim for the integration of language and culture learning. Teaching and learning about acculturation involves teaching and learning the language and terms that come with it. Students can expand their vocabulary to learn terms that could help them express their feelings. In order for students to do this, we need to give them the necessary linguistic tools. Therefore, one of the first lessons should be how to express feeling in English. I consider learning to express one's feelings a crucial first step in any classroom, for it signals to students that such expressions are encouraged and welcomed. One way to do this is to brainstorm and elicit adjectives and to create cards with "I feel + adjective" statements, which students can then match with a situation (on cards), e.g., "I feel happy when I talk to my parents on the phone." The cards can be posted in the classroom; whenever the students encounter more adjectives or need to find more ways of expressing feelings, more cards can be added. I found that students responded very positively when I gave them these tools, which again showed me their need and willingness to describe their emotions.

These four functions of language—participation, description, interpretation, response—not only point to cultural content areas (products, practices, perspectives, communities, persons), they indicate language content areas, as well. Specifically, the language of participation requires communicative exchanges and expressions involved in social interactions of participants in the practices in question. The language of description calls for specific vocabulary and expressions related to literal and figurative description. The language of interpretation encompasses the vocabulary and expressions associated with critical thinking or rigorous inquiry into perceptions, values, beliefs, and attitudes. The language of response involves the words and expressions needed to voice one's opinions, feelings, intentions, and other responses to the cultural phenomena under study.

To summarize, language, as a product of culture, is infused with culture. Language-and-culture are two sides of the same coin, especially—and always—when we immerse ourselves in the culture. Each mirrors the other, and one is inseparable from the other—when we are in the culture. Members of the culture use their language to portray their culture, to put their cultural perspectives into practice, to carry out their way of life. Language thus unites products, practices, perspectives, communities, and persons. On the other hand, when we, as language teachers, bring language-and-culture into the second language classroom, it changes. To help learners, we tailor the language-and-culture to be more accessible. This necessarily involves separating language from culture and working separately on the language to learn culture. While there are many ways to do this, the experiential cycle is particularly effective.

Suggested Readings

The National Standards in Foreign Language Education Project (NSFLEP, 1999) proposes a framework of three communicative modes—interpersonal, interpretive, presentational—the language functions that learners need to learn language and culture and to communicate. The book contains lesson plans in Chinese, classical languages, French, German, Italian, Japanese, Portuguese, Russian, and Spanish that show applications of these three modes. One of the most comprehensive and practical resources for teaching and learning language-and-culture that I have found is the Summer Institute of Linguistics (http://www.sla.org). Most of their material is designed for self-study of language and culture but is easily adapted to the classroom.

5
CULTURAL PRODUCTS

*Stepping off the airplane into the equatorial climate, I breathed
my very first impression of Côte d'Ivoire. When I inhaled, the air
smelled different, thicker, more pungent, somehow more fertile,
aromatic. From the airport to the hotel, a spellbinding display of
things assailed my senses. The form and sensation of the seats in the
bus, the sweltering heat, the stampede of odors, the cacophony of
sounds, the blur of sights rushed by as the bus bounced and swerved
toward the hotel. Even though much was similar to my own culture, everything seemed new, different. All the people, with very
few exceptions, were black. Many were wearing western clothes that
I instantly recognized, while others wore garments that I had never
seen before: flowing robes, headscarves, small pillbox hats, skull-
caps. I saw vegetation unknown to me, houses with thatched roofs,
French automobiles. The roadway, instead of being reserved for cars
and trucks, was filled with people engaged in all sorts of activity
alongside the road—walking, stopped in groups at roadside stands,
buying, selling, talking, and, I noticed right away, carrying things
on their heads, things I could never have imagined. A man dressed
in dark shorts and a sweat-stained khaki shirt stepped quickly along
the shoulder of the road, carrying a bicycle perched sideways on his
head, one arm swinging in rhythm with his gait, the other lightly
touching the bicycle frame. As the bus pulled up to the hotel, I
noticed the way the natural vegetation had been landscaped around
the small hotel, how the grass was a species I had never seen before.
The hotel room seemed similar, but the bed, the bureau, the closets,
the electrical outlets were designed differently. I walked into the
bathroom and lifted the seat on the toilet. Suddenly a lizard as long
as my foot lunged out of the bowl, landed on the floor, scuttled up
the wall, over to the open window, and leapt outside into the green
trees and bushes that brushed against the building.*

Products, the visible dimension of culture, are the gateway to the new culture,
the new way of life. They are the first things that greet our senses when we
enter the culture, and the differences stand out. We can see, hear, feel, smell, or
taste these cultural products, the creations of members of the culture. They
range from isolated objects such as trowels, mortar, and bricks to complex constructions such as buildings and neighborhoods and even further to the intricate,
multifaceted systems of social institutions situated within these buildings and
places. Products run the gamut from tools you can hold in your hand to complex material and ideational creations such as law, economics, religion, and art.

In this chapter, I present an organization of cultural products into four categories based on increasing complexity: artifacts, places, institutions, and art forms. Artifacts are situated within places, which are set within institutions, all of which are interpreted through art forms.

Visible cultural products often appear discrete or isolated. However, if we look more closely at them, we see that they are almost always related to other products, and that these collections of objects are ultimately linked to sets of cultural practices, set within specific communities, involving particular persons, and are carriers of meaning—cultural perspectives. Thus, I propose two strategies for examining cultural products: to study their relationship to other products, and to study their connection to the other dimensions of culture—practices, perspectives, persons, and communities.

Figure 5.1: Cultural Products

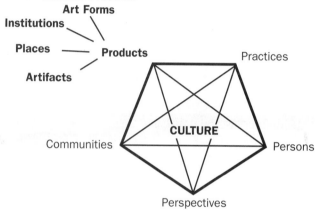

As a rule, products are tangible forms of cultural phenomena, perceptible through the five senses: sight, hearing, touch, smell, or taste. In the case of many cultural products, especially objects and places, this perceptibility is quite obvious. For other products, this perceptibility is not as apparent. The larger systems or institutions that cultures create—politics, economics, education, religion, family—are certainly perceptible in the sense that they have tangible aspects, but they can be quite complex and occur in different physical settings. Take the social institution of education, for instance. There are thousands upon thousands of tangible artifacts associated with this product, from large school buildings and associated facilities in many varied places and locations to other artifacts—such as curricula, textbooks, audiovisual materials, official documents, clothing styles, uniforms, and the like—to the many concrete objects that are found in classrooms and in students' desks.

ARTIFACTS

Artifacts are individual objects created, adopted, or adapted by members of the culture. They are the "things" of the culture, commonly known to language teachers as "realia," "authentic material," and to anthropologists as "material culture." For any culture, the list of artifacts is long.

Many artifacts are unique to a specific culture (such as Nigerian wooden masks, Japanese kimonos, Guatemalan weavings) and not found in other cultures. However, due to trade, emigration, intercultural exchange, conquest, colonization, displacement, and other international interactions, many artifacts are imported and exported among cultures and nations. These are not creations of the culture but are adopted as they are, or are adapted to fit the new culture.

Consider currency—money. All national cultures have bills and coins, making these artifacts similar, yet each nation has adapted them, using different materials of differing sizes, with distinct imprinted or engraved images. Newspapers are another common artifact in literate cultures, but format, content, size, and presentation differ. Or consider footwear, where the basic elements of shoes, sandals, or boots are similar across cultures, but also distinctly different in terms of materials, design, or construction. These differences point toward the cultural practices and perspectives. I remember my surprise in northern Mali when I first saw a pair of leather sandals made by the Tuareg, nomads of the African Sahel and the Saharan desert. Unlike the open-toed design of many sandals, the Tuareg sandal was fashioned with a wide piece of leather attached to the front that looped over the toes. When I used them to walk in the desert, as the Tuareg do, it didn't take long to understand the purpose behind the design: to divert sand from one's toes.

In cases of adoption of artifacts, the cultural aspects tend to lie less with the nature of the artifact itself and more with the ways in which members of the culture use it, in the practices they develop around it and the perspectives that inform these practices. An artifact that appears in one or more cultures, such as the television, is essentially the same product, although there may be superficial differences. Basically, though, everyone recognizes the artifact and its function. Operating the television set is essentially the same. The similarities are reassuring, but they can be misleading, since our tendency is to assume that the members of the other culture share not only the artifact but also our own practices and perspectives related to its use. We assume similarity. In teaching culture, we need to examine the differences. The important distinctions come from the use of television by members of different cultures, through practices. Where is the television set located in the home? Who watches it? When? For how long? What is watched? What kinds of programs are broadcast? What procedures are followed? What role does it play in their way of life? What meaning does it have for them? And so on.

Artifacts, whatever their source, are not necessarily restricted to one place or one set of purposes within the culture. Many, if not most, artifacts can appear in numerous places and social situations. They may be used in the same ways for the same purposes or they may take on a different form and be used for slightly different purposes. Consider the pencil. Small children in school use thick ones. Artists use a variety with different hardnesses of graphite. Architects use mechanical ones. Carpenters use flat ones. Editors use blue pencils. Makeup artists use pencils with washable colors. These varied forms of the pencil reflect different uses determined by occupations.

Artifacts also involve assemblages of objects, like the contents of a tool box, a street vendor's cart, a businessperson's briefcase, a hiker's backpack, a refrigerator, or the articles of clothing and adornment one wears to work.

Each artifact is used in specific ways, and this is essential information. At the same time, as man-made objects, artifacts are involved in various manipulations or transactions. Artifacts are designed, manufactured, bought, sold or traded, maintained, lost, damaged, and so on. Adding to the description of artifacts from these viewpoints expands our knowledge about them and leads to more cultural information. Consider the fact that many French store their wine in the cellar, for example, or that many Americans decorate their automobiles with bumper stickers.

5.1 *LEARNING CULTURE: ARTIFACTS AND PRACTICES*

Choose an artifact from the list below (or another from the culture you teach). Provide a detailed description of the artifact from each of the practices listed on the diagram below. If the practice is not applicable, explain why, and identify other, more appropriate practices for the artifact. Following this, list connections to perspectives, communities, and persons.

Figure 5.2: Artifacts and Practices

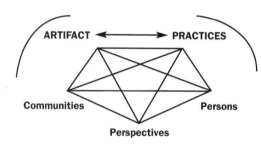

automobile
book
computer
telephone
eyeglasses
dishes
household pet
house
jewelry

making/creating
designing
decorating
buying
selling
trading
losing
using/operating
maintaining
storing
damaging
repairing
discarding
recovering

5.2 *TEACHING CULTURE: ANALYZING ARTIFACTS*

Ask your students to bring in an object from their homes, one of their personal possessions. Put the pentagonal diagram of culture on the blackboard and ask students to describe the object using the four dimensions, following these key questions:

Product: What is it? Where do you find it?

Practices: How do you use it? When?

Persons: Which people use this?

Communities: Which groups of people use this object?

Perspectives: Why do people use this? What significance does it have in the culture?

PLACES

Places or physical settings are also cultural products. Places encompass use or interpretation of the physical features of the natural environment. The ways in which members of the culture integrate or manipulate their environment through shelter, villages, agriculture, and cities also constitute places.

Man-made settings are populated with numerous artifacts, arranged in particular ways within the physical space. The organization, layout, or interpretation of this physical space is a critical feature of places, just as much as the artifacts and their arrangement in these places. A place can be as small as a desktop, a room in the house, a garden, a campsite, or as large as a building, a public park, an airport, a neighborhood, a city, or as vast as a region, or even the country itself.

Investigations

5.3 *LEARNING CULTURE: MAPS*

One useful strategy for examining the cultural dimensions of places is mapping. Aerial views of the place, and including all important objects within the map, provide a visual representation that can lead to an exploration of the artifacts, the activities that occur in the place, as well as the significance of the place itself.

Draw a floor plan of your house, apartment, or residence. Include the objects in the various rooms and label them. Show your drawing to a partner. Describe the rooms and name the objects in them. Explain the use or purpose of each room. Do the same for each object and why it is in a particular room. Make statements about the relationship of objects and rooms based on the above descriptions and explanations. Discuss practices that are conducted in each of the rooms of the house, and identify corresponding cultural perspectives. In what ways is your residence cultural?

In addition to man-made places, cultures also organize or interpret the natural environment. They situate their houses, farms, villages, towns, and cities within this environment. They also put boundaries around certain tracts or features of this natural environment, including geography, plants, and animals. The ways in which members of the culture construct relationships between and among places, natural and man-made, constitute the ecology of their culture.

Bridget Adams (1990), teaching ESOL at the teacher training college in Niger, made use of photographs and postcards that portrayed places and activities in Niger in her conversation and composition classes. Through "photo elicitation" she asked her Nigerien students to describe these photographs and to explain their significance. The students became cultural informants, telling Bridget about the products, practices, and perspectives of Nigerien culture. She chose photos that depicted apparel, facial scarring, nomadic cattle herders, markets, and recreational areas, among others. She describes the results of this inquiry:

Teachers'
Voices

Bridget Adams

The photo elicitation sessions often provoked very emotional responses from the students, especially during discussions on development and changing Nigerien traditions. The students pointed out that "our reality is not the same." As they began to delve more deeply into their feelings and beliefs—something they hadn't done before, especially in a classroom situation—the very bases for their internal struggle came to the surface. They pointed to the scars on their faces and the outfits they were wearing (*pagnes* and *fonctionnaire* suits), as well as the changes they had seen just in their lifetimes, brought about in large part by drought and foreign involvement in the country's affairs. They feared that they were losing their customs and that the traditions that bound them together in separate ethnic groups or as countrymen were being lost forever in the popular rush to be more like people from places they'd probably never visit.

These discussions prompted many of the students to take an in-depth look at their beliefs and at how, as the teachers of Niger's future generations, their beliefs would affect their teaching as well as those they were to teach.

Opportunities for teaching and preserving national customs and traditions, as well as for promoting the value of individual choice and thought, are many. The photo elicitation sessions gave the students a chance to ponder this and to begin to formulate their own teaching beliefs. The work with photo elicitation not only allowed the students time to explore their own cultural identities, it also brought them to a better understanding of their classmates as well as their teacher.

The photo elicitation technique that Bridget describes illustrates how perspectives are embedded in cultural products and how, with a teacher's guidance, members of the culture can bring these perspectives to awareness, and use this awareness to articulate personal responses.

INSTITUTIONS

Cultures create social institutions to deal with "the business of living" (Klopf, 1998, p. 156). These institutions are formal, organized systems that define and regulate the practices of members of the culture. Consequently, these institutions exert a significant enculturating force on members of the culture who participate in them. Politics, law, economics, education, religion, family, or kinship are the institutions most commonly cited, but others include institutions of health, social welfare, and mass media (Stern, 1983), as well as intellectual-esthetic and humanitarian institutions such as leisure and recreation (Nostrand, 1978). Institutions are complex, intricate constructions that comprise multiple products and associated practices and are situated, more often than not, in numerous locations.

Because they tend to govern and structure the activities of the culture as a whole, institutions are intricately linked to practices. Consider the many facets of the political institution of a culture—all the many practices and procedures related to government and governing, from the village to the nation. At the same time, institutions overlap and intersect in complex ways. For example, politics, economy, religion, and family all come into play in matters of education.

5.4 LEARNING CULTURE: FLOWCHARTS

Institutions involve many cultural practices. A strategy for understanding institutions is to list the procedures they require through a flowchart. Flowcharts map the procedures (practices) one needs to follow, from beginning to end. Using your native culture, list the steps for each of the procedures listed below and put them on a flowchart.

- getting a driver's license
- getting medical treatment
- reporting a crime
- establishing a law

- getting married
- getting a bank loan
- religious rituals
- paying taxes

What connections do you see to perspectives, communities, and persons?

ART FORMS

Art forms are complex products that pervade the culture and exist beyond particular social institutions. These include language and its creative manifestations, as in literature. Also in this category are music, dance, painting, sculpture, theater, cinema, architecture, design, decoration, clothing styles, and adornment.

Art forms reflect the esthetic outlook, sensibilities, and philosophy of the culture, and thus enter the territory of cultural perspectives. In and of themselves, such ideas are not tangible; they are mental constructions, inventions, or creations. As such, we can make an argument that they are cultural products. In the intersection of products, practices, and perspectives, esthetics and philosophy represent the gray area where products and perspectives fade into one another, where material culture becomes ideational culture. For example, consider the notion of "style" in clothing or fashion, how members of a culture choose or use their possessions to reflect a certain style or esthetic.

Traditionally, the esthetic and artistic accomplishments of a culture—particularly literature, along with history and geography—are part of civilization courses, a common cultural content area in language courses. Like other cultural products, any work of art can be studied from the five vantage points of the cultural pentad. A literary work—for example, a novel—can be examined in terms of the person of the author, from the cultural communities it reflects or portrays, from the cultural practices it describes, from the cultural perspectives it manifests, and from the relationship of the novel to other cultural products, such as bookstores and libraries.

Gary Allen, a high school French teacher, describes how he dropped a textbook for his Advanced Placement class and devised his own curriculum based on art forms, which he categorized as "the rich tradition of France."

Gary Allen

> This particular French textbook was recommended to me as being very good. It really addressed more about the francophone world than just France, which was interesting to me. But as we were doing it, I found that I was losing a lot of "me" in it. I was losing a lot of creativity, things that I had normally done with these students.

The weekend when I made the decision to drop the textbook, I went home and I said, "If I were an upper-level advanced student of French, what are some things that I would like to learn?" I also asked myself, "What is it about French that is attractive to me?"

So, I made a list. It was very much what I enjoy about French. It was personal contact, the creation of friendships, how I enjoy film, how I enjoy theater, the opera, reading and literature, and cuisine. I figured that, by taking a look at myself and what I enjoy about French, what I enjoy in each of those different realms, it would be a lot easier for me to share it with the students. Since the themes are so general—film, opera, literature, drama, and even cuisine— these are themes in which the French have a very rich tradition. Also, these are themes that the students can actually—hopefully— enjoy and use in the future.

So I took the list to class. I told the students, "I was thinking about your class, and I was thinking about what we're currently doing. This is not something I typically do in the middle of the year, but I want to see what you think. I was thinking about my reasons for studying French, the reasons why I still enjoy it after all these years. These are the things I enjoy about learning French. What do you think about these things? Can you see that my enjoyment of French comes out of the language, but underneath all the aspects of language are these subtopics, these subthemes? These are what they are. Do you see how I can enjoy French beyond the study of language?" They said, "Yes, we can."

Then I asked them, "Is there anything on this list that could apply to you? If you could put yourself in my place, if you had been studying French for 25 years, what might be interesting to you?" They mentioned things like sports—some of them are athletic—and things like that. Then we discussed the questions, "Of all these things, where would you like to go with it? Where would you like to improve? In what areas do you find yourself not having a lot of knowledge?" One topic they mentioned was opera.

Our discussion of opera was very interesting. I said, "I know several French operas. When I went to my very first opera, I didn't have a very good experience of it." They asked, "Why?" I said, "Because I had no concept of what opera was. I remember *La Traviata* in Caen, when I was there. I just didn't know anything about it." We had a nice discussion about how we have a tendency to make things wrong or bad out of our own ignorance, out of not knowing. I told them, "Maybe, if just by doing *Carmen* this year, you gain a little bit more appreciation of what opera is, maybe sometime you'll go see another opera. It might not be a French opera, but maybe just out of the initiation that we'll do in class this year, you'll be a little bit more interested in that, for your life in the future."

To teach these particular products of culture, Gary Allen describes the importance of his personal relationship to them. Is personal relationship to cultural content a factor in your teaching of culture? Explain your answer.

Products, in sum, include identifiable artifacts, assemblages of artifacts, places, social institutions, and art forms. Together, they constitute the visible, material culture, immediately recognizable to visitors. Products lead to practices, communities, persons, and when examined closely, they reveal cultural perspectives.

Suggested Readings

I recommend all of anthropologist Edward T. Hall's books for penetrating insights into tacit culture. In the classic *The Hidden Dimension* (1966), he shows how the construction of places reflects cultural perspectives. Photographer Peter Menzel, in *Material World: A Global Family Portrait* (1994), shows dramatic photographs of families from 30 countries around the world: their homes, and their possessions, situated in their communities, neighborhoods, and villages; his book is a gold mine for examination of cultural products. In "Out of House and Home," John C. Condon and Fathi Yousef (1975) contrast housing structures and activities in the home of five cultures: U.S. American, Japanese, Swahili, Middle Eastern, and German. The process that the authors use to connect products to practices and perspectives is still relevant and instructive (although the content is dated). *The Trans-Cultural Study Guide* (1987) by Volunteers in Asia (www.volasia.org) provides an excellent guide to studying the social and cultural institutions (and practices) of any culture; it's a book of down-to-earth research questions. Based on his years with student exchange programs, J. Daniel Hess (1994) has compiled a wealth of practical experiential culture learning tasks in *The Whole World Guide to Culture Learning*, including "A Plaza Study," "Studying Institutions," and "A Study of Religious Institutions.

6

CULTURAL PRACTICES

One of the most challenging cultural practices I have had to learn—and teach—is the conversational style of the French (and other francophones)—specifically, how they participate in casual conversations or discussions. Their style, broadly speaking, stands almost in direct opposition to the mainstream American conversational participation I grew up with. The first time I encountered this style was at a faculty party in Bondoukou, Côte d'Ivoire. A collection of teachers had gathered at a teacher's home for the apéritif. *The group included a combination of French nationals, Ivorians, a Ghanaian, and me, the sole American. We sat around the courtyard, drinks in hand, nibbling on hors d'oeuvres, and, of course, talking. The conversation was in full force, and it was like nothing I'd ever experienced before.*

I could not follow what was being talked about. Topics seemed to jump from one theme to another, arising from everywhere around me. I didn't know where to put my attention. Everyone was talking at once, except for me and perhaps Kofi, the Ghanaian. As soon as I turned my head to follow what I thought was the thread of the conversation, talk erupted behind me, or to one side or another. People there seemed to be able to listen and talk at the same time, sometimes actually speaking to more than one person at once. I saw absolutely no way to enter the conversation. I heard no hesitations, no moments of silence. The direct questions I awaited to bring me into the conversation were never asked. Nursing my drink, I sat silently, nodding, showing attentiveness and interest, feeling intensely uncomfortable.

At that time, I concluded that my French was simply not fluent enough, and that I needed more work on vocabulary and listening comprehension. Eventually, after becoming more proficient in the language and encountering many more such conversations, I realized that it was not really a matter of speaking French, but rather a matter of knowing how to speak like the French. Language was only one part of this cultural practice.

Cultural practices comprise all the actions that members of the culture carry out as part of their way of life, including language. These can be silent, solitary activities, such as preparing breakfast, doing household chores, taking a siesta, or walking the dog, as well as highly interactive exchanges with other people, such as negotiating a purchase price, making conversation over a meal, participating in formal meetings, or gossiping. In addition, there are collective tasks, such as organizing and carrying out a parade, a criminal investigation, a concert, or a civic demonstration. These actions involve people engaged in communication, giving and receiving messages, transacting meaning, achieving ends. Practices, as with products, are infused with perspectives. The kinds of practices cultures employ and the way people enact them embody their cultural perspectives.

In this chapter, I present a framework for organizing the practices based on their inherent structure and features. As language teachers, if we emphasize language for communication, we are necessarily involved with cultural practices. Practices call for the language of participation in the culture—to do as those of the culture do.

Figure 6.1: Cultural Practices

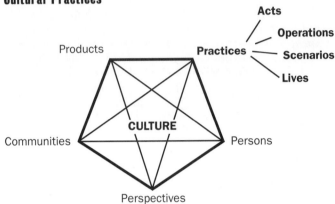

The term *practices* includes these cultural concepts: customs, traditions, folkways, or everyday culture (small "c" culture). Practices tend to be ritualized and follow an established series of steps—sometimes explicit, sometimes not. Almost always, practices involve language, products, specific social settings, and people. In highly ritualized practices where certain procedures must be rigorously followed, such as playing the national anthem, swearing in witnesses in a trial, or participating in a folk dance, we might even consider these practices as products. Indeed, taken to an extreme, certain practices can be seen as an art form, as in an athletic performance, an intellectual debate, a public speech, a play, a dance, or a song. However, even ritualized practices such as these are organized within larger sets of practices or contexts, which are also part of the cultural picture.

ACTION CHAINS

One useful approach to mapping practices is to examine their structure, how they are constructed. Sociolinguists, interculturalists, and anthropological linguists have all examined practices from a structural standpoint. Not surprisingly, in their examination of practices, linguists and sociolinguists tend to emphasize language—speech, to be exact—as the central feature of these practices. They categorize speech practices as "speech acts" (Chaika, 1994) set within "speech events," which are in turn set within "speech situations" (Stern, 1983, pp. 222–23). Looking beyond language, E.T. Hall proposed a scheme called "action chains"—"established sequences of events in which one or more people participate—and contribute—to achieve a goal" (Hall and Hall, 1990). Hall did not draw a distinction among action chains, and his examples run the gamut from "greeting people" to "floating a stock option" (ibid., p. 24). This concept is similar to the notions of scripts and schemata (Chaika, 1994), scenarios (Palmer, 1996), frames (Agar, 1994; Tannen, 1986), or social episodes (Lustig and Koester, 1999).

All these various views hold that there is both an expected set and an expected sequence to cultural practices. In other words, practices are organized and implemented in preordained ways according to the expectations of members of the culture. They involve a linguistic dimension (written or spoken language), an extralinguistic dimension (paralanguage and nonverbal language), manipulation of products, and specific social circumstances, and often occur in particular physical settings or places.

6.1 *LEARNING CULTURE: WRITING INSTRUCTIONS FOR PRACTICES*

Investigations

List the steps in inviting and receiving guests in your home (in your native culture) as if you were writing instructions for a visitor from another country. Number each step and underline those that must be performed in the proper sequence (or at the same time). Once you complete this, review the steps and identify the kinds of dialogues or communicative exchanges that would take place for each step.

Do this exercise again for another culture that you know, or interview someone from another culture about this practice. Compare the steps, the sequence, and the communicative exchanges. What connections do you see to products, perspectives, communities, or persons?

A structural approach to practices allows us to dissect them into their component parts, but language teachers need additional ways of approaching the complexity of cultural practices. We need to be able to distill practices into accessible cultural content areas, a way to distinguish greetings from floating stock options. We can begin by considering different kinds of action chains, different ways of organizing cultural practices.

I propose the following framework for practices: operations, acts, scenarios, and lives. In a nutshell, *operations* describe practices that involve manipulation of cultural artifacts. *Acts* are specific communicative functions with both linguistic and extralinguistic features. *Scenarios* are practices enacted in specific social situations, involving operations, acts, and other sets of specific practices. *Lives* are sets of practices organized by individuals through the way they live their lives in the culture. For example, a significant part of the cultural life of an automobile mechanic involves scenarios associated with the work of fixing cars: interacting with customers, salespeople, coworkers, superiors and subordinates, parts distributors, not to mention following certain procedures for diagnosis and repair. Within these scenarios, the mechanic needs to be able to carry out acts such as explaining mechanical problems, requesting payment, defending the work done, thanking customers, and so on. Participating in the practice of auto mechanics also entails many operations where mechanics manipulate tools and other artifacts, from socket wrenches to invoices.

Figure 6.2: Operations, Acts, Scenarios, Lives

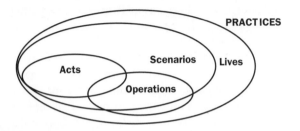

OPERATIONS

Operations involve **manipulation of cultural products** by individual members of the culture. For the most part, the interaction is between a person and the product, and often does not require language. Operations can be conducted apart from scenarios, as solitary practices, like tending a garden or cleaning a room. Operations are negotiations of the material world of the culture, carried out in an appropriate manner. They include practices such as manipulating eating utensils, making a sandwich, operating a vending machine, riding a horse, using a video camera, decorating a room, shopping at the market, changing a flat tire, putting on makeup, preparing meals, playing the guitar, or filing a tax return. Operations also include avocations or pastimes: fishing, hunting, gardening, photography, painting, and the like.

6.2 *LEARNING CULTURE: OPERATIONS*

The word "operation" comes from a language teaching technique originated by Ray Clark (1980), where the procedures for manipulating artifacts become the basis for language (and culture) lessons. For one of the operations listed in the paragraph above, write a set of procedures. Repeat this process with another operation that is specific to the culture you teach, such as preparing meals, doing folk dances, calligraphy, or the like. How does this operation reflect the culture?

ACTS

These action chains consist of **ritualized communicative practices** involving other people. Language—verbal and nonverbal—is essential. Acts are usually brief utterances and responses that consist of established language expressions and accompanying nonverbal language, although they can also be entirely nonverbal. Language teachers know these as functions or as speech acts. Examples are greetings/leave-takings, expressing enjoyment, making/declining invitations, thanking, requesting clarification, asking for the price, complimenting, reprimanding, teasing, and so on. Acts, along with operations, are the building blocks of scenarios. Ultimately, all acts need to be situated within scenarios.

Answer the following questions using your native language. After you've finished, do the same in your second language. What cultural comparisons can you make?

A. List as many different statements as you can to express the act of expressing thanks.

B. List as many different gestures or body movements you can also use to express this act.

C. List combinations of language and body movements to express thanking.

Scenarios

Scenarios are **extended communicative practices** that involve a series of interactions, including operations and acts. They are scenarios in that they follow an expected sequence of practices within particular settings and social circumstances. They can be relatively simple, with clear boundaries, as in buying a train ticket, making a telephone call, or conducting a job interview. Scenarios can also be more complicated, with a number of sequenced exchanges and practices, such as going through immigration and customs, participating in a wedding, putting on a school play, or buying an automobile. They can also be even more complex, involving numerous practices, communities, and products over extended periods of time, such as teaching a course, running a business, caring for the aged, building a subway system, conducting a military campaign, instituting educational reform, or governing a country.

Scenarios, therefore, are not isolated or discrete sets of practices, but tend to be situated within broader networks. Because they are embedded in social settings and circumstances, one way of categorizing scenarios is from the viewpoint of social situations. There are many possible viewpoints, but I will propose five types of scenarios: time-based, event-based, group-based, institution-based, life-cycle-based.

These categories are not necessarily mutually exclusive, but are simply viewpoints. While many scenarios may be unique to a particular category (such as testifying in a trial—institution-based, or naming ceremonies—life-cycle-based), many more can appear in any or all of these categories. The scenario of a birthday celebration, for example, can be seen from multiple viewpoints, each of which defines the scenario differently. These multiple viewpoints ultimately expand our understanding of the scenario and the culture.

Time-based Scenarios

Practices are organized in time. By arranging practices according to time—hours, mornings, afternoons, evenings, days, weekends, weeks, months, years or other chronological measurements, like seasons—scenarios are grouped and given meaning. As with all practices, these scenarios often take the form of routines—sets of predictable and expected practices that are consistently repeated. Examples include scenarios related to agriculture—planting, weeding, watering, harvesting, storing; the academic year—registration, orientation, classes, vacations, examinations; weekly or daily routines—mail carriers, homemakers, secretaries.

Figure 6.3: Types of Scenarios

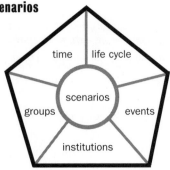

The important distinction is that time is the controlling element in the scenario. That is to say, the procedures in the scenario depend on changes in time. Admittedly, this can be somewhat confusing, since all scenarios unfold in time; however, many scenarios depend on the passage of time in order to occur.

Event-based Scenarios

Practices are also organized through events. These events are usually restricted in time, with clear beginnings and ends. Countless scenarios can be classified as events, ranging from holiday celebrations to automobile accidents, political rallies, sporting events, dances, or burglaries. Event-based scenarios, if they involve several participants and many cultural communities, necessarily involve different perceptions of what occurs. The case of the celebration of a national holiday in a small town, for example, might consist of a number of events, some sequential and others simultaneous, such as parades, public speeches, musical performances, banquets, and fireworks displays.

Group-based Scenarios

Practices are organized through social groups or communities. Members of particular groups have identifiable sets of practices that they enact as part of the activities and purposes of their group. Groups are many and varied, including those related to occupation or profession, age, region, religion, ethnicity/race, gender, personal interests, or other formal or informal associations. Consider the scenarios that members of a particular family carry out as they go about their daily lives, such as earning a livelihood, maintaining a home, raising children, preparing and sharing meals, socializing, participating in leisure activities, and enacting other traditions or customs that are part of their way of life.

Institution-based Scenarios

Practices are organized through social institutions. Members need to enact certain scenarios to participate in these formal, organized systems of the culture. These include systems and institutions of education, politics, economics, religion, as well as health and welfare and communications. Consider, for instance, all the scenarios associated with entering another country: going through customs and immigration, including those special scenarios when something goes wrong, such as not having a visa, losing one's passport, or not declaring imported goods.

Life-cycle-based Scenarios

Practices are organized through perceptions of the life span, from birth to death—and even beyond. There are scenarios associated with birth, infancy, childhood, adolescence, adulthood, old age, and death. Such scenarios take their definition from the various life stages, as defined by the culture. Many cultures mark passages from one stage to another with certain scenarios. Take the infirmity that comes with old age as an example, and all the scenarios associated with caring for elders, or involving them in the affairs of the community. Or consider childhood and the games, chores, or other scenarios associated with raising children or with being a child in a particular culture.

6.4 *LEARNING CULTURE: MAPPING SCENARIOS*

Most scenarios can be examined from many points of view. Consider a marriage ceremony, which can be time-based, life-cycle-based, event-based, or institution-based, depending on how you choose to perceive it. Using the semantic map below, list the operations, acts, and accompanying scenarios that comprise a marriage ceremony in your culture of origin. Repeat this exercise with other scenarios. What do you notice about the process of analyzing scenarios from multiple viewpoints?

Figure 6.4: Semantic Map of Scenarios

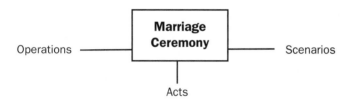

6.5 *TEACHING CULTURE: WRITING SCENARIOS*

Scénario means screenplay in French, and this is one useful way of presenting cultural practices. First, ask students to brainstorm the possible practices, using a semantic map. Then have them write a screenplay for a five-minute scenario of a marriage ceremony, using one of the options described above. Have them research the scenario and identify setting, props, characters, plot, and dialogue, complete with nonverbal behaviors. After they have written their scenario, have them perform it.

LIVES

If culture is a way of life, we can benefit from looking at lives, **stories of members of the culture**, through biography and drama. These stories provide a means of bringing together practices as individuals or groups of people have lived them. Operations, acts, and scenarios are grounded in individuals' experiences in specific communities. Biographies can offer important insights into the historical dimension of cultural practices, how they might have changed over a lifetime. These can be historical lives, biographies of people in the past, or biographies of the living—actual people. Or they can be fictional lives portrayed through literature, drama, or film. Drama has the advantage of showing the interactions between characters based on specific social circumstances that mirror the way of life of a particular culture.

Tae Kudo, a Japanese teacher in a U.S. high school, uses film as a means of showing cultural practices and perspectives in her Japanese classes. The life of the main character in one film and the events in his fictional story illustrate how practices can be organized through lives.

Tae Kudo

I showed my novice Japanese class the film *Shall We Dance* (in Japanese with English subtitles), and we used it to explore Japanese values and compare them with U.S. values. It's about a Japanese man who decides to take dance lessons. He lives the life of a Japanese businessman, and he feels that there is something missing. On his way home one day, he sees a dance instructor through his subway window; she looks so unreal and pretty that he decides to take a dance lesson. As he goes to dance lessons, he gets involved in dancing itself—not with this woman. He doesn't tell his wife or family about this. His wife suspects that he is having an affair and hires a private detective to find out what her husband is doing. When she discovers that he is taking dance lessons, she doesn't say anything to him. They eventually have to face the situation, and they come to an understanding.

To me, this film highlights many Japanese behaviors that are interesting points of comparison for my American students. The husband took dance lessons, which is quite unusual in Japan. Also, the husband did not share this with his family, which is not unusual in Japan. The wife did not directly ask her husband what he was doing and instead hired a private detective. The wife did not tell her husband or ask him directly about the dancing lessons once she found out. Other behaviors I focused on were the relationship between the dance teacher and the students, relationships among family members, relationships among coworkers, Japanese attitudes toward a person who is different or does something different, and how the direction of Japanese people's lives is already decided, just like the railroad cars on a train. These behaviors show differences in values.

Students had difficulty with the fact that in Japan one doesn't necessarily share many things with one's family. The Japanese attitude of not wanting to stand out or be different from others and to instead try to be the same as others was hard for them, too. Also, they couldn't understand that many Japanese men are more focused on their work than on their home life—and that Japanese women seem to accept this. Finally, the students didn't understand the importance Japanese place on not having eye contact when they are having an argument.

Ask students to describe a marriage ceremony that they have attended (possibly their own). Have them describe what happened, using operations, acts, and scenarios. When they finish, ask them to explain the significance of this ceremony to the lives of the participants they know. Have them tell about the meaning of this ceremony in their own lives.

As described, practices can be categorized in the above ways, but there is more to take into account—namely, doing them. What does it mean to participate in cultural practices? This brings up the task of participation in the manner that members of the culture expect, in the ways that they themselves participate in cultural practices.

FEATURES OF PRACTICES

Many analyses of culture examine the forms we use to communicate. These features of practices appear in many texts on intercultural communication (Samovar and Porter, 1998; Lustig and Koester, 1999; Dodd, 1998; Ting-Toomey, 1999). To enact practices, one must manipulate linguistic and extralinguistic features, which are summarized in Table 6.1 below.

Linguistic

Linguistic features obviously include speech and script, but they also involve more than oral and written language. Social interactions include all the vocalizations that accompany spoken words, phrases, and sentences. Silence, pauses, and hesitations are also part of the linguistic dimension, since they are defined in relation to speech.

Language

Language teachers know well this dimension of practices: syntax, lexicon, phonology, and the many forms they take in different social situations.

Paralanguage

Paralanguage is the term that describes all sounds that affect the speech utterances themselves, such as pitch, tone of voice, rate, and volume. It also includes other vocalizations that parallel or punctuate speech, such as coughs, laughter, sighs, gasps, groans, hemming and hawing, swallowing, throat-clearing, whistling, tongue-clicking, humming, sniffing, and the like. Other examples of paralanguage include the use of onomatopoeia—words invented to mimic sounds such as bow-wow, moo, whoosh, blam, boing, rata-tat-tat, wham, and interjections or exclamations including ouch, oops, oh, psst, hey, whew, etc. (Damen, 1987, pp. 166–69).

Extralinguistic

The extralinguistic dimensions of practices, in addition to actions and behaviors associated with manipulation of products, involve many forms of nonverbal communication.

Table 6.1: Features of Practices

Linguistic	written language	script	• syntax • vocabulary • pronunciation, accent
	oral language	phonology	
	para-language	voice	• tone • volume • pitch • rate of speech
		vocalizations that accompany speech	• interjections ("ouch," "oops," "psst") • onomatopoeia ("bow-wow," "bam," "whoosh") • coughing, laughing, gasping, whistling, groaning, humming, sniffing, swallowing, throat-clearing, tongue-clicking, etc.

APPROPRIATENESS

Extralinguistic	kinesics	body movements	• facial expressions • gestures • posture • gait
	oculesics	eye movements	• eye contact • winking
	haptics	touching	• hands • lips • arms
	olfactics	smell	• body odor • use of perfume, fragrances
	proxemics	use of physical space	• distance between people • positioning of people
	chronemics	how actions occur in time	• polychronism—many at once • monochronism—one at a time • synchrony—coordination of actions in time
	context	the role of social situation	• low context—directness in speech (more explicit) • high context—indirectness in speech (more tacit)

Kinesics

The use of the body in cultural practices includes many dimensions beyond the movements connected to spoken language and social interactions, such as gestures and facial expressions. Kinesics also involves how people carry themselves and how they move. Demeanor, posture, gait, stance, and seated and reclining positions are also part of body movements.

Oculesics

Eye behaviors include eye contact, gaze, blinking, winking, glancing, squinting, and other eye movements that are used in cultural practices.

Haptics

Touching behaviors involve certain parts of the body and include aspects such as duration, intensity, and frequency.

Olfactics

Odors are also part of practices, whether they are natural body or environmental smells or fragrances that are fabricated as cultural products.

Chronemics

The use of time, chronemics, plays into actions and speech in many ways. If practices are sequences of events or actions, then the nature of the sequence itself reflects concepts of time. Do events or actions occur sequentially or simultaneously? Are they separate or overlapping? Are there clear beginnings and ends, or are they blurred? E.T. Hall (1983) proposed the notion of monochronism and polychronism to describe the relationship of practices to time. He proposed that cultures can be categorized along a continuum between these two poles. In very simple terms, these poles run from doing one thing at a time to doing many things simultaneously.

For instance, the French style of conversation tends toward the polychronic. This is what caused me difficulties when I first experienced it at the faculty gathering in Bondoukou. My monochronic outlook and practices did not mesh with the polychronic practices of that conversation. People were not doing what I tacitly expected from a conversation: one person talking at a time, taking turns, allowing people to finish, creating pauses, asking questions to engage people. What I took for outright interruption of another's speech in French was in fact a form of overlapping, which for a brief moment meant that two or more people were indeed talking at once.

In addition to these two poles of time, Hall (1983) also proposed the concept of synchrony. Through synchrony, members of a culture coordinate their actions and speech in time. When members are in sync, or in interlocking rhythms with one another, the practices unfold in concert, as expected. When participants are out of sync, awkwardness and misunderstandings occur.

When I teach greetings in French to beginning-level students I present the language forms as well as the gestures, handshaking, and *la bise*, kissing on the cheeks. Once students have gained control over the language and the gestures, respectively, I ask them to put everything together. The task is one of synchrony, since in French greetings (as in all languages) you talk and do at the same time.

The challenge lies in coordinating your words and actions with those of the person you're greeting in a seamless, rhythmic fashion—the way that native French speakers orchestrate speech and movements.

Proxemics

The use of space or spatial orientation in cultural practices is commonly known as proxemics (Hall 1966). Space is most obvious in the cultural setting itself, where products occupy a particular space by virtue of their design and construction, as in the case of buildings. Products also occupy space in relationship to one another, as in the layout of buildings and structures in a downtown area or in the arrangement of furniture and other artifacts in the rooms of a house. In terms of practices, however, proxemics relates to the physical positions that people take in relationship to one another as they participate in practices. Do they face one another? Are they side by side? How much space separates them? Does this distance remain the same throughout the practice, or does it change?

6.7 *LEARNING CULTURE: PROXEMICS*

With a colleague, stand facing each other about ten feet apart. In unison, taking one step at a time, walk toward each other. Pause for a few seconds before taking each step. As you proceed toward each other, carry on a conversation about the weather or another everyday topic. Continue in this way, talking and stepping, until you are almost touching one another, then stop. (If, at any point along the way, either of you feels uncomfortable about continuing, stop.) After stopping, share your observations and feelings about space that this exercise generated. What can you say about your culture?

Another feature of practices relates to the degree of explicitness of the messages conveyed. To what extent do the words convey all of the message—literally, in no uncertain terms? Or to what extent do the words (if there are any) suggest, imply, or refer to the intended message?

CONTEXT

E.T. Hall (1977) proposed the notion of **low context** and **high context** to differentiate between two ends of a continuum. On one end are low-context messages, where the context or situation plays a minimal role in the communication. Low-context messages are explicit, direct, and conveyed primarily through spoken language. ("It's cold in here. Would you please turn the thermostat up to 74°?") High-context messages are on the opposite end of the continuum. They are implicit, indirect, conveyed primarily through the context or the social situation. (In silence, one person shivers slightly and glances quickly at an underling, who immediately turns up the thermostat to an understood setting.) Hall cites numerous examples that illustrate these two extremes. Low-context messages include communication between two U.S. trial lawyers in the courtroom or two politicians drafting legislation. High-context messages, in Hall's examples, are the unspoken messages expressed and understood by twins, or by people who have extensive networks with others, where the circumstances of the social situation carry the messages.

Another way of looking at the low-context/high-context distinction is to see messages in degrees of explicitness, from explicit to tacit, direct to indirect. Seen this way, some practices require greater explicitness or visibility in the messages, meanings, or understandings, whereas others call for less. In other words, low-context practices like courtroom exchanges or air-traffic control tower communications require explicitness. High-context practices like folk dancing, buying and selling at a cattle auction, or learning through apprenticeship may call for more tacit messages.

The following diagram illustrates how perspectives, underlying meanings, and messages are more tacit in high-context situations and more explicit in low-context situations.

Figure 6.5: Context in Practices

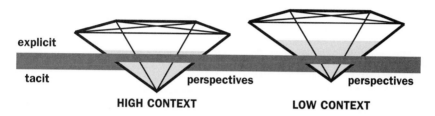

Looking exclusively at the linguistic dimension in terms of high/low context leads us to degree of directness in language, an important feature of practices. In direct communications, people tend to say what is on their minds and to mean what they say, to "tell it like it is." In indirect communications, people tend to not say what is on their minds and to rely more on suggestion and inference. Craig Storti (1999) offers a useful comparison of interpretations of the same language items by speakers from direct and indirect cultures. When direct communicators say "yes," for example, they are conveying agreement, approval, acceptance, or understanding. When indirect communicators say "yes," however, they are expressing politeness and respect and acknowledgment of having heard what the other has said.

A common cultural misunderstanding in language classes involves conflicts between direct and indirect communication style. Tom Kuehn describes a situation where he expected Mexican and Korean students in his ESL class to ask questions in class when they needed clarification, a classic form of direct communication.

> I was frustrated with a low-English-level Korean student who never asked questions in class. My goal was to equalize classroom participation, and one aspect of it was to have students ask questions when they didn't understand something during class. I taught techniques of how to ask a question, which the students from Mexico readily adopted, but not the Korean student. At the end of the course, I interviewed the Korean student (with a translator) and learned, in her culture, that asking questions in class is an insult to

Tom Kuehn

the teacher. Furthermore, she reported, "To learn English one must listen very carefully to the teacher and study hard after class." Through interviewing her, I realized that she was being a good student by not asking the teacher a lot of questions. She could work hard with the homework to grasp a concept she couldn't get in class. Numerous questions would show a disrespect for the teacher. Listening to the teacher is a sign of a good student. There is also the concept of losing face if one is seen as not knowing something the teacher is talking about. It reflects on the student, who must not have studied enough. I realized that I hadn't addressed the underlying values of her culture or mine, and that just teaching techniques wouldn't produce the behavior I was hoping for.

Tom Kuehn's account shows, again, how practices are intimately linked to perspectives. It is not simply about learning how to formulate questions in the new language and observing others perform this practice in class; it's about recognizing that there are cultural perspectives attached to these practices and that these need to be named as well to help students learn to participate appropriately in practices.

Appropriateness

A critical feature of practices is appropriateness, or doing and saying the right thing at the right time in the right way. Knowing what to say and what to do depends on a number of factors, all related to the social situation and the people involved. Not observing the agreed-upon procedures in the proper sequence causes misunderstanding, even conflict. Saying or doing the right thing at the wrong moment, or the wrong thing at the proper moment, also provokes problems. For instance, I have consistently blundered when it comes to *la bise*, kissing the cheek in greetings or leave-takings in France. I know that I need to *faire la bise*, and I know how to do it. However, I'm not always sure how many times to do it—two, three, or four. In fact, one of my exasperated French relatives still announces to me beforehand how many times I should kiss her on the cheek (twice). This does ease some pressure to do the right thing, but at the same time, I'm reminded that I still haven't got it figured out.

Valerie Hansford describes the challenges of teaching the cultural practice of apologizing in a foreign language context: ESOL in Japan.

Valerie
Hansford

I teach a required course in ESOL to non-English majors at a university in Japan, and I am required to use the resources selected and/or approved by the program and department, including texts. I am limited in many ways by the textbook. In this particular textbook, there were a number of communicative aspects (complaining, making requests for personal possessions, etc.), but I chose the function of apologizing to give a specific focus, and also because the manner, style, and timing of an apology varies from culture to culture.

I designed a unit on apologies that spanned four 45-minute lessons and focused on both language and cultural objectives. The primary language objective was the difference between the meaning of *because* and *so*, in the context of apologizing. ("I'm sorry. I'm late because there was a train accident" or "I'm sorry I'm late, so I'll come early tomorrow and help you set up the desks.") Cultural objectives included identifying similarities and differences between Japanese and North American styles of apologizing, including when to apologize. We also explored appropriate nonverbal behaviors for each of the styles.

I started to observe both in class and out of class that the "when," or timing, of the apology was also a factor. As the students and I worked through the unit, I learned more about the Japanese cultural aspect of apologizing as well as the styles of a few other Asian countries. (In one of my classes there were six international students.) I also discovered that there are times when my students would use the apologizing form that I had labeled "North American style," but they told me that their parents might not use that form in the same situation.

The most challenging aspect is having students work with "knowing why": to explore the reasons for North American or Japanese apology styles. It is difficult to get students to understand that the objective is for them to make their own guesses and/or share their ideas rather than to know the "correct" answer. This is especially challenging in this academic setting in Japan where students are hesitant to stand out and generally want to "know" the correct answer before being willing to answer. Two ways I found to address this were: (1) having students work in small groups and then presenting their group's ideas; and (2) having the students write their ideas for homework by giving them specific questions to address. I am still working on ways to address this challenge as I feel that this is an important area for students to develop and/or broaden their critical thinking skills and because it is an important element in the experiential learning cycle.

The reality is that there are very few opportunities for the students to have experienced the cultural element that I'm focusing on and thus they cannot talk about any previous experiences. Also, once students have learned about/how/why, they have very limited opportunities to use it outside of class. Even so, after completing the unit, the students demonstrated a clear understanding and awareness of the different apology styles. Before class started for the day, in fact, when students came to tell me why they had been absent or that they hadn't completed the homework, they would do so in one of the two styles studied. Other students who were in the room at the time would shout "Ah, Japanese style" or "Ah, North American style". The same occurred after class if a student was late. In effect, the students were making conscious choices in how to apologize.

Sociolinguists have developed various systems for analyzing the language of social interactions (Chaika, 1994). I find that the simplest strategy for identifying the factors that determine appropriateness is to use the journalistic approach: asking the key *wh-* questions.

Table 6.2: Questions to Determine Appropriateness in Cultural Practices

Who?	Who are the persons involved in the practice? How many are they? What roles do they play? What is their relationship? What status do they have?
What?	What topics or messages are expressed or exchanged? What are the tacit messages? the explicit messages?
Where?	Where does the practice occur? What is the place? The physical setting? The social circumstances or situation?
When?	In which season, year, month, week, or day does this occur? At what time of day or night? Which events or circumstances immediately precede this? Follow this?
Why?	What explicit purposes do people bring to this practice? Why are they interacting? What are their shared intentions? What tacit intentions or purposes do individuals bring to this practice?
How?	How is the practice enacted? What are the key features? What kind of language is used: verbal, nonverbal, spoken, written? Eye contact? Touching? Use of space and distance? Silence? What is the style of communication? Formal/informal? Direct/indirect? Serious, solemn, ironic, comic?

6.8 *LEARNING CULTURE: DETERMINING APPROPRIATENESS*

To explore the implications of appropriateness, use the following illustration of an act. Identify the language for each exchange, based on your native language. Write these questions or statements down. Then use the wh- *questions in Table 6.2 above to create situations, roles, messages, and so on. Having specified these scenarios, identify the linguistic, paralinguistic, and extralinguistic forms needed to enact the scenario appropriately. Repeat the exercise by answering the journalistic questions in a different way in order to involve different people and social circumstances. What do you notice about appropriateness?*

Figure 6.6: Avoiding Unwanted Attention

Moran (2001)

Practices encompass a vast cultural expanse. Virtually anything or everything that members of the culture do or say falls into this territory. By conceptualizing practices as predictable sequences of actions—as operations, acts, scenarios, and lives—we can analyze and organize them in language-and-culture lessons.

Suggested Readings

Chaika (1994) has written a highly readable and informative introduction to the field of sociolinguistics, *Language: The Social Mirror*, which addresses the linguistic component of cultural practices. Deborah Tannen has written a number of books that describe gender differences in language, such as *That's Not What I Meant!* (1986), with the implication that men and women comprise distinct cultural communities with different communicative practices. She also points to differences in direct and indirect communication between men and women. E.T. Hall's "Map of Culture" in *The Silent Language* (1959) is a helpful comprehensive matrix of categories of cultural practices. More recently, Donald Brown (1991) in *Human Universals* makes a convincing argument for the commonalities of cultural practices; in his chapter "The Universal People," he lists many practices that all cultures have in common. Even though he didn't intend it for language teachers, it is a very useful reference. In *Figuring Foreigners Out* (1999), Craig Storti outlines an excellent series of practical culture-general exercises in a workbook format that contrast many aspects of intercultural communication practices, such as directness/indirectness, low-context/high-context, and other generally tacit features of cultural practices.

7

CULTURAL PERSPECTIVES

Il n'est pas propre? My French sister-in-law's question floated in the air. I pretended not to hear, waiting for my wife to answer. She was asking about our two-and-a-half-year-old son, who had just scampered by her, chasing a ball on the beach in Normandy. I wasn't exactly sure what she was asking. He isn't clean? What could she mean by that? When my wife answered, it became clear. It was about the diaper he was wearing, and the fact that he was not yet toilet trained. Wasn't he getting a little old for diapers? This conversation, and the implication that our American toilet training practices were somehow inadequate, bothered me. I knew there were cultural differences in play, but the only explanation I could come up with in the moment was a simplistic notion about informality, or different traditions. Truthfully, I was struck more by how bothered I was. My emotions were triggered, and I couldn't figure out why.

Later, I came across a comparison of the differences between French and American child-rearing practices (Wylie and Brière, 1995). In the authors' view, the French perceive that humankind—all people—contains both good and evil, and that children therefore need the guiding hand of rational adults in order to prepare them to participate properly in society, to bring out the positive in them and to control their innate negative tendencies. Children must follow the rules, so to speak. Americans, in contrast, tend to view humankind as basically good, and are consequently more tolerant of children finding their own way, learning from mistakes, trusting them to do what is right.

What helped me most in this comparison was the realization that the fundamental differences in views between my sister-in-law and me could be explained in terms of cultural perceptions, that these perceptions were submerged deep within, and that it was not really a matter of right and wrong between the two of us. I question whether I could have come to this understanding by relying on my own experience. I needed others' views.

Practices, products, persons, and communities embody cultural perspectives, and vice versa. Perspectives are the explicit and implicit meanings shared by members of the culture, manifested in products and practices. These meanings reflect members' perceptions of the world, the beliefs and values that they hold, and the norms, expectations, and attitudes that they bring to practices. To name the perspectives that underlie practices is to answer the question, "Why do the people of this culture do things in the way they do?"

In this chapter, I examine the nature of cultural perspectives. I present perspectives as a combination of perceptions, values, beliefs, and attitudes, as explicit and tacit, as emic and etic. I also propose three different orientations to perspectives, or views of culture: functionalist, interpretive, and conflict.

Figure 7.1: **Cultural Perspectives**

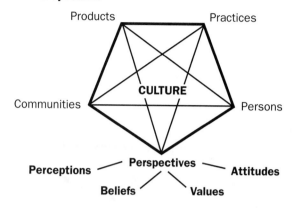

EXPLICIT AND TACIT PERSPECTIVES

Like the other dimensions of the cultural pentad, perspectives can be tangible. Perceptions, beliefs, values, and attitudes can be explicitly stated in oral or written form. These explicit perspectives are expressed through sayings, proverbs, creeds, proclamations, myths, mottoes, principles, guidelines, mission statements, scholarly studies, cultural studies, or other explicit forms of expression. These overt perspectives, the shared public outlooks, guide practices.

As an example, consider the perspective of "the American Dream"—a cultural perspective that reflects a **belief** that anyone can achieve fame and fortune in the United States through hard work, self-reliance, and sacrifice. This belief is based upon **values** of equality, individualism, achievement, competition, and materialism. These values, in turn, derive from a cultural **perception** that people possess free will, and can control their destinies and the environment, and that the future is more important than the past. **Attitudes** of competitiveness, ambition, determination, self-centeredness, and resilience follow. Accordingly, U.S. culture has many practices that reflect the pursuit of the American Dream, including establishing certain relationships, developing a career, and acquiring wealth, status, or respect. Products accumulate with such practices: possessions, goods, capital, status, and recognition.

Many explicit perspectives are found in the history of a culture and in social and cultural studies and commentaries. The histories of political, economic, religious, educational and other formal institutions both reflect and propagate cultural perspectives. For example, the belief that "every man is presumed innocent until proven guilty" pervades the judicial system in the United States, and has its origins in the American Revolution as a conscious response to the political institutions in Europe. Likewise, U.S. history books are filled with stories of "self-made men," "rugged individualists" who "pulled themselves up by their own bootstraps," "left their pasts behind," and went from "rags to riches" to attain the American Dream, "proving," in effect, that "God helps those who help themselves." (Depending on the Americans you talk to, this perspective may be seen as myth or reality.)

7.1 *LEARNING CULTURE: EXPLICIT PERSPECTIVES*

Research the following explicit perspectives from these different cultures. Use reference materials or find an informant, a native of that culture or someone who knows about it. Find out what the perspective stands for and how it is reflected in cultural products, practices, communities, or persons.

Sanuke (Thailand)
Panache (France)
Filial piety (China)
On (Japan)

Perspectives are thus explicit, but at the same time they can be tacit, or outside awareness. Members of a culture carry out practices, but when asked to explain them, they often cannot specify why they engage in these practices; they frequently reply "That's just the way it is," or "We've always done it this way." This is not to say that people are unable to specify perspectives, but rather that people tend not to be aware of them. They take them for granted. The maxim "If you want to know about water, don't ask a fish," often used in intercultural circles, makes this point.

Even though most cultural perspectives are tacit, they can be brought to the surface and made explicit, as anthropologists, among others, have demonstrated. It can demand a significant effort to uncover the tacit perspectives that govern practices. While this discovery is possible, it is questionable whether all tacit perspectives can in fact be surfaced. Some (or many, who knows) remain imprinted in the depths of our reptilian and mammalian brains, beyond the reach of language.

7.2 *LEARNING CULTURE: PROVERBS*

Examine the following North American proverbs to identify underlying cultural perspectives and, from there, practices. In your examination, follow this sequence:

- list as many meanings as possible;
- for each meaning, give concrete examples from the culture;
- describe situations in which you have used this proverb or heard others use it;
- following these concrete illustrations, confirm the original meanings or add new ones;
- state whether you personally hold the meanings of the proverb.
    Time is money.
    Cleanliness is next to godliness.
    The early bird catches the worm.
Repeat this exercise with proverbs from other languages and cultures.

CULTURAL VALUES

In the fields related to the study of culture, there are numerous views of the content and nature of perspectives. They are variously referred to as meanings, attitudes, values, ideas (NSFLEP, 1999); beliefs, values, thought patterns (Weaver, 1993); values and assumptions (Althen, 1988); values, beliefs, attitudes, assumptions (Damen, 1987); cultural patterns (Stewart and Bennett, 1991); perceptions, values, attitudes, belief/disbelief systems (Singer, 1987); value dimensions (Hofstede); and value orientations (Kluckhohn and Strodtbeck). Many terms are the same, although they are sometimes defined differently.

PERCEPTIONS, BELIEFS, VALUES, AND ATTITUDES

I have listed perspectives as consisting of "perceptions, beliefs, values, and attitudes" (Samovar, Porter, and Stefani, 1998). I present each of these as a discrete aspect, because, to a certain extent, they can be examined independently. More often than not, however, they intertwine and overlap, making it difficult to separate them. For this reason, others have grouped them as patterns, systems, or orientations. Despite the overlap, I believe that the distinction is useful. I define these terms as follows:

Table 7.1: Perceptions, Beliefs, Values, Attitudes

Perceptions	What we perceive, what we ignore; what we notice or disregard
Beliefs	What we hold to be true or untrue
Values	What we hold to be right/wrong, good/evil, desirable/undesirable, proper/improper, normal/abnormal, appropriate
Attitudes	Our mental and affective dispositions—our frame of mind, our outlook—charged with feeling or emotion

Placing these aspects along a continuum from tacit to explicit, we have perceptions on one extreme and attitudes, visibly manifested in practices, on the other.

Figure 7.2: Tacit and Explicit Perspectives

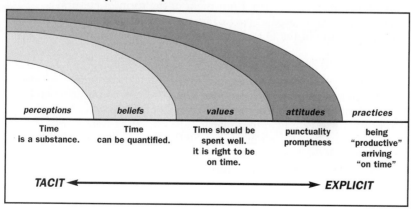

Using the notion of time as an illustration and reading the above diagram from right to left, perspectives move from explicit to tacit, observable to invisible. At the most explicit level, perspectives are expressed most often as feelings that are associated with attitudes, revealed in the words or deeds of practices. For the most part, these feelings are either positive or negative ("This person is not arriving when I expected. I feel OK about this" or "I don't feel OK about this"). The attitudes enclose values, which can be made explicit ("I don't feel OK about this, because it's not right for someone to do this; a normal person wouldn't do this"). Values are closely linked to beliefs, what we hold to be true or false, which also can be made explicit, with reflection. ("I believe that time is precious. We should spend it well, and not waste it. We only have so much available.") Beliefs are based on perceptions, and these are almost always tacit, although they too can be brought to awareness, upon reflection or research. ("I perceive time as a substance, as material; it can be measured, quantified, and handled like any other commodity").

Issues related to time, especially punctuality, illustrate the explicit and tacit nature of perspectives. If I'm waiting for someone to arrive at a prearranged time, I begin to feel vaguely uncomfortable as the expected hour passes. The more time elapses, the more irritated I become. It takes conscious effort to remind myself that my perception of time and the beliefs and values associated with it are in full force. I tell myself that I need to drop my belief that the person I await possesses deep, irreversible character flaws. To move through the emotions and attitudes to discover values, beliefs, and perceptions takes work, especially if the emotions are strong. Strong emotional reactions generally signal that an important cultural perspective has been touched, called into question, or threatened in some way.

Joe Barrett, high school Spanish teacher, describes a critical incident experienced by one of his students during an exchange program, where values, emotions, and behaviors intersected and clashed.

Teachers' Voices

Joe Barrett

Our school offers a term abroad in the Dominican Republic, where students have homestays with Dominican families. Their experiences in these families and in other situations outside the family inevitably lead to cultural conflicts. We ask students to write them up as "critical incidents" and bring them to class for discussion and analysis. Later in the term, I put them in the form of cultural assimilators to be used as part of final exams as well as materials for orientation of the D.R.-bound group the following year.

Here's one critical incident written by "Mary" about her sister Luz:

"I brought a Sony Walkman and three of my favorite tapes with me to the Dominican Republic because I like to listen to music when I go on long trips. The other day, when my homestay sister Luz asked to borrow my Walkman to do her English listening homework, I said yes because I wasn't using it at that moment. Later that night, I saw her with the headset on, the Walkman in her hands, and she was dancing *merengue*. She returned the Walkman to me that night but every day since then, she takes the Walkman to listen to music. What bothers me is that she doesn't even bother to ask; she just takes it without my permission. I would loan it to her sometimes but the way it's going, the batteries will soon run out and I won't be able to listen to music on the trip this Sunday. What should I do?"

The conflict here is a difference in cultural values and beliefs. In the beginning, Mary didn't realize that her Dominican sister saw her as a member of the family, literally. As a member of the family, in the Dominican view, family possessions are shared by everyone. Luz was acting as most Dominican sisters would in borrowing without asking every time.

Once Mary understood that there was a different way of looking at this, she became more accepting. However, she still experienced the same frustration when this happened again. Even though she understood what was going on, Mary still couldn't really accept the behavior. She had to find ways to cope with her own emotional cultural reaction as well as her practical problem (the batteries running out). In the class we discuss a variety of options to clarify the cultural element in all this as well as to avoid the unpleasant conflict if possible.

7.3 *LEARNING CULTURE: FINDING CULTURAL PERSPECTIVES*

Joe Barrett mentions one difference in cultural perspectives in the conflict Mary experienced. What other contrasting cultural perspectives may have caused this conflict?

WORLDVIEW

One way in which perceptions are commonly described in cultural studies is as "worldview." Literally, worldview is what it suggests: perceptions of all that surrounds one. Worldview is varyingly defined as a belief system (Dodd, 1998), a fundamental cognitive orientation (Palmer, 1996), a reality set (Gee, 1990), and an orientation toward such philosophical issues as God, humanity, nature, the universe, and the others that are concerned with being (Samovar, Porter, and Stefani, 1998). The assumption underlying the notion of worldview is that of a unified, shared outlook on the world. Worldview is used most often to describe the fundamental perceptions shared by members of a culture. Perceptions, in other words, are the organizing element in culture. Beliefs, values, attitudes, practices, and products follow. Perhaps the most obvious illustration of worldviews is religious institutions. Religions propose perspectives on humankind, deity, nature, and the universe. These views engender beliefs, values, and attitudes, which are manifested in the sets of specific practices developed by members of the religion. If they adhere to these practices, members will lead a proper way of life.

EMIC AND ETIC PERSPECTIVES

When discussing perspectives, we need to recognize that there are two kinds: emic and etic (Damen, 1987). **Emic perspectives** are those articulated by members of the culture to explain themselves and their culture, while **etic perspectives** are those of outsiders to the culture who use their own criteria to explain the others' culture.

Etic perspectives include those of visitors to the culture, the criteria they use to describe and explain what they encounter, as well as categories for cross-cultural description and analysis established by anthropologists and other cultural researchers to describe many cultures. At one end of the continuum, etic perspectives consist of simple explanations from one's own cultural background. This is a common reaction to cultural phenomena—explaining them in terms of perceived similarities or differences to one's own culture, better known as *ethnocentrism*. At the other end of the spectrum, etic perspectives consist of categories that can be used to describe any and all cultures. Some of these categories are drawn from notions of cultural universals and read like the table of contents of introductory cultural anthropology textbooks. They reflect cultural practices and products: institutions like family, kinship, economy, leisure, music, or government. Other etic classifications come from theories of cultural perspectives: value orientations such as individualism/collectivism, low-context/high-context, polychronic/monochronic, and the like.

Etic perspectives, therefore, provide frameworks to describe, analyze, and explain a culture from the outside. Each etic category carries assumptions about the nature of culture, and it is important to bring out these assumptions.

Emic explanations are perspectives that members of the culture use to describe or explain their own way of life. These perspectives do not necessarily correspond to etic categories, nor does the terminology that the members use for their explanations. When asked, members may easily express the reasons for cultural products and practices. Or, given that many fundamental cultural perspectives are outside awareness, like the submerged bulk of the cultural iceberg, members may have difficulty finding words to fully explain them, just as I had no explanation on American toilet training practices.

Parfait Awono illustrates the insider/outsider perspectives on the same touching behaviors seen from two different cultures, his native Cameroon and the U.S. students in his French class.

Parfait Awono

In my French I class, we were reviewing greetings. After the usual *bonjour, salut,* etc., I introduced handshaking. I asked them how often they shake hands with their friends. The answer was rarely to never. I then explained to them how friends in Cameroon would shake hands several times during the same day. Whenever they would meet, they would shake hands. Students said they would really be uncomfortable to be touched. We explored the possible reasons why Cameroonians shake hands so much, with the main one being the limited personal space people allow themselves in Cameroon.

To make things worse, I told them that friends, brothers, sisters walk hand in hand—literally—in Cameroon, without that having any connotation. When they heard this, most students were shocked, except for a Korean-American student. He said that on a trip to South Korea he noticed people holding hands everywhere, and he thought everybody was gay. He said he refused to hold hands with his cousins, and they thought he was just a weird American kid. Students admitted they'd try holding hands only if they had to.

As a Cameroonian living in this country, I have noticed that people in the United States don't touch each other a lot. The rare occasions that I have observed people touching others are when expressing approval or satisfaction for a job well done; a tap on the shoulder (usually from a superior/coach, etc.); when sealing a deal (handshake); for a farewell (hug); friends giving each other a hug to comfort one another. I have also observed that holding hands occurs in the following situations: parents hold younger kids when crossing roads; lovers hold hands as a sign of intimate affection. Although not explicit, when two individuals of the same gender are seen holding hands, people in this country always consider them love partners.

In view of the unfortunate and biased negative perception of gay and lesbian life in many American cultural circles, students do not want people to think they are gay or lesbian. The issue of use of personal space also comes into play here. In general, people in the United States need a large personal space. Touching infringes that freedom.

My goal was to show students the different interpretations the same personal behavior can have according to cultures. One behavior can be marked in one culture and unmarked in another. I wanted to stress the fact that people in Cameroon are closer, and they tolerate being touched by and touching acquaintances. I think my students became aware of the difference. I hope that if they ever find themselves in Cameroon or surrounded by a bunch of Cameroonians, they'll remember that shaking hands is OK and even expected, and that holding hands does not mean people are intimate. Lovers in Cameroon seldom hold hands! I don't recall seeing my own parents holding hands, let alone showing any other sign of affection to each other!

So hopefully my students will not say "Gross!" or "That's gay!" when they see such behavior in a Cameroonian setting, or even in a Korean one, as we learned from the Korean-American boy.

7.4 *LEARNING CULTURE: ETIC AND EMIC PERSPECTIVES*

Review Parfait Awono's account and identify the emic and etic perspectives. Based on the cultures you know, what other perspectives (emic or etic) can you add to the touching behavior he describes?

Etic Perspectives: Perceptions

It is a daunting task to identify the perspectives of a culture. Fortunately for language teachers, anthropologists, interculturalists, and others have devised frameworks for examining cultures. These frameworks, because they apply to all cultures, are examples of etic perspectives.

A number of models of etic perspectives are prevalent in the field. In essence, these models presume that there is a finite set of realities that all cultures must address. These realities are part of the human condition. Different cultures perceive these realities in distinct ways. These distinct perceptions, in turn, lead to different beliefs, values, attitudes, and practices—in a word, to different worldviews. For example, a fundamental reality of the human condition is nature. Therefore, a basic etic perspective is the perception of humankind in relationship to nature. Do the people of a culture see themselves in control over nature? Or do they see nature as controlling them? Each of these perceptions will lead to different values, beliefs, attitudes, and practices. By determining how cultures perceive this and other aspects of the human condition, we are able to identify worldviews.

For models of etic perspectives, see Appendix A, p. 157.

The models of etic perspectives are thus very useful in attaining cultural understanding. These models include perceptions of humankind, humankind and nature, time, activity, social relationships (Kluckhohn and Strodtbeck, 1960); perceptions of self and others—"individualism/collectivism" (Hofstede, 1984); perceptions of uncertainty—"uncertainty avoidance" (Hofstede, 1984); perceptions of inequity—"power distance" (Hofstede, 1984); "masculinity/femininity" (Hofstede, 1984), and others.

To summarize at this juncture, cultural perspectives are both explicit and tacit. Members of the culture have their own explanations, emic perspectives. Outsiders bring etic perspectives, their own ways of explaining others' cultures using criteria that they apply to all cultures. The interplay between emic and etic perspectives is crucial to cultural comparisons and to cultural understanding. The central challenge in this process is to make tacit perspectives explicit.

VIEWPOINTS ON CULTURAL PERSPECTIVES

Once these emic and etic perspectives are brought to light, however, there is still a significant obstacle in the pathway to cultural understanding: point of view. To illustrate this obstacle, let me describe a research task I assigned to a group of language teachers.

Their task was to research the culture surrounding football at a nearby high school. We all attended a game on a windy, frigid night in October and observed the action that unfolded, on and off the field of play. From this observation, the teachers decided on persons to interview about football. They supplemented their interview findings with readings and discussions, and attempted to make explanations about U.S. culture based on their research. The task was to discover and articulate cultural perspectives, using the framework of products, practices, communities, and persons.

The teachers chose a wide variety of involved people to interview: coaches, players, parents, a referee, pep band members, student bystanders, even a radio announcer at the game. As the teachers shared their results in class, an intriguing picture began to appear. Informants, members of the culture, expressed some shared perspectives on football, which was to be expected. However, divergent, even conflicting, views also emerged.

Band members were critical of football and the amount of money that the school devoted to this sport at the expense of other extracurricular activities for other students. Some disliked the attitude of certain football players and the status they enjoyed in the school as they walked down the halls. One coach talked about the importance of character-building, teamwork, discipline, achieving goals, and learning other lessons for responsible adulthood, which were secondary to football itself. The only female member of the football team saw her task as one of achieving equality with the boys, gaining acceptance. A teacher/coach recognized the inherent contradiction of valuing the physical violence of the game and educating for citizenship at the same time. One student cared little about the game and was only interested in the event as an opportunity to socialize with friends and to meet girls. A parent saw the competition as a necessary evil, something that her son would have to do if he was to succeed in life after graduation from high school, even though she disliked the aggression of football and worried about her son getting hurt.

This posed a dilemma for many of the language teachers, who did not know how to resolve this multiplicity of perspectives. Americans seemed to hold different perceptions, values, beliefs, and attitudes about the cultural practice of football. What was the "American" perspective on football? What was the answer?

Part of the difficulty in determining such a unifying perspective is that there are many points of view, multiple perspectives on the nature of culture. Earlier, I described an examination of cultural anthropology that I carried out and the many schools of thought, or theories of culture, that I encountered. Although there are many differences among these various schools, they differ most significantly in the area of perspectives. That is to say, these schools offer different explanations of cultural meaning—the perceptions, values, and beliefs of the culture. These varied explanations can be abstract and philosophical. For example, cultural materialism holds that the values members share derive ultimately from the economic realities of their culture, whereas structuralism maintains that culture consists primarily of the myths created by members of the culture and the duality of mental constructs such as raw and cooked, male and female. How to reconcile such points of view?

Understanding perspectives, in my opinion, represents the most challenging aspect of teaching culture. The task, simply put, is to identify the perceptions, values, beliefs, and attitudes of the culture. However, culture consists of numerous communities, all coexisting under the umbrella of a national culture. These communities, in theory at least, share common perspectives. In fact, by its very nature, the national culture presumes such common perspectives. In practice, on the other hand, these various communities often hold different perspectives. Some of them are in opposition—sometimes in open conflict, as in pro- and anti-abortion communities, pro-environment and pro-development groups, criminals and police, or vying political parties.

It boils down to this: Cultural perspectives depend on your point of view. I'm using point of view literally, in terms of how you choose to view cultural perspectives. Given shifting points of view, how can language teachers hope to offer accurate explanations of cultural perspectives?

THREE POINTS OF VIEW ON CULTURE

The working solution I propose is to present alternative viewpoints as part of knowing why, or discovering interpretations. Although there are many viewpoints and theories of culture, I will reduce these to three broad approaches (adapted from Martin and Nakayama, 1997) to explaining cultural perspectives: the **functionalist view**, the **interpretive view**, the **conflict view**. In simple terms, these can be defined respectively as culture as a unified whole, culture as distinct communities, and culture as a competing communities.

Figure 7.3: **Three Points of View on Culture**

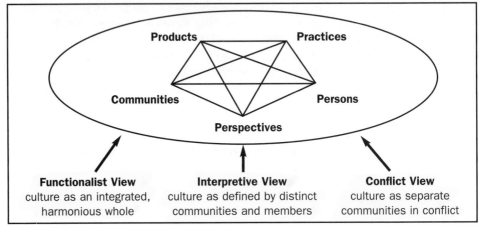

THE FUNCTIONALIST VIEW

The functionalist view takes the broad view of culture, most often at the national level, using the nation as the focal point. Drawn from social science theory, it assumes a national cultural community, a national way of life. This perspective holds that a society constructs systems or structures—institutions— to ensure the harmonious functioning of that society. Accordingly, the institutions of the culture establish the key products, practices, and perspectives of the culture as a whole, as the following diagram illustrates.

Figure 7.4: **The Functionalist View of Culture**

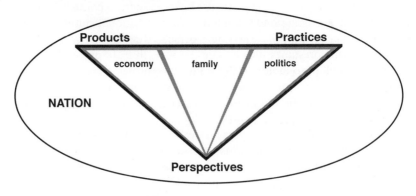

The functionalist view pertains at the most general level, culture and society at their broadest—what tourists or visitors are likely to encounter, such as an experience with the educational system, involvement with the laws and government, encounters with the health care system, participation in the economic system, and the like. The functionalist view assumes that the culture is an integrated, harmonious whole, and that it tends to be static. There is also an assumption of peaceful coexistence, of resolution of conflicts for the common good. It is at this level that politicians talk about "the people"—an appeal to those who supposedly constitute the heart of the culture, or to that dimension that unites all members of the culture.

Even though the functionalist view bypasses the existence or role of other communities within the culture, it does address a common question that arises in culture learning. This question is about national culture. What makes the French French? Mexicans Mexican? Italians Italian? And so on. Broad generalizations about the way of life apply to this national community. We have to assume that there is something that all members of any national culture share, to varying degrees, by virtue of having participated in its social institutions. The history of a culture or nation, particularly in terms of its political, social, and economic development, reveals much of its cultural perspectives. The functionalist view, in effect, is the culture that dominates most language/culture textbooks and materials.

Also, most of the etic perspectives discussed earlier tend to address the functionalist view; they are often applied to national culture. Applying these etic perspectives to the national culture leads to generalizations like these: "Americans tend to be individualists, monochronic, low-context, future-oriented, activity-oriented, informal, and tend to value equality;" "Japanese tend to be collectivist, high-context, being-oriented, formal, and tend to value hierarchy." Similarly, the notion of worldview is often presented at the level of the national culture community; hence it supports a functionalist view of culture.

In the case of the high school football study, the functionalist point of view would seek to identify the broad national culture perspectives and determine where and how they are reflected in this microcosm of the larger culture. The belief that sacrifice, hard work, competition, and teamwork make for success, for example, would be used as a predictor of the perspectives held by all those associated with the sport in the high school.

Key Questions

- What are the cultural perspectives portrayed in the institutions of the culture?
- How are these perspectives reflected in the cultural phenomenon under study?
- How are these perspectives reflected in groups or communities?
- How are these perspectives reflected in individuals?

7.5 *Learning Culture: National Characteristics*

Find a source that describes the "national characteristics" (See Brake et al., 1995) of your culture of origin. Being honest, apply each of these national characteristics to yourself to see which ones are relatively accurate. Apply these characteristics to members of your family or others you know from your culture. To contrast this, find a source of characteristics from another national culture and apply these to yourself. What observations can you make about the functionalist view?

The Interpretive View

The interpretive view assumes that cultural meanings or perspectives are defined by the members of the culture in the circumstances in which they find themselves, either as individuals or as members of communities. Since many communities comprise a culture, there are an equal number of cultural perspectives. The interpretive view does not address the notion of a national culture community. All culture, in the interpretive view, is local (Geertz, 1973).

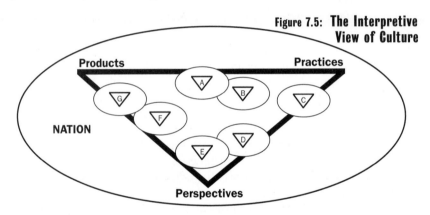

Figure 7.5: The Interpretive View of Culture

The interpretive view places great emphasis on the emic perspective, the insider's view, and assumes that this is the view that matters most. Insiders are exactly that: those who are members of the communities in question. If members of the national culture are not members of a particular community, they are not really insiders of that community and are not in a position to offer views on behalf of that group.

In the football research project, taking the interpretive point of view would assume that each of the groups associated with the phenomenon of football has a valid perspective. The band members have their view, just as the players, the coach, the referees, the booster club, families, or others do. It is the perspective that the participants in the phenomenon bring that matters. In fact, the interpretive point of view presumes that there will be multiple perspectives, as many as there are participants.

Key Questions
- What are the groups or communities involved in this phenomenon?
- How do the participants in these groups or communities view the phenomenon?
- How do individual participants view the phenomenon?

7.6 *Learning Culture: Interpreting Communities*

Draw up a list of a few groups or communities of which you are a member. For each community, describe an event sponsored and carried out by its members, including yourself. Compose a brief speech in which you briefly recount this event and explain its importance to this community and to you as a member. Work with a colleague. Deliver your speeches to one another, and then ask each other questions about the perspectives held by this community and their manifestations in the event. Following these interviews, compare the perspectives of your communities. What observations can you make about the interpretive view of culture?

THE CONFLICT VIEW

The conflict view puts the emphasis on the communities that make up the culture, particularly on their interactions with the core culture and its institutions and among themselves. Although this view accepts that each community has its own perspectives, it does not assume harmonious relationships among them. To the contrary, it assumes that these groups are in competition or conflict with one another, vying for influence, power, or control. The conflict view perceives power as the central feature and views culture as a place where struggles for power among communities are played out.

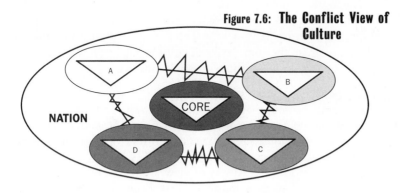

Figure 7.6: **The Conflict View of Culture**

The **core culture** is the community that controls the institutions of the society. Microcultures, cocultures, or other cultural communities consist of groups of persons who possess distinct sets of practices and perspectives. They participate in the core culture yet their perspectives come into conflict with those of other communities in the culture. This view underscores the dynamic, evolving nature of culture. The conflicts are points of potential change in cultural perspectives and practices.

Looking at the football project in terms of the conflict point of view, it appears that the band program and its members are in competition with the football program for school funding, status, and influence in the school. There also seem to be issues of equality between the male players and the female player.

Key Questions

- What are the groups or communities involved in the cultural phenomenon?
- How do these groups or communities perceive themselves in relation to other participating groups?
- What are the issues of power (authority, dominance, or influence) between or among these groups?
- How do individuals perceive issues of power (authority, dominance, or influence) in this phenomenon?

Investigations

7.6 *LEARNING CULTURE: COMMUNITIES IN CONFLICT*

Scan a few newspapers, both local and national. Make a short list of the disagreements, conflicts, competitions, disputes, negotiations, confrontations, alliances, or collaborations described in the news. Next to each item on your list, identify the groups or communities involved. If the community has an official name or title, write this down; otherwise, assign a name. As best you can, list the issues of power that are involved, from the viewpoint of each of the communities. What observations can you make about the conflict view of culture?

The advantage of these three perspectives is that each offers a distinct viewpoint on cultural phenomena. When we look at culture from different viewpoints, our understanding is increased. By acknowledging and seeking multiple perspectives, we begin to grasp the complexity of culture. We begin to see that there are many possible explanations, not just one right answer.

Suggested Readings

James Banks (1991), in *Teaching Strategies for Ethnic Studies*, has developed an approach to teaching a multicultural curriculum that is based in part on examining events from multiple perspectives. He describes how an issue such as social protest can be explored from a variety of viewpoints: the political system, social institutions, literature, language, music, and art. Even though Brake, Walker and Walker (1995) wrote *Doing Business Internationally: The Guide to Cross-Cultural Success* for businesspersons, they present an excellent synthesis of 10 cultural orientations (etic perspectives) drawn from a number of researchers in cultural studies, anthropology, and intercultural communication. They explain these in a clear, succinct manner and use them as a frame for comparing cultures of Africa, the Middle East, Europe, North America, Asia, and Latin America. The Peace Corps (1998) has published a culture learning workbook, *Culture Matters: The Peace Corps Cross-Cultural Workbook*, written for Peace Corps volunteers about to embark on their service and intended to be used during the volunteers' stay abroad. It's filled with critical incidents, vignettes from former volunteers, and exercises to elicit cultural understanding. The sections on cultural perspectives are particularly informative, with enlightening contrasts between the United States and other cultures. Many texts on intercultural communication provide overviews of cultural perspectives; one I have found particularly helpful is *Intercultural Competence: Interpersonal Communication Across Cultures* by Lustig and Koester (1999), particularly the chapters "Cultural Patterns and Communication Foundations" and "Cultural Patterns and Communications: Taxonomies," in which they offer a comprehensive synthesis of various viewpoints on perspectives, drawing a useful distinction between Western and non-Western views. Stella Ting-Toomey (1999) also provides an excellent summary of these various views in the chapter "Value Orientations and Intercultural Encounters" in her book *Communicating Across Cultures*. She displays a value orientation in a table and classifies various national cultures for each one.

8

CULTURAL COMMUNITIES

Quelle famille! *Over the years, I often heard members of my wife's family in France describe themselves using this expression, usually in reference to some quirky behavior, or as a way of laughing at a shared memory or poking fun at someone, like my father-in-law, who tended to leave early at family gatherings outside the home. Eventually, it dawned on me when I heard "What a family!" that I was included. I was part of this family. I realized that they were no longer a group of people in a foreign country who were related to my wife. My experiences were part of their experiences. I was part of their history just as they were part of mine.*

In the beginning, my wife would instruct me on what I should and should not do in her parents' house, watching my every move to see that I followed the rules. I learned how to act at the table, how to participate in the family events and activities. I had the hardest time remembering to close the doors; I left them open only to have people either get up and close them or make a remark about the draft in the room, *le courant d'air*. I tried to be helpful by repairing things around the house, like the sagging hinge on the front gate, but learned that this was not really part of my role. We made the obligatory visits to the local cemetery to pay our respects to the relatives under the headstones. In the early years, I didn't know any of the deceased, but as time passed and others passed away, I did know them: *Tata Rose, Georgette, Charlotte, Mado.*

As we all got to know each other better, I learned what I was supposed to do, what my roles entailed—as son-in-law, brother-in-law, uncle, cousin, or acquaintance—what kinds of relationships were expected, and how being a member of this family affected my cultural identity.

Communities consist of the specific groups of the culture in which members, through different kinds of interpersonal relationships, carry out practices in specific social and physical settings. Such groups of people range from broad, amorphous communities like nation, language, gender, race, religion, socioeconomic class, region, or generation to more narrowly defined groupings: a workplace, a neighborhood, an alumni association of a particular school, a local political party, a religious social club, a sports team, a charity organization, coworkers, or one's family. All cultural practices are grounded in social settings of some kind that reflect the communities that participate in those settings.

In this chapter, I describe different kinds of communities within a culture, national and coexistent, and discuss how these communities affect relationships and cultural practices, including variations in language.

Figure 8.1: Cultural Communities

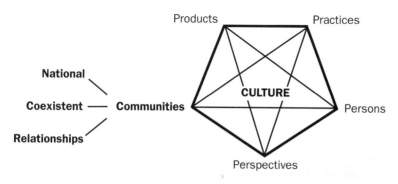

THE NATIONAL CULTURE COMMUNITY

At the broadest level, the social institutions of the culture define communities and accompanying practices for everyone within the borders of the "national culture." Economic, political, educational, health, and other institutions exist for members of the national culture as a whole. Accordingly, these institutions establish and maintain many practices that members of the culture need to enact in order to go about a large part of their daily lives. Getting an education, finding a job, starting a family, participating in the economy, obeying the law, paying taxes, and maintaining health all require certain practices that hold, broadly speaking, for virtually all members of the culture.

In many second and foreign language textbooks, the community of the national culture sets the scene for much of the cultural content presented to language learners. The social institutions of the culture and its systems tend to reflect the dominant cultural communities, that is, those groups that have the most influence. The communities associated with these public institutions also tend to be the communities most accessible to language learners. Consequently, many practices (operations, acts, and scenarios) are placed within this broad, public community. Public places like airports, bus stations, post offices, restaurants, markets, parks, stores, stadiums, government offices, and the like all provide the physical settings for communities and the many associated practices needed to participate in them.

Consider the setting of a supermarket, where shoppers fill their shopping carts with groceries and proceed to the checkout counters to make their purchases. In this case, the community is defined by the economic institutions of the culture, that is, members as the general public. Almost any shopper, even including visitors from other cultures and countries, can be considered a member of this community and is welcomed into the store to buy groceries. The actual practices are defined by the particular supermarket, but are also the same shopping practices enacted in other supermarkets and stores. The culture and the language needed to participate in the culture at this broad level are defined with relative ease and, significantly, apply to many institutions. Equally important are the kinds of interpersonal relationships that are formed in such broad, public communities

Viewed more narrowly, toward the other end of the spectrum, take the much smaller community of the immediate nuclear family. Here, membership is necessarily restricted to family members and others they might include in this group. Family members' roles, relationships, and practices are defined by family life—how the family earns its livelihood, activities associated with the various family members, the dwelling and its surroundings, as well as its place within the larger community. At the family level of community it becomes much more challenging to generalize about cultural practices, especially in national cultures that are comprised of many ethnic, linguistic, religious, political, or socioeconomic groups. The differences among families and other smaller communities can be significant, to the point where certain groups appear to inhabit different worlds even while sharing the same national culture.

COMMUNITIES AND PLACES

Communities are closely connected with places, namely, physical settings. However, these settings may or may not be essential to the community. Many communities do not require a specific place and are able to enact their practices in many different physical settings. For example, a writer's circle could hold its meetings in a local coffee shop, a restaurant, or a meeting room in the public library. A political party could hold its rally on a street corner, in a sports stadium, in a public building, or in a community center. Families can carry out many practices outside the home, in the larger community.

This said, however, many physical settings and communities are intimately connected to the point where one depends on the other. Consider the local hospital, a physical setting that includes many specific places within and around it as well as a number of specific communities. There is the large group that makes up the organization itself: doctors, nurses, aides, support staff, administrators, trustees, and community outreach workers and volunteers. Thus, the hospital itself is a place and a community, with a particular set of practices. At the same time, each of the members of this larger unified hospital community represents separate communities, defined by occupation and roles. Within the communities of doctors, nurses, and support staff, for example, other sets of practices and relationships unite these members. Likewise, for outsiders who enter the hospital, there are norms and expectations for participating in the services that the hospital offers. There are also certain kinds of relationships, such as the doctor-patient relationship, which call for specific practices.

COEXISTING COMMUNITIES

As mentioned above, there are communities associated with the social institutions of the culture, and these serve to support the functioning of these institutions. Consider, for instance, the thousands of groups that are associated with the educational system, especially public schools. There are the many occupational groups: teachers, administrators, service staff, policy-makers, fundraisers, counselors, nurses, doctors, social workers, and so on. Within the school there are student groups, associations, and special interest clubs or organizations. Linked to the school are ancillary groups: labor unions, parent associations, school boards, certification boards, curriculum committees. And there are groups that serve to change or improve the institution, although not necessarily by promoting the status quo: school improvement committees, alternative schools, model schools, school reform committees, or special interest groups that seek to change curriculum in accordance with their own views through banning certain books or promoting specific topics for inclusion in schools.

In addition, there are overt groups that exist alongside or in opposition to this institution, such as the private school system, home-schooling groups, or other alternative education associations and programs. There are also covert groups, such as gangs, secret societies, or organized groups of nonconformists, in or outside school, often referred to as "deviant" groups in the sociological literature.

Coexisting communities, in other words, are in relationship with one another in the national culture. They may be physically isolated from one another, or they may exist next to one another but be separate, with no interaction between them. They may have a harmonious collaborative relationship or they may oppose one another, possibly in open conflict.

DISCOURSES

These many communities exist alongside one another within the larger culture, the national culture. Some call these communities "microcultures" within the "macroculture" (Klopf, 1998; Dodd, 1998; Banks and Banks, 1997) or "co-cultures" within the "dominant culture" (Samovar, Porter, and Stenia, 1998). The macroculture or dominant culture is also referred to as "mainstream culture" or "umbrella culture" (Samovar, Porter, and Stenia, 1998, p. 37), or as "core culture" (Banks and Banks, 1997). Linguist James Gee (1990) calls these communities "Discourses" as a way of emphasizing the "social practices" they carry out: "ways of behaving, interacting, valuing, thinking, believing, speaking, and often reading and writing" (p. xix). Gee contends that individuals are members of many Discourses and that each one calls for a distinct set of practices for membership, what he calls "an identity kit."

8.1 *LEARNING CULTURE: CULTURAL DIFFERENCES AS COMMUNITIES*

One approach to identifying the communities in a culture is to use existing differences among members of the culture. Create a chart like the one below. For each category, list examples of specific communities that you know about—their members, and practices they employ—using your culture of origin.

	Communities	Members	Practices
Religion			
Age			
Education			
Profession/ Occupation			
Social Class			
Gender			
Race			
Region			
Neighborhood			

Review the information you have listed. Identify similarities and differences in cultural practices and perspectives between and among these communities.

COMMUNITIES AND RELATIONSHIPS

Inside any given community, a person plays certain roles and carries out certain practices according to the norms and expectations of that community. In almost every case, people enact these practices with others through specific interpersonal relationships appropriate to the social setting and the community. These practices include language, particularly the sociolinguistic variations that a person uses in order to say and do the appropriate things in a given relationship. Consider the workplace, where an individual performs a specific job alongside coworkers performing the same job. As fellow workers, they develop certain relationships on the worksite. If they are members of a labor union, this leads to another set of relationships. Some coworkers may become friends and get together after work for leisure activities, informally, or in organized groups. The workers probably have another kind of relationship with their job supervisors, and yet another sort of rapport with the owners of the company where they work.

Communities, therefore, in physical settings and social circumstances, form a basis for relationships in the culture. The kinds of relationships that members of the culture establish and maintain are connected to the kinds of communities in which members participate. Communities exist for a wide variety of purposes and they use certain practices to achieve their respective ends, which in turn affect the kinds of relationships that are possible or expected.

Investigations

8.2 *LEARNING CULTURE: RELATIONSHIPS IN COMMUNITIES*

Make a list of three groups or communities of which you are a member. For each community, write the names of other members with whom you have a relationship. Describe each relationship in terms of your interactions with the other person, as practices—the things you do. Following your descriptions, characterize each relationship by giving it a name or title. What cultural aspects do you see in these relationships?

The important point here is that relationships are practiced according to the cultural perspectives that underlie practices in these communities. Strangers, acquaintances, friends, romantic partners, rivals, enemies, family members, and group-based relationships are all defined accordingly. In simple terms, you relate to people according to the norms, the unwritten rules, of that particular community.

Ani Hawkinson, a Swahili teacher, describes how she seeks to provide her students with an experience of community from an African perspective and to foster the kinds of relationships this demands. She draws on her own experiences in East Africa as a guide.

The key is an Afrocentric pedagogical process, one which I have only recently begun developing, and can only develop in the company of native members of Swahili communities and—where there is commonality between African cultural communities—with other African language and culture teachers. This work was begun when I taught Swahili at Indiana University. It included a conscious effort on the part of all of the teachers to organize a classroom community and to devise learning activities that embodied certain aspects of African consciousness. We all agreed that these aspects were common to the cultures of the African languages we were teaching and also that they were distinct from the cultural consciousness of dominant U.S. cultural values.

Ani Hawkinson

In the classroom, what linked the two was the experiences and contributions of African heritage learners. What we deemed essential to the consciousness of the African communities we were inviting students to learn about was also apparent in the communities whose African ancestors came to this country much earlier, either as slaves or as free citizens.

As a specific example, in terms of consciousness carried through to behavioral artifacts and pedagogical process, I would point to the experience of life and of others as "inclusive," as opposed to "exclusive." Marimba Ani, in her book *Yurugu,* has a quite detailed analysis of European consciousness, as opposed to an African-centered one. In this, the exclusivist consciousness is characterized as one where self is defined in opposition to "other," in that it gains its sense of who it is through domination of the "other."

For most, if not all, members of African communities, membership in a family is a visible manifestation of an inclusivist consciousness. So, to create a classroom process that embodies the experience of being in a family—a family where everyone is seen fully and included regardless of individual behaviors that may offend or annoy other learners or even the instructor—is a difficult and complex task. This is especially so in the context where the learners spend the majority of time in exclusivist situations, i.e., their other classes on campus. To create such a family community became a primary goal for me.

It was much easier to create this during the summer intensive program, where learners spent six hours a day together and had no other course obligations. The lessons in this situation were set up so that students first, as a group, chose the course syllabus, choosing topics from a larger list of topics that had been generated by students in the whole program during the academic year.

Then, in pairs and individually, students were responsible for teaching new materials and for facilitating sessions for their peers to demonstrate what they had learned. It was a truly inclusive process. Students who had a better grasp of material were asked to help others who did not. Those who had less of a grasp were still asked to conduct classes and were given the necessary support to experience success. They were required to create lessons that were experiential, to set up activities where their peers had to experience the material being taught in actual use. Our classroom was a town, complete with different buildings and streets one day, a market another day, and a restaurant another.

There were no conditions that had to be met in order to be part of the community. As long as you show up, then you are part of what happens. What happens is cooperatively created, through a process of active experimentation with some cultural artifact—material, linguistic and/or behavioral—and inquiry into how that artifact fits into the larger whole.

As an American of European descent living in a Swahili family in East Africa, I acquired the sense of being a part of something much larger. I was included as I was, with all my differences and lack of understandings of many things that were part of the cultural ethos that surrounded me. This was quite transformative for me. I knew then, and I know now, that I am still a member of that family. I knew that I would always be taken care of, that I would never be alone, and that no matter what I did, I would still be part of that unit. It is this that I am trying to bring into my classroom pedagogy: It is the awareness that if you show up, you are part of what is there and you will be taken care of. An exclusivist consciousness does not say this. It says instead that if you show up and act a certain way, then you can stay. It doesn't even say, necessarily, that you will be taken care of, just that you can stay. This is quite different.

The challenge that I faced in my Swahili classes was one of getting students to *show up*, and I don't mean just attend the class. Students can physically show up and not be present, and apparently this works in many of their other classes, presumably larger lecture classes. It doesn't work in a community where everyone is included and is therefore mutually responsible for everyone else. So one of the behavioral artifacts of an inclusivist consciousness is mutual responsibility. This is something that can be infused into pedagogical processes. Then, once students have had the experience, this can be linked through discussion to the cultural consciousness from which it emerges.

8.3   TEACHING CULTURE: CLASSROOM COMMUNITY AND CULTURE

Ani Hawkinson seeks to create an African community consciousness in her Swahili class. What kind of cultural community do students experience in your language classroom?

Communities require different practices. Coworkers in a restaurant may engage in communicative practices that are quite different from those they employ with their supervisors or those they employ when requesting a loan at the bank. When examining cultural content, it is helpful to situate phenomena within specific communities. Even if this is at its broadest level, the national culture community, making this distinction helps learners put the content into perspective.

Suggested Readings

I have found the works of linguist James Gee especially useful in understanding the role that group membership plays in identity and how individuals manage membership in multiple groups, or Discourses. In *Social Linguistics and Literacies: Ideology in Discourses* (1990), he shows how Discourses interact in political terms, with power as the pivotal factor. He also explains how learners can become aware of the structure of Discourses to communicate across groups.

9

CULTURAL PERSONS

"I'm not like other Japanese. I'm different," Yuko announced with determination in her voice. She had come up to me after class to clarify the assignment I'd given, and we were engaged in small talk when she made this comment. In the cultural autobiography assignment, she put this same statement in writing as the theme of her paper. This statement was somewhat of a mystery to me, but she went on to describe how she did not share certain Japanese cultural perspectives, nor did she accept certain Japanese cultural practices. She saw herself as different, with a different identity: Japanese-but-not-Japanese.

I begin this course on culture and language teaching with a cultural autobiography. Since so much of culture learning depends on self-awareness, I find that this is a good place to begin: telling one's story. There are a number of assignments that ask language teachers to reflect on their language and culture learning experiences, such as a timeline and critical incidents. In addition, there are assignments that focus on identity: a family tree, group membership. For each of these tasks, students discuss the results in a small group. Through readings on these topics, reflection, writing, and talking, they put together a self-portrait of themselves as cultural beings.

Like Yuko, all see themselves as part of their culture(s) of origin, but as distinct in some way, even if it is only to say that they are different from their parents or from other members of their families. There are no surprises here. However, when these teachers share their autobiographies with their peers from the same national culture, most are often surprised to see how similar they are, how many values and beliefs they share, in spite of their differences.

Culture resides in persons, in individuals. Each member of a culture, like a minuscule twist in a kaleidoscope, refracts and reflects the common colored lights of their culture in a unique display, recognizably similar yet unquestionably different.

When we enter another culture and participate in its practices, we do this through our interactions with individuals, with the people of that culture. We form relationships with these persons. We work with them. We live with them. We participate in their lives. As outsiders, our initial tendency is to see the similarities among persons and to assume that they are representative of their culture, that they are "typically" Japanese, Chinese, or Spanish. Yet as we get to know these persons, we begin to discern the differences, the idiosyncrasies, the quirks, the personalities, the special characteristics that set them off from others in their culture. The unique ways that people have lived their lives, their histories, their experiences, their interests, outlooks, and intentions—all these blend together in a single person with a distinct and dynamic cultural identity.

We see that each person has a story, a cultural autobiography. Everyone has a life history that portrays a unique interpretation of the culture—one way of living a shared way of life.

In this chapter, I discuss culture and persons from two viewpoints: identity and life history.

Figure 9.1: **Cultural Persons**

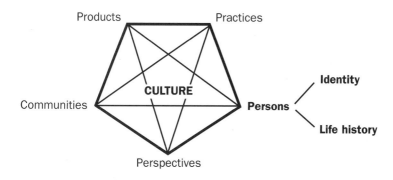

IDENTITY

Identity is a complex topic, and I do not pretend to address it fully here, just two dimensions of it. Individual members of the culture have their own distinct identities, derived in part from their unique characteristics, experiences, and outlooks and in part from their membership in particular groups and communities.

Like other aspects of culture, identity is both explicit and tacit. There are aspects of ourselves that we can describe or put into words and there are others that we cannot express, or that are simply outside our awareness. Not until we find ourselves in situations where our sense of self—our values, beliefs, practices—is called into question do we perceive the tacit dimensions of our identity. This a common occurrence in culture learning, where our worldview meets another.

Friederike Weiss, a German ESOL teacher, describes how she discovered her cultural identity and how she applies this awareness to her language teaching.

> In my eyes, students need to become aware of their identity before
> they can step outside their own culture to explore another way of
> looking at the world. Most students are not aware of their own
> cultural self-concept until they leave their culture behind. Thus I
> did not discover my "Germanness" until I came to the United
> States. And although I experienced myself as a "German" and
> therefore different, I did not start to discover and explore my
> Germanness until I took a culture class at the University of Missoula
> in Montana. In this class, the readings and conversations with other
> international and U.S. students helped me realize that I could not
> just absorb the new culture I chose to live in for a while. Instead,
> I needed to look at who I was and how my self was shaped and
> defined by my Germanness. I had always considered myself a
> unique individual and had rejected labels like "feminist" and

Friederike Weiss

"German." Therefore I felt an inner resistance to acknowledging the presence of such a label inside me.

Small incidents showed me, though, that I could not deny that my self was influenced to a large extent by culture. One example was the relationships I tried to establish with Americans. We lived in a family housing apartment complex on campus, and I did not think that it would be hard to make friends. After all, I had lived in Germany for the last four years, and I had found many close friends. I soon realized that my expectations were not met, and that I could not transfer my German way of looking at my surroundings to the United States. My efforts to get to know my neighbors (who had a small child and were both students, like us) failed, or did not turn into the relationships I wanted and needed. I remember one incident when I brought doughnuts to my neighbor's house, as I went there so that our children could play together. She thanked me for them and left them on the table. Being German, I had expected that she would make us some coffee and that we would just have a nice time together. My husband told me afterwards that this is not an American custom and that I should stop expecting things to be "my way." Incidents like these helped me to become aware of my own cultural identity, my "German" way of thinking, of interpreting the world.

But it was a painful process, which I was not prepared for. This is why, as a teacher, I consider it important to raise students' awareness of their culturally shaped selfhood and acknowledge the likelihood of some emotional disturbance during their cultural adjustment.

9.1 *LEARNING CULTURE: NATIONAL IDENTITY*

Follow the example of Friederike Weiss. Put "-ness" after your national culture or culture of origin (e.g., your "Canadian-ness," "Chinese-ness," or "Peruvian-ness"). Describe yourself in these terms. What do you notice about your ability to express your cultural identity in this way?

National culture identity is one form of identifying ourselves in terms of groups or communities. When we look more closely at the groups to which we belong, we begin to see how membership in these groups affects who we are—to ourselves and to others. Cultural identity, in other words, depends on our similarity to others.

CULTURAL IDENTITIES

In depicting cultural identity, Singer (1987) relies on group affiliations. He distinguishes between two types of groups: perceptual groups and identity groups. **Perceptual groups** consist of groups of individuals who perceive aspects of the external world in a similar manner yet do not communicate these perceptions among themselves. Once they do communicate these common perspectives, they become an **identity group**. This distinction helps explain how persons may see the world from a perspective of gender, religion, marital status, or race, yet until they communicate their shared perspective, they do not necessarily identify with others of this particular group. An important feature here is that the definitions of membership or identification originate with the individual. Martin and Nakayama (1997) refer to this self-identification as *avowal* or *avowed identities*. We identify with others who think as we do.

Our identification with others, however, is only part of the role of groups in identity. The other part is outside our control and depends on others. Based on their perceptions, others in the culture assign persons to groups. Observable features such as skin color, appearance, age, gender, dress, mannerisms, accent, vocabulary, possessions, or even locale all serve as means of classifying persons as members of particular groups. In a word, we are labeled by others. These labels or assignations may or may not correspond to the avowed identity groups of these persons. Martin and Nakayama (1997) call these *ascribed identities* (p. 70).

The avowed and ascribed dimensions of identity turn around two distinct perceptions: how individual members of the culture perceive and identify themselves, and how other members of the culture perceive and identify these individuals. These two perceptions do not necessarily coincide. For example, because of their skin color, certain persons may be perceived by others as black, brown, or white, whereas they might not consider themselves in these terms.

9.2 *LEARNING CULTURE: AVOWED AND ASCRIBED IDENTITIES*

Using the column format below, make two lists about your identity. In one column, list your avowed identities—how you perceive yourself. In the other, list ascribed identities that others have assigned to you, naming those groups or individuals who see you in this way. As much as possible, try to separate the avowed from the ascribed.

Table 9.1: **Avowed and Ascribed Identities**

Avowed Identities	Ascribed Identities
I see myself as:	Others see me as:

When you've completed your lists, compare the two. Are there identities that appear on both lists? If so, explain why. Are there identities that appear contradictory? If so, explain why. Review all items on both lists. What cultural aspects are present in the identities you have listed?

What observations can you make about your cultural identity?

As this investigation may have shown, identity is a complicated overlay and interplay between the psychological and the social, between the idiosyncratic characteristics of a person and the groups in which that person participates (Gee, 1990). Identity springs from this intricate mix of others and self. In this way, persons can be said to belong to certain groups or communities in a culture, but at the same time, they may or may not take their full identity from these groups.

The diagram below (adapted from Brake et al., 1995) illustrates the mix of social groupings or communities that can go into making up a person's cultural identity.

Figure 9.2: Cultural Identity Groups

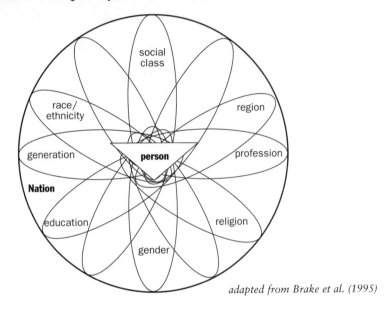

adapted from Brake et al. (1995)

9.3 LEARNING CULTURE: CULTURAL IDENTITY GROUPS

Use the diagram in Figure 9.2 to identify the groups or communities to which you belong in your culture of origin. Within each of the titled categories, identify yourself using a name, title, or other description. Review these categories. Rate the importance of each group to you and your own sense of identity by putting "+" marks at the ends of the ellipses. The more marks, the more important this group is to your identity.

Add other ellipses to the diagram to include other groups to which you belong. These groups can be formal and organized, such as an association or a club, or general and less well defined, such as Spanish speaker, or Canadian. Put the names of the groups into these new ellipses. As above, rate the importance of each group to you and your own sense of identity by putting "+" marks at the ends of the ellipses.

Study your identity groups as you've portrayed them in the diagram. What do you notice about yourself, your identity, and culture?

Repeat this exercise with a second culture that you know. When you've finished, compare this analysis with your analysis of your culture of origin. What observations can you make about your cultural identity?

CULTURAL MARGINALITY

Depending on how you filled out the diagram, you may have identified yourself as part of the dominant cultural groups, or identified with nondominant groups and communities, or even both. Janet Bennett (1993) describes cultural identity in terms of individuals' relationships among identity groups, in particular in relationship to dominant groups. She uses the notion of marginality to describe the rapport that persons of nondominant communities have with dominant communities, suggesting that there are two essential responses, **encapsulated marginality** and **constructive marginality**. Encapsulated marginals are persons who allow the dominant groups to ascribe their identity. Constructive marginals are persons with avowed identities with a relativistic outlook, not dependent on particular group affiliations, who are capable of moving among all communities. Her analysis is useful in considering how group affiliations affect a person's identity, particularly in situations that may be oppressive or diminishing to a person.

LIFE HISTORIES

One means of understanding identity is through life histories. Individuals and the way they lead their lives within the larger way of life of the culture as a whole reveal identity. Through biography and autobiography, we elicit life histories. Life histories not only instruct us about the culture and how individuals situate themselves within it, they also bring us closer to these people.

One approach to life histories is to study the famous persons of the culture, or cultural heroes (Stewart and Ohtake, 1999) through biographies, autobiographies, or other historical documents. In addition to the life histories of the famous, there are also stories of ordinary persons of the culture, published as biographies or autobiographies. If read from the point of view of identity, these stories can be equally compelling and revealing of the cultural identity of individuals, as well as of the culture itself. In fact, the life history method is a widely used research tool in sociology and anthropology. Such accounts are designed to reveal the culture in the individual, and vice versa.

Beyond these published accounts, there are also the life histories of the people we meet as we enter another way of life. As we listen to them tell their stories, we build our relationships with these persons, and their lives illuminate our understanding. My French professor at the university told our class an unforgettable story over coffee in her home. To make conversation, I had asked her about a crude charcoal drawing of a thin woman with a broom which hung on her living room wall. "That's me," she said. "A friend made this drawing when I was in Ravensbrück." And then her story emerged, how she was a member of the French Resistance in Paris during World War II, how her husband had denounced her to the Gestapo, how she had survived two concentration camps, and made her way to the United States to teach French literature. Suddenly, the history of this period in France came alive, and I understood her in a new way.

9.4 *LEARNING CULTURE: CHRONOLOGY*

Make a list of all the places you have lived or worked, and arrange them in chronological order, beginning with the place where you were born and ending with the place where you now live and work. Assign dates and time periods to each of these places. Next to these dates and places, list significant events in your life that occurred during those time periods. Explain each significant event, from the beginning to the present. For each time period, next to your significant events, list significant events that occurred during the history of your culture or country of origin. When you've finished, compare your autobiography with the history. What do you notice about your cultural identity?

Identities become even more complex when persons of one culture and language enter other cultures and learn other languages. The degree to which they do or do not integrate these new ways of thinking, acting, and interacting affect cultural identity. For those of us who are nonnative teachers, these dimensions of our identity emerge in our language classrooms.

Joe Barrett, a high school Spanish teacher, describes how he developed his identity as a "Hispanic" person and how this identity emerges in his language classes.

Joe Barrett

> To paraphrase a famous computer game, "Who in the world is José Barretto?" He carries no passport, pays no taxes, and yet displays allegiance to several countries on three continents! His close friends are mainly Hispanic and his "extended family" includes folks with names like Luli, Pito, Rubia, and Gorda. His students stare incredulously when they hear him speak English for the first time ("I never knew you knew English!"). Most find it hard to believe that he is really from Philadelphia, not some foreign country.
>
> "José," in point of fact, is the persona I've developed over the past 30+ years since college, my acquired cultural identity. José was born in 1968 in the Dominican Republic during my hitch as a Peace Corps volunteer. I learned Spanish for the first time through a process of total immersion while living with a Dominican family. The transformation was complete. I salivate at a plate of rice and beans. I can't keep my body still if I hear *merengue* music. I boast of the exploits of Dominican baseball players Pedro Martinez and Vladimir Guerrero, Manny Ramirez and Sammy Sosa, just as any other Dominican does.
>
> When I first started to teach Spanish, the "I" who showed up for class was José, decked out in a fancy *chacabana* (*guayabera* to the initiated, a barber's gown to *gringos*). José wouldn't dare go to class without shined, leather shoes. Even his nonverbal gestures were

Dominican, down to the nose blink and the chin point, to show incomprehension and direction. His students found all this amusing (strange?) but figured it was par for the course for some non-English-speaking foreigner who asked to be called "*el Señor Barretto.*"

In the 1980s, I twice lived for two months with a family in Burgos, located in the heart of Castilian Spain, where José soaked up his Hispanic cultural identity #2. He now wears a *boina* to and from class, cooks *paella* in class, and shares pictures of his stint as a hooded *penitente* in a Catholic *cofradía* during Holy Week, as a member of a religious men's group marching in a parade. José started to use the *vosotros* forms naturally in class, as in "*¡Levantaos!, Hacédmela para el lunes*" (Stand up! Do it for Monday). I knew this new cultural identity had taken over when I recognized that José frequently imitated without thinking the speech patterns and nonverbal gestures of our good friend, Segundo Carpintero, and his elbows-out, palms-open shoulder shrug.

Things got really out of hand in terms of my cultural identity in 1999 when I lived for two months in Argentina. José #3 appeared: a *gaucho* who teaches my students to dance *la chacarera* and a *porteño* from Buenos Aires who teaches them the basic dance steps of *el tango*. "*Pues, mira vos*" and "*¡Meta!*" (Well, how about that! and Good!) became his favorite expressions during class and he added the *vos* forms to all my Power Point verb conjugation charts. *¿Comprendés?*

The result of all these (mixed-up?) cultural identities? Well, in class, the students and José share cups of Dominican coffee—*tacitas de café dominicano*—today, sip on strong Argentinean tea—*hierba mate*—tomorrow, and enjoy *café cortados*—strong coffee laced with milk—the day after that. They'll cook fried plantain bananas, *fritos verdes*, this week, *empanadas*, meat pies, next week, and *tortilla española*, a Spanish omelette, the week after that. For snacks, José likes *turrón*, almond candy from Spain, and *mentas*; his students prefer *los alfajores*. They listen to singers Juan Luis Guerra and Carlos Gardel (but José isn't a big fan of Julio Iglesias or Ricky Martin, *lo siento*—I'm sorry to say).

But what does it all mean? José's students learn Spanish by experiencing it. Just as I assume a different cultural identity in the class, he asks that they do likewise. José wants them to feel relaxed, to enjoy our social time together as if we were all just sitting on rocking chairs on the *galería*, *conversando*, chatting on the front porch. We ask them to *portarse* or behave like Spanish speakers: to not take off their *zapatos*, shoes, in class when the weather gets nice out of *respeto propio* (self-respect), to sit on a *silla*, a chair, rather than on the floor or a desktop to show that they are *bien educados*, well-mannered, to share everything, *compartir todo*—candy or *fruta* or whatever they bring *a la clase*, to loudly greet the student *que viene* late to class as a courtesy, *una cortesía*, and to immerse themselves 100 percent in the language by *expresar* every question, every statement, every need *en español*—expressing everything in Spanish.

José makes my classroom into a little Spanish-speaking *país* (a country—not a Spanish classroom) where Hispanic cultural norms and *el español* are the ways we relate to each other. José expects his *estudiantes* to get up and try to dance *salsa* even if it is embarrassing to them as *gringos*. He expects them to eat *morro de guandules* even if rice and pigeon peas doesn't look very appealing. Since José doesn't understand *el inglés*, my students have to use Spanish even to request *permiso para pasar al baño*, permission to go to the restroom.

All this is to get students to leave who they were at the classroom door and assume a new *identidad cultural*, a new cultural identity, to (consciously at first) suspend who they were in order to try on a different set of values, interests, behaviors, and language, and to (unconsciously eventually) enjoy being Hispanic and *comunicarse en español*.

Incidentally, some also become very good dancers.

9.5 *TEACHING CULTURE: A CULTURAL PERSONA*

Joe Barrett represents Spanish-speaking cultures to his students through his Hispanic "persona." Reflect on the persona that you present to your language students. What are the cultural dimensions of your persona? What are the conscious and unconscious dimensions? What effect does this have on the students in your classes?

Persons are at the nexus of culture learning. Through life histories and personal relationships, we can see both the commonality and the diversity of culture, the individual variations on themes, how persons define themselves and are defined by others.

Suggested Readings

In "Culture Heroes in Intercultural Training," Stewart and Ohtake (1999) propose a useful strategy for using culture heroes as a vehicle for culture learning. They offer a detailed procedure for studying recognized heroes of a culture based on the assumption that such persons reveal much about cultural identity and help learners understand this concept. In *Beyond Experience* (Gochenour, 1993), Don Batchelder's article "Preparation for Cross-cultural Experience" shows how to structure a culture learning curriculum based on five questions that relate to identity (Who am I? Where do I come from? Where am I going? What for? What am I willing to attempt?). In the same volume, Lise Sparrow, in "Examining Cultural Identity," describes three techniques to provoke self-awareness (a values inventory, cultural autobiography, and an exploration of one's ancestry).

10

CULTURE LEARNING OUTCOMES

Denis looked at me with furrowed brows, as if he hadn't under-stood my question. I repeated it: Est-ce qu'il y a une différence entre les joueurs de hockey francophones et les joueurs anglo-phones? *I asked Denis this question, based on the assumption that there was a difference in play that was culturally based. In other words, a francophone Québécois hockey player would approach and play the game differently from an anglophone Canadian player due to distinct cultural values, beliefs, or attitudes. This was the focus of my research as a fledgling ethnographer.*

My cultural research project had led me here to Denis' office behind the bar he owned in a small town in southern Quebec. A former coach and now director of a hockey school, he was one of several people that I interviewed in French, trying to find out if and how francophone culture was reflected in the national sport of Canada. All in all, I made seven trips north from my home in Vermont to this small town. I interviewed Bertrand, the coach of a *pré-novice* hockey team, and watched him conduct team practices with children at the local *aréna*, the skating rink. I interviewed one of the parents who oversaw the team within the overall league hierarchy. As a participant observer scribbling in my notebook, I attended a midget hockey game that filled the stands of the arena in town. I read books on hockey, on the history of Quebec, on the influence of Catholicism in *Québécois* culture, on the role of René Cavalier, the legendary francophone broadcaster who ensured a French version of the vocabulary of hockey during a time of encroachment of English into French (*lancez la rondelle* instead of *shootez le puck*).

Denis didn't answer my question directly. As it turned out, my question, like so many outsider hypotheses about culture, was not really relevant for the insid-ers, all the *Québécois* to whom I spoke. In fact, when I asked Bertrand, the *pré-novice* coach, he didn't hesitate at all. "*Non,*" he said. When I heard this, my carefully constructed inquiry fell apart like a house of cards. I had to drop my hypothesis and concentrate instead on figuring out how these people perceived the relevance of hockey to their way of life.

Bertrand told me his story in the locker room of the *aréna*: 25 years old, mar-ried with two children, an unemployed cook, trying to raise his family and to impart a love of the game of hockey, of playing for the joy of it and for the com-panionship, as he had learned it as a child.

And in reading about how Catholicism had forged certain values and attitudes in the worldview of certain *Québécois*, I was surprised to see these implications in my own upbringing in the Catholic faith. I also pushed my French to new limits as I struggled with new vocabulary and the different rhythms and sounds. I experienced again feeling like an outsider, looking and sounding like one, wanting to fit in, to pass unperceived, and knowing that I couldn't.

I carried out this project as part of a course on cultural studies where the goal was to do an in-depth study of a cultural group, employing observation and interviewing strategies. Despite my dubious results and the many mistakes that I made, I learned a lot about approaching culture learning using ethnographic techniques. Since then, I have used this approach as a training tool in my courses for language teachers, as it includes many key culture learning outcomes.

Outcomes engender and guide cultural content and learning activities. As teachers, we need to articulate our intentions in teaching culture, which outcomes we seek for students in our language classes, or which outcomes they seek for themselves.

Numerous outcomes for culture learning are currently in circulation in the field of language teaching, as well as parallel fields of intercultural communication, multicultural education, literacy education, and critical pedagogy. There is great overlap in these varied outcomes. I see six different emphases, summarized in the chart below. In this chapter, I describe each of these differing emphases, and end by proposing a framework for organizing them.

Table 10.1: Cultural Learning Outcomes

Outcome	Emphasis	Examples
Culture-specific understanding	Intellectual insight and empathy regarding a specific culture	• history, literature, the arts • area studies • products, practices, perspectives, communities, persons
Culture-general understanding	Insight into general concepts of culture and culture learning	• analysis of critical incidents • values clarification exercises • cultural simulations
Competence	Verbal and nonverbal cultural behaviors and skills	• language proficiency • communicative competence • cultural competence • intercultural competence
Adaptation	Entry and adaptation to a specific culture	• integration • assimilation • acculturation
Social change	Critical thinking and action regarding the target culture	• social justice • cultural change
Identity	Transformations in the learner's self-concept	• a second language "self" • bilingualism • multiculturalism

CULTURE-SPECIFIC UNDERSTANDING

Culture-specific understanding involves both intellect and affect, thoughts and feelings. Essentially, the intended outcome is that learners be able to recognize and explain cultural phenomena, and that they exhibit certain attitudes toward the culture. To achieve culture-specific understanding, therefore, learners not only acquire information about the culture, they also develop the ability to make valid cultural explanations based on this information. In order to make such explanations, learners need an awareness and understanding of their own cultural perspectives, etic or outsider views, which they consciously contrast with those of the target culture, emic or insider views. Through this knowledge and understanding, learners can ultimately develop appreciation and empathy for the people of this culture and their way of life.

These intellectual and attitudinal outcomes are often listed separately by language and intercultural educators (Seelye, 1994). It is useful, however, to see them as connected, even interdependent. In other words, an increase in cultural knowledge and understanding contributes to changes in attitudes. The more learners know about a culture and its people, the more likely they are to empathize, to see the world from another perspective and, ultimately, to accept this perspective.

Minhee Kang is a Korean teacher of English as a Foreign Language (EFL). She describes her approach to teaching language-and-culture and the outcomes she seeks. In her estimation, many of her Korean students associate English with U.S. culture and place it on a pedestal. She sees this as a hindrance. Consequently, she seeks culture-specific understanding of a different sort for her students.

Minhee Kang

> *Validate learners' views toward their home culture*: I believe that an English class should serve as a forum for students to explore and discuss their home culture, society, history, language, values, customs, and practices. In Korea, like other EFL locations, it is not uncommon for English learners to idolize the images of the target culture, mostly U.S. culture. Such a message that their home culture is inferior to the U.S. and European culture is often transmitted to people. This is partly due to the common English class environment, where these target cultures are predominantly introduced and heavily projected while the learners' home culture is not actively included. Therefore, in order for English learners to prevent a sense of inferiority and possibly cultural abandonment, and to develop a sense of pride and value in their home culture, language teachers should regularly provide a platform for them to explore their views about their home culture. Like other aspects of culture, identity is both explicit and tacit. There are aspects of ourselves that we can describe or put into words, and there are others that we cannot express, or that are simply out-of-awareness. Not until we find ourselves in situations where our sense of self—our values, beliefs, practices—is called into question do we perceive the tacit dimensions of our identity. This is a common occurrence in culture learning, where our world view meets another.

CULTURE-GENERAL UNDERSTANDING

Outcomes of culture-general understanding emphasize learners' insight into the nature of culture in general, the processes of entering other cultures, cultural relativity, and themselves as cultural beings. Like culture-specific understanding, they stress intellectual and attitudinal outcomes, but with different cultural content. Instead of acquiring information about a specific culture, learners concentrate on generic aspects of culture, such as perspectives, practices, products, and communities. In general, learners end up identifying perspectives from their own cultures, which they contrast with those of other cultures.

Models of culture-general understanding come primarily from the field of intercultural training and education, where people are prepared to enter other cultures. Culture-general learning activities are designed to underscore the process of entering another culture, namely, encounters with differences. Learners' reactions to these simulated differences are explored and linked to theories and models of culture, cultural adjustment, or crosscultural communication. The primary learning activities are simulations, critical incidents, case studies, and awareness inventories.

A significant emphasis in culture-general learning outcomes involves learners' recognition of their own perspectives, both personal and cultural. In the intercultural field, culture learning outcomes in this category are often phrased as cultural awareness, or crosscultural awareness, or intercultural awareness (Kohls and Knight, 1994), or intercultural sensitivity (Bennett, 1993). Through awareness, learners come to realize or recognize the cultural dimensions of their own behaviors and background—that they possess culture, that they are cultural beings, and that they tend to react to the unknown from the perspectives of their own culture.

Minhee Kang offers a slightly different version of culture-general understanding.

Minhee Kang

Promoting multiculturalism: If the teacher promotes the sense of uniqueness of learners' home culture in her language class, she also should be willing to provide an opportunity for her learners to be exposed to different cultures around the world, including the target culture. However, this practice in teaching multiculturalism shouldn't end with displaying the facts or outdated customs in different countries, thus reinforcing learners' stereotypes and prejudices. In other words, she should consciously avoid teaching "tourist-multiculturalism." She should teach multiculturalism in such a way that her students can become aware of and examine their own stereotypes and prejudices, and affirm a sense of equality among cultures by appreciating the uniqueness of each culture and embracing differences across cultures. This is a broader definition of teaching multiculturalism in a monocultural classroom.

COMPETENCE

Outcomes in this category focus on behaviors of the culture—acting, doing, saying, and interacting as people of the culture do. They emphasize learners' development of appropriate cultural behaviors—verbal and nonverbal means of expression and communication—and they assume learners' involvement and interaction with members of the target culture. To be competent, learners need to be able to interact and communicate both effectively and appropriately with people from other cultures.

A number of models of competence apply to language-and-culture learning. Some come from the field of language education and emphasize, understandably, language proficiency and communicative competence. Other models, from the field of intercultural communication, emphasize the cultural and intercultural aspects of competence. These models are summarized in the chart below:

Table 10.2: Views of Competence

Competence	Emphasis	Proponent
Language proficiency	Developing fluency and accuracy in a second language in listening, speaking, reading and writing. An emphasis on using language for communicative purposes, with the educated native speaker as the goal.	ACTFL Proficiency Guidelines (Omaggio-Hadley, 1993)
Communicative competence	Developing language abilities for effective and appropriate communication within cultural contexts of the target language-and-culture. Includes other specific language competencies: grammatical, sociolinguistic, discourse, strategic.	Canale and Swain (1980) Savignon (1983)
Cultural competence	Developing the ability to act appropriately (alongside communicating appropriately) in the target culture. Gestures, body movements, action sequences such as nonverbal greetings, table manners, manipulation of cultural products.	Steele and Suozzo (1994) Damen (1987) Stern (1983)
Intercultural competence	Developing the ability to interact effectively and appropriately in intercultural situations, regardless of the cultures involved.	Lustig and Koester (1999) Samovar, Porter, and Stenia (1998) Fantini (1999)
Intercultural communicative competence	Developing intercultural competence and communicative competence	Byram (1997)

As I read the literature, models of competence are still evolving. In the view of some language educators, one of the recent models, intercultural communicative competence, joins language and culture as key ingredients. Byram (1997), in fact, has expanded the notion of competence to encompass cultural understanding and identity. This is the exception, however, since other models place the emphasis on developing behaviors. The important dimension of competence-based culture learning outcomes is that they all, to varying degrees, depend on participation in the culture, real or simulated. They feature engagement in cultural practices.

Minhee Kang addresses competence by combining language-and-culture, but in an expanded manner:

Minhee Kang

> *English for communication and intercultural understanding*: The outcome that the teacher should pursue in her English class, by helping her students affirm their self-identity, develop a sense of pride and value in their home culture, and expand their worldview through the learning of multiculturalism, is the view of English for communicative purposes and intercultural understanding. In Korea, English (more specifically American English) is widely viewed as a means to succeed in society. This nationally prevailing view toward American "Standard English" as, so to speak, the International Language, results in the concept of the hierarchy among languages and cultures held by many Korean people. This also accounts for their feelings of inferiority toward white North Americans and Western Europeans and their feelings of superiority to people from other countries. I believe that English teachers, Koreans as well as native speakers, should keep this phenomenon in mind and make a conscious effort to promote the true meaning of English, whose first and foremost purpose is to communicate with people from different languages and promote their mutual understanding.

ADAPTATION

See Appendix B: Models of Culture Learning, p. 161.

Outcomes in this category are all based on learners' actual entry into a different culture with the goal of living and/or working there for an extended period of time. The emphasis is on learners' adjusting, fitting in, living, and working within the way of life of the host culture. Models of cultural adaptation all present adaptation as the eventual outcome of a lengthy and involved culture learning process. Depending on the model, learners' journeys from cultural ignorance to cultural adaptation follow different paths.

Different adaptation models describe the ultimate outcome in different terms. Gochenour and Janeway (1993) propose the "conscious establishment of self-sustaining and meaningful relationships in the host culture" as the culmination of "seven concepts of cross-cultural interaction." In his acculturation model, Brown (1994) proposes two possible outcomes, assimilation and adaptation, without drawing much of a distinction between the two. Kim (1997) speaks of the ultimate outcome as "internal growth" though an ongoing "stress adjustment," where learners cycle in and out of periods of stress as they adapt to the new culture. Hoopes (1979) proposed four options for outcomes: assimilation/acculturation, adaptation, biculturalism, and multiculturalism. Martin and Nakayama (1997) follow somewhat similar outcomes, suggesting a range of "modes of adaptation": assimilation, separation, integration, and marginalization (pp. 180–182).

Again, the outcomes here essentially advocate accepting the culture on its terms and adapting to it, not attempting to change it in any way. In general, this means that the learner will probably have to change his or her accustomed ways of thinking, feeling, and doing in order to function effectively and appropriately within, alongside, or even separated from the target culture.

1. *Look back on an extended stay that you made in another culture. Use Martin and Nakayama's modes of adaptation, listed below, to describe your experience. Why did you favor this mode? What were significant factors in your choices? (If none apply, offer your own definitions.)*

   ### Separation
   Culture learners choose to retain their original culture and language and at the same time avoid interaction with other groups in the host or target culture.

   ### Assimilation
   Individual culture learners do not want to keep a distinct cultural identity or retain their cultural heritage but rather seek to establish and maintain relationships with other groups in the target culture. Learners give up or lose many aspects of their original culture, including language.

   ### Integration
   Learners seek to maintain their original culture and language and also to maintain daily interactions with other groups in the target culture.

   ### Marginalization
   Learners show little interest in maintaining cultural ties with the dominant groups in either the target culture or their culture of origin. They live on the margins of the dominant culture, not fully able to participate in its political or social life due to cultural differences.

   Adapted from Martin and Nakayama (1997, pp. 180–82)

2. *Interview second language teachers about their students (who are learning the language in the culture). Ask these teachers which of these modes of adaptation characterize their students, and why. If none apply, ask for their own definitions.*

SOCIAL CHANGE

The viewpoints associated with this outcome all essentially involve learners' taking action to modify aspects of the target culture, based on a critical examination of that culture and guided by their own beliefs and principles. Learners consciously evaluate perspectives or practices in the target culture and take them into account as they seek to achieve their own ends or, if they disagree with these perspectives and practices, set out to change them. Learners thus act as change agents, and the overall learning outcome is learners' social action.

Critical examination does not mean criticizing the culture, done without an insider's understanding of the culture ("Why can't these people be more like us? If they could just get the trains to run on time, things would be a lot better in this country."). Critical examination instead assumes that learners have some insider understanding of the culture, coupled with a values-based interpretation or critical stance regarding some aspect of that culture. Learners do not necessarily seek to accept the products, practices, and perspectives of the culture as they are and adapt to them, but rather to take steps to change them ("I understand the origins and importance of this cultural practice, but I choose not to accept it and, furthermore, I will try to change it, based on my own strongly held beliefs.").

Such outcomes can be controversial, especially if they call into question the authority of dominant groups or perspectives within the culture, as in challenging unfair labor practices on behalf of immigrant workers, or advocating women's rights in male-dominated cultures. At the same time, social change outcomes can also privilege dominant groups within a culture, as in the promulgation of technological innovations among the middle class, or establishing educational programs for the wealthy. Culture learning for social change, in other words, does not necessarily mean social justice. Rather, it can represent any effort to change the culture by learners, be they religious missionaries seeking converts, businesspersons seeking new markets, environmentalists seeking pollution controls, health workers seeking disease prevention, educators seeking school reform, or immigrants challenging a landlord's rental practices.

In the language teaching field, the participatory or problem-posing approach to ESL literacy education (Wallerstein, 1983; Auerbach, 1992) advocates social change outcomes of "critical thinking and action" (Auerbach and Wallerstein, 1987). For learners, the intended outcome is both perception of the "social, historical, or cultural causes of problems in one's life...[and]...actions and decisions people take to gain control over their lives" (ibid., p. vii). This outcome originates in the work of Paolo Freire (1973), the Brazilian educator who sought to encourage learners to gain awareness of themselves and their social circumstances, to think critically about these matters, and eventually, through heightened self-confidence, to take action in the culture.

Critical thinking outcomes for culture learning are also advocated by Claire Kramsch (1993) in her "critical foreign language pedagogy." In her viewpoint, a central learning outcome in language and culture learning is reaching "a third place," a psychological space that learners construct for themselves. This third place is neither of their first culture/language nor of the second one they are learning. From this third place, learners can not only participate appropriately and effectively within the target culture, they can also gain "critical distance" from this second culture/language. With this distance, learners attain the means to critically examine the culture and to decide whether or not to act to change it.

From the field of multicultural education in the United States, James Banks (1991, 1997) advocates a number of scaffolded culture learning outcomes based on the integration of diverse ethnic and cultural views. The culminating outcome is "social action," which requires learners to "make decisions on important social issues and take actions to help solve them" (1991, p. 27). Ultimately, the goal is to help learners "acquire the knowledge, attitudes, and skills needed to participate in the reformation of the world's social, political, and economic systems so that peoples from diverse ethnic, cultural, and religious groups will be politically empowered and structurally integrated into their societies" (ibid., p. 28).

Other social change outcomes derive from intracultural education, where culture learning occurs as learners engage with members of other communities within their shared national culture. The primary culture learning outcomes in this area relate to overcoming prejudice and other forms of discrimination, with the intention of transforming social institutions and cultural practices. Diversity training, prejudice reduction, teaching tolerance, and unlearning racism are educational efforts designed to help learners not only face discriminatory beliefs and practices in themselves but also take action to eliminate them in the culture.

10.2 TEACHING CULTURE: SOCIAL CHANGE

You are a second language teacher. The following groups of immigrant students need language-and-culture classes to do their jobs in the culture. List possible social change outcomes they might undertake in the culture. Which groups would you consider teaching? Explain your choices.

- missionaries
- health workers
- business executives
- union organizers

- environmentalists
- animal rights activists
- migrant workers
- sales representatives

IDENTITY

These culture learning outcomes emphasize the psychological transformations that learners can undergo in culture learning. In one way or another, such outcomes result in a learner's enhanced or transformed sense of self. These involve notions of identity—linguistic, cultural, social, ethnic, racial, gender, and otherwise.

Viewpoints that concentrate on language as the agent of transformation revolve around the notion of becoming another person when using a second language. This is referred to in various ways: a new person (Brown, 1994), a language ego (Guiora, 1972), or a language personality (Grosjean, 1982) that learners develop as a result of increased proficiency in the language and engagement in the culture. Tacitly or explicitly, the model for these second language identities is often the native speaker, becoming like the people who speak that language—using the language as they do, sounding like them, dressing like them, and acting like them. Other viewpoints broaden the single language identity outcome to becoming bilingual—where learners' linguistic identity is of neither one language nor the other, but of both, or in the case of learners who speak more than two languages, a multilingual identity.

In contrast, Byram (1997) argues that a primary outcome of language learning ought not to be the native speaker, since this is not only impractical but, in fact, impossible. There are far too many variations of native speakers in a culture. Instead, he proposes that learners become "intercultural speakers," that they "see their role not as imitators of native speakers but as social actors engaging with other social actors in a particular kind of communication and interaction which is different from that between native speakers" (ibid., p. 21). Intercultural speakers bring their "social identities" to intercultural interactions, and these provide a frame of reference for "establishing relationships, managing dysfunctions, and mediating" between people of different origins and identities" (ibid., p. 38).

From the intercultural field come other versions of identity. Hoopes (1979) describes a "multicultural identity," in which a person develops a relativistic outlook on self. Janet Bennett (1993) proposes an identity outcome of "constructive marginality," describing a person who is on the margins of two or more cultures and is able to move among them. Kim (1997) puts forth "intercultural personhood," a perception of oneself that allows for a connection to humanity and "growth beyond the perimeters of one's own cultural upbringing" (p. 435). Adler (1982) describes a "multicultural man," whose "orientation and view of the world profoundly transcends his indigenous culture" (p. 411).

Minhee Kang describes how identity figures into her culture learning outcomes for her Korean students.

Teachers' Voices

Minhee Kang

Affirming learners' self-identities: I strongly believe that self-expression is one of the major purposes and functions for learning a foreign language and for communicating with people. Therefore, a language teacher should be aware that acknowledging and affirming self-identity is an integral part of teaching and learning L2. Designing lessons and providing tasks that invite students to share their individual identity is essential for each individual student to acknowledge that she or he is a unique and valuable being. Self-identity and appreciation are the starting points that inspire students to embrace differences and the uniqueness of other people and that prepare them to transcend labels of people. This is a smaller definition of celebrating diversity in a nondiverse classroom.

Investigations

10.3 *Learning Culture: Ranking Learning Outcomes*

Rank your own culture learning on a scale of 1 to 5 (least to most significant). Circle the number that corresponds most to the outcomes you have pursued in your formal culture learning experiences. For each ranking, write a brief explanation or rationale.

Culture-specific understanding	1 . . . . 2 . . . . 3 . . . . 4 5
Culture-general understanding	1 . . . . 2 . . . . 3 . . . . 4 5
Competence	1 . . . . 2 . . . . 3 . . . . 4 5
Adaptation	1 . . . . 2 . . . . 3 . . . . 4 5
Social change	1 . . . . 2 . . . . 3 . . . . 4 5
Identity	1 . . . . 2 . . . . 3 . . . . 4 5

10.4 *Teaching Culture: Ranking Teaching Outcomes*

Frameworks

Rank your own culture teaching outcomes on a scale of 1 to 5 (least to most significant). Circle the number that corresponds most to the culture learning outcomes you emphasize in your teaching. For each ranking, write a brief explanation or rationale.

Culture-specific understanding	1 . . . . 2 . . . . 3 . . . . 4 5
Culture-general understanding	1 . . . . 2 . . . . 3 . . . . 4 5
Competence	1 . . . . 2 . . . . 3 . . . . 4 5
Adaptation	1 . . . . 2 . . . . 3 . . . . 4 5
Social change	1 . . . . 2 . . . . 3 . . . . 4 5
Identity	1 . . . . 2 . . . . 3 . . . . . . 4 5

Examine your rankings for your learning and teaching above. List any similarities or differences you see in these two lists. Ask yourself these questions:

• What influences have my culture learning experiences had on my emphasis of culture teaching outcomes?

• What has had the most influence on the culture learning outcomes I now emphasize in my language classes?

As the preceding exercise may have demonstrated, many outcomes can overlap and intertwine in practice. Again, all these culture learning outcomes are interrelated and are integrated by individual learners. Each individual learner engages in the culture, acquires information, develops effective and appropriate behaviors, discovers explanations, and ultimately responds in a unique way. The overall, organizing outcome in culture learning is this individual response: knowing oneself.

Learners thus attain more than cultural or intercultural knowledge, skills, and understanding. They develop a capacity that goes beyond the specific culture(s) they are learning—an ability to respond to differences and overcome them, whatever these differences may be. This ability grows from specific language-and-culture learning and, in fact, depends on such learning. To capture this capacity of knowing oneself, I will use the term *personal competence.*

PERSONAL COMPETENCE

Earl Stevick (1986) coined the term personal competence (p.18) as a companion to linguistic competence and communicative competence, based on his view that language learning involved much more than language. Learners also gain competence in learning; they develop abilities that transcend subject matter, which Stevick classified as more within the domain of education. As I have adapted it, the concept of personal competence applies to culture learning, in this case, becoming a skilled language-and-culture learner.

A number of models address culture learning outcomes related to personal competence. From the field of learner strategy training (Cohen, 1990; Oxford, 1990; O'Malley and Chamot, 1990), outcomes feature learners' development of their abilities as language learners. In fact, Oxford (1994) makes a direct connection between acquisition of specific learning strategies and the development of cultural awareness. Stern (1983) lists similar outcomes, including enhanced self-esteem, self-confidence, willingness to take risks, acceptance of errors, broadening of one's horizons, seeing one's potential, and self-actualization (p.436). Paige (1993c) proposes related outcomes, such as tolerance of ambiguity, curiosity, and openness (pp. 190–191). Along these lines, I would also include culture learning outcomes that feature self-awareness (Fantini, 1999) or developing mindfulness (Ting-Toomey, 1999). Again, I put such outcomes as central, as personal competence, as the diagram below (adapted from Fantini, 2001) shows.

Figure 10.3: Culture Learning Outcomes: Personal Competence at the Core

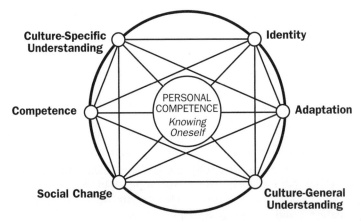

Personal competence, therefore, is the capacity that transcends or informs the learner's work in any of the other outcome areas. Personal competence can apply to any focus—language, communication, culture, or intercultural interactions.

The diagram on p. 119 illustrates how personal competence, as a dimension of knowing oneself, organizes the other culture learning outcomes discussed earlier.

The organizing outcome is personal competence, the capacities and abilities of the learner. Personal competence transcends any particular content area, such as language, culture, or communication. Through personal competence, the learner brings to bear knowledge, awareness, attitudes, and strategies appropriate

Figure 10.4: Hierarchy of Culture Learning Outcomes

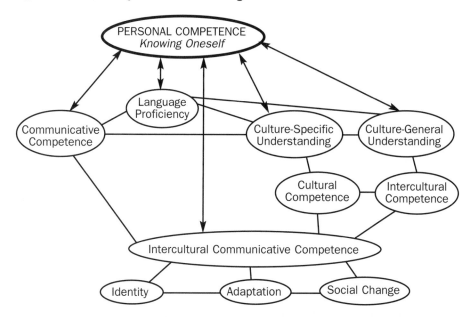

to the task at hand. Through language proficiency, the learner develops communicative competence, cultural understanding, or cultural and intercultural competence. These outcomes meld into intercultural communicative competence, from which other potential culture learning outcomes emerge—identity, adaptation, social change. These potential outcomes depend upon learners' personal goals, priorities, and circumstances. They also depend on the emphases that the teacher brings to the language classroom.

To generalize further across all these culture learning outcomes, I would say that all intend that learners confront, comprehend, accept, and overcome cultural differences. This process involves an interplay of mind, body, heart, and self—or, in technical terms, cognition, behavior, affect, and identity. As part of mastering the language, learners need to change the way they think, act, feel, and perceive themselves and their roles if they are to function effectively and appropriately in the other culture. Some models emphasize thinking, some stress acting, others highlight feeling, and some underscore being. Virtually every model features all four emphases, but in different proportions and for different purposes—all under the rubric of overcoming cultural differences.

Perhaps the key distinction among these models lies with differing notions of "overcoming" cultural differences. These range from simply changing one's mind or feelings about a given culture (*culture-specific understanding*) through recognizing how one's own culture affects acceptance of other cultures (*culture-general understanding*), learning to communicate appropriately in the second language/culture (*competence*), integrating oneself into another language and culture (*adaptation*), developing a distinct sense of self (*identity*), to taking action to transform a culture based on one's own beliefs (*social change*). Ultimately, the individual learner decides how to respond and develops skills as a culture learner (*personal competence*).

Seen from the perspective of the cultural knowings, these outcomes can be stated in broader terms. These four knowing outcomes overlap, intertwine, and are interdependent. The more you participate in a culture and use its language, the more know-how you acquire, and the more you know about it. The more information you acquire about the culture, the more accurate your cultural explanations become. In turn, the more perceptive and accurate your explanations are, the more thoughtful and empathetic you become in your responses to that culture. On the other hand, these outcomes can be separated and emphasized differently, depending on the learning circumstances. Nevertheless, in my view, knowing oneself is the dominant, organizing outcome. Learners encounter, process, and integrate all cultural information, behaviors, and explanations through self-awareness.

To a large degree, these varied outcomes are due to differences in learning contexts, such as a second language or a foreign language context, the overall purposes of language/culture curricula learners encounter in schools, or learners' individual goals. Outcomes shift considerably depending on whether learners are to engage directly with people of the culture or are to learn their language and learn about their culture from afar. Learners' attitudes toward the language and culture also exert an influence on outcomes. On another level, the distinction in outcomes reflects different philosophies of education that teachers and learners encounter in schools and institutes.

Given these contextual variations, teachers themselves still need to come to their own decisions about culture learning outcomes. As language-and-culture teachers, not only do we need to articulate culture learning outcomes for our students, we need to do the same for ourselves.

Minhee Kang describes how she, as a Korean teacher of English, needs to present herself to her Korean students.

Minhee Kang

Portraying myself as a role model: As a Korean teacher of English, I see myself as my Korean students' role model. At one point, while learning English as a teenager, I idolized the American and European cultures, and absorbed any information about this culture. However, thanks to some of my English teachers in college (Koreans and native speakers) and my own inquiring process, I began to revalidate my self-identity, to appreciate the beauty of my culture and language, to become fascinated by the function of English as a means for intercultural communication, and to expand my worldview beyond the American and European white upper-class cultures.

For this reason, I see a great value and advantage in portraying myself as a role model for Korean students so that they can relate to me. Aiming at teaching diversity in both the definitions I describe above and promoting multiculturalism, I will strive in my daily teaching practice to promote my core beliefs and principles in teaching and learning English—helping my students affirm their self-identity, validate their view about culture, and expand their worldview.

Review Minhee Kang's statements of culture learning outcomes in this chapter and compare them with the list of culture learning outcomes on page 108. Answer these questions:

- What factors influenced Minhee Kang's decisions about culture learning outcomes?

- What are the significant connections between her own language and culture learning and her principles and beliefs as a language/culture teacher?

- Put yourself in Minhee Kang's situation. Describe how your response would be similar or different.

Learning language-and-culture can take us in many directions, to many destinations. If we are nonnative speakers of the language we teach, like Minhee Kang, our own learning experiences deeply influence the culture learning outcomes we present to our students. Whatever our background, we need to attain awareness of the possibilities from our own experiences and those of others, and at the same time, we need to decide which outcomes to foster in our language-and-culture classes. These decisions depend on the language, the students, and the realities of the schooling context.

Suggested Readings

With the publication of the National Standards for Language Learning (NSFLEP, 1999), the language teaching profession in the United States has articulated important culture learning outcomes for language learners in the areas of communication, culture, comparisons, communities, and connections. These are the basis for foreign language curriculum revisions in many states, and I believe that they can be applied to ESOL curricula as well. Michael Byram (1997), in *Teaching and Assessing Intercultural Communicative Competence* provides a detailed discussion of language and culture learning objectives, along with teaching and assessment strategies.

11

THE CULTURE
LEARNING PROCESS

It was the first afternoon of my weekend homestay with an Ivorian family in West Africa, and I had just been introduced to everyone. I was sitting on a low wooden stool with the family and their guests on benches in the shade of a large mango tree in the courtyard of their compound, trying hard to recognize any of the few words in Dioula that I had learned. As the adults talked, I noticed a child of about five years sitting cross-legged next to me, his brows knit, his gaze hard upon me. He was studying me intensely, looking me up and down. After a time, he reached out, touched my arm, and lightly rubbed his fingers against my white skin. Slowly, he withdrew his hand and resumed his contemplation. A few minutes later, his face cleared. He looked at me and said in a low voice, touching his skin, "Ça, c'est bon." He then pointed to my skin and said, "Ça, ce n'est pas bon." He then turned away and joined the other children.

"This is good. That is not good."

My jaw dropped. I guessed that I was the first white person this black child had seen up close. Confronted with an undeniable difference between the two of us, I figured that he needed to reconcile this for himself. I couldn't tell if he was expressing reassurance for himself or pity for me, a white man obviously out of place in his world. Whatever he was thinking, his observations reminded me that he was black and I was white. Up until this point in Africa, I had not fully recognized that I was indeed white nor had I realized that this would make a difference in my experiences in Côte d'Ivoire.

This experience has stayed with me, because this child's reactions captured so dramatically and honestly the initial encounter with difference that lies at the heart of culture learning. Since that time, I have witnessed similar reactions in students in my language classes, and in language teachers in my culture classes—novice and experienced alike. And I have seen them in myself. Unlike the Ivorian boy's terms, the words used may not be "good" and "not good," but are euphemisms for the same. The new—the unknown, the extra-ordinary, the different—is perceived as right or wrong, comfortable or uncomfortable, interesting or boring, fascinating or weird. The challenge is to move beyond such reactions to acceptance of difference and ultimately, if possible, to integration of another language and way of life into our own. What is the process of culture learning that leads to such outcomes?

In this chapter, I propose that the process of culture learning be made explicit and that it be included in the language-and-culture curriculum. The process, in other words, becomes part of the content. Learners' experiences with learning language-and-culture need to be verbalized and compared with existing models of culture learning. The model that I propose for this process is based on the experiential learning cycle.

MODELS OF CULTURE LEARNING

As I said in Chapter 1, there are many views about the nature of culture learning. In Appendix B, I summarize seven models of culture learning: Hanvey, Brown, Hoopes, Gochenour and Janeway, Bennett, Kim, and Paige. In one way or another, these models feature encounters with cultural differences and how learners tend to respond to these encounters. These models of culture learning are based on learners' direct experiences in the host culture and interaction with people of that culture. They highlight the adjustment process as learners learn about and change to meet the requirements of the culture, while they are immersed in it. If they progress, learners pass through stages, phases, or passages, gradually accumulating knowledge about the culture, appropriate cultural behaviors, fluency in the language, and ultimately changing their attitudes—toward the target culture, their own culture, themselves, and cultures in general.

See Appendix B, p. 161.

These models are instructive in that they provide frameworks for situating learners along the continuum from initial contact to full adaptation. They are particularly relevant for second language classrooms, where learners are surrounded by the target culture and language and are in the process of cultural adjustment. In foreign language classrooms, on the other hand, learners do not generally have access to direct experiences or interactions in the culture. Nonetheless, their indirect encounters with cultural differences can also be compared with these models (Mantle-Bromley, 1992).

Taken together, these models of culture learning describe a similar process, but from different perspectives, with different emphases and different outcomes. All stress that the culture learning process involves changes within learners—changes in the ways they think, feel, and act. Almost all models emphasize that this process involves psychological intensity, stress, or shock of some kind, which learners need to manage in some way. The process also involves learners' finding ways of establishing and maintaining relationships with members of the new culture. These relationships depend not only on the learners but also on the members of the host culture and their perceptions of the learners, and the degree of receptivity they display. Also, the process, as a few models suggest, is idiosyncratic; all learners go through the process in unique ways, leading to different outcomes.

For the relationship between culture learning models and outcomes, see Chapter 10, beginning on p. 107.

With a few exceptions, all models attempt to describe a process that is essentially an unconscious one, especially in the early phases. In other words, culture learners tend not to know what is happening to them, or why they feel the way they do—that they are experiencing cultural conflict or stress. They tend not to recognize that they are in such a process. Because so much of culture is tacit, this lack of awareness is understandable. Indeed, most models seem to suggest that the culture learning process is one in which learners move from an unaware state to one of awareness as they discover their culture, their cultural conditioning, and recognize the same circumstances in the other culture.

The key to "teaching" this unique experience is self-awareness, knowing oneself. At some point in this process, learners need conscious awareness of themselves. They need to recognize what they are going through and to purposefully take action. As teachers, we can help learners bring their experiences to the surface, to expression and articulation, so that they can decide how to respond to the culture. When learners do name their experiences—what they perceive, think, or feel—we need to be ready to help them situate this within a larger framework. This is the point at which established models of culture learning prove most useful. When learners can place their experiences against these models, they gain additional perspective and clarity.

I propose that the process of culture learning be conscious and explicit, following the stages of the experiential learning cycle. I have liberally adapted Young Yun Kim's model of stress-adaptation-growth (1998) to include these stages. With this model, I do not propose that this is how culture learning occurs, but that this is a way to process it in the classroom.

Table 11.1: Culture Learning in the Classroom

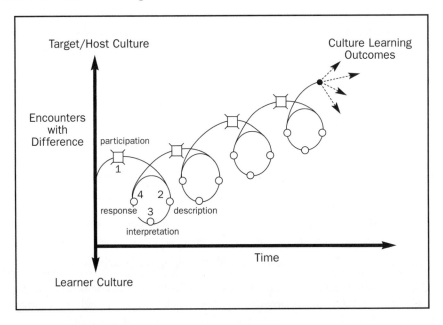

In this model, the process of culture learning consists of an ongoing series of encounters with cultural differences presented through structured participation in the language-and-culture curriculum (products, practices, perspectives, communities, persons). These differences can trigger emotional reactions. Guided by the teacher, the learners engage in description, interpretation, and response, consistent with the stages of the experiential learning cycle and cultural knowings. Over time, through repeated encounters and explicit reference to models of culture learning, learners acquire more knowledge of the target culture, develop more appropriate linguistic and cultural behaviors, attain greater understanding, and enhance their awareness of their own culture, their intentions, and their competence as culture learners. Depending on learners' intentions and their learning circumstances, the ultimate outcomes will vary. This process features a constant back-and-forth between the learners' culture and the culture they are learning. This relationship, in fact, is critical. The extent to which learners feel welcomed, accepted, or included by members of the other culture exerts great influence on their process.

This model is based on the following assumptions:

1. Culture learning can be a conscious, purposeful process.

In the language classroom, we have a forum for examining the culture learning process (Archer, 1986). We can present models and theories of culture learning as a part of the language-and-culture curriculum. We can invite learners to share their experiences, and help make sense of them, using these models and theories. By triggering awareness and understanding of this nature, learners can articulate their intentions and identify appropriate strategies to advance their culture learning (Oxford, 1990).

In this regard, Gochenour and Janeway (1993) propose a model for culture learning that is distinct from others. They present this process as an intentional one, very much as a series of tasks that learners need to go through in order to establish themselves in the culture, ranging from observation and communication all the way to consciously choosing to change. Originally developed as a crosscultural training tool for professionals going abroad, it provides a valuable set of guidelines applicable for language-and-culture learners.

2. Culture learning requires managing emotions.

Encounters with cultural differences frequently evoke emotional reactions. These emotions run the gamut from euphoria to anxiety, from feelings of excitement when faced with the new culture to disorientation, shock, and anomie (a loss of identity). Our emotions are the gatekeepers to our cultural perspectives, guardians of our worldview. Our perceptions, values, and beliefs are an awesome force—as they should be. After all, they hold our world together. It takes a conscious effort to step outside of them, and to do so calls for recognizing and managing these emotions.

While easily recognized, emotions are not always easily managed. This is where the stages of the experiential cycle aid. Once ignited, emotions need to be separated from the encounters that engendered them. The stage of description allows learners to dispassionately recount the source of their feelings; the stage of interpretation allows them to come to an understanding of the cultural differences in play; and the stage of response permits them to reassess their original feelings, this time with greater insight.

All models acknowledge the role of emotions, but Paige (1993b) addresses them most squarely through what he calls "intensity factors" or predictors of emotional stress. These factors are useful in that they provide concrete points of reference that learners can apply to their experiences.

Bennett (1993) also addresses emotions; his model is helpful in naming and explaining the specific attitudes that learners may hold toward themselves and the culture they are learning, particularly the stubborn entrenchment that can occur in his ethnocentric stages of denial, defense, and minimization.

3. Culture learning depends on cultural comparisons.

The culture learning process runs back and forth between the learner's culture and the culture under study. There is an ongoing series of encounters with differences in cultural products, practices, perspectives, communities, and persons. There are similarities as well, but it is the differences that evoke the learner's culture or worldview. To learn the new culture, learners need to purposefully construct an understanding of the other worldview, a separate reality, so to speak. They need to consciously navigate back and forth between the emic and the etic perspectives and ultimately come to a point where they can see the world from the other's perspective. Eventually, as learners attain an insider's understanding, there may be less need for explicit comparison.

In terms of learning, this process of constructing another worldview involves going from the known, one's own world, to the unknown. Schema theory (Carrell and Eisterhold, 1983) offers practical approaches here. Activating learners' schema—their own knowledge of their world—as a basis for comparison and contrast is an effective teaching strategy. Asking learners to describe what they know about their own culture before moving to the same topic in the target culture can help them make comparisons from a place of greater awareness.

Kim (1998) calls this a process of "deculturation and acculturation" that consists of discarding cultural behaviors or attitudes that do not fit the new culture while at the same time acquiring new ones. In contrast, Fantini (1999) sees it as a transformative process where the intersection of two worldviews can produce a recognition of both differences and similarities, which could be cultural universals (p. 178). In other words, constructing the new worldview may uncover shared perspectives and practices.

4. Culture learning requires making the tacit explicit.

The tacit lies within learners, and the task here is to help them express their opinions, thoughts, feelings, questions, concerns, and intentions. Their culture and their experience are evoked and voiced as they work through the cycle of participation, description, interpretation, and response.

Weaver (1993) has a captivating image of cultural conflict. He depicts it as two icebergs, the learner's culture and the target culture, coming into contact with one another. Because of their bottom-heavy structure, the icebergs crunch against each other beneath the water's surface, out of sight, with shock waves rippling upward to the peak. Like iceberg collisions, most culture conflicts occur outside conscious awareness, at the tacit level of culture. The learning task is to peer underwater with the learner so as to pinpoint the source of the conflict, the place where the learner's cultural perspectives collide with those of the other culture, and to bring this to the surface through words.

5. Learner characteristics affect culture learning.

Learners bring their own orientations to the culture learning process. In addition to their goals and intentions, and their previous experiences, there are also other factors that relate to learners' attitudes toward themselves and others.

Kim (1998) speaks of the learners' "predisposition" or "mental, emotional, and motivational readiness to deal with the new cultural environment," (p. 300) which she labels as "personality traits: openness, strength." (ibid.) She also talks about their "ethnicity" (ibid.)—a term that she uses broadly to describe learners' "distinctiveness" as persons, since this will affect how they are perceived by members of the host culture. Hanvey (1979) speaks of "a readiness to respect and accept, and a capacity to participate" and a "plasticity, the ability to learn and change" (p. 51). Not all learners come with such predispositions. The teaching challenge, consequently, is to help such learners develop these outlooks and orientations.

6. The relationship between the learner's culture and the target culture affects culture learning.

Kim's model, more than others, underscores that culture learning is a shared undertaking. It depends on both the learner and the members of the culture. She names the "receptivity," the "conformity pressure," and the "ethnic group strength" of the host culture as key factors in the learner's ultimate experience—in effect, the degree to which the culture welcomes or otherwise involves the learner in the culture. Along the same lines, Brown (1994) cites "social distance"—the perceptions of similarity or difference that the learner has of the target culture—as an influential factor. In simple terms, this means bringing the perceptions of the target culture into the process: how people of this culture perceive learners and their actions in a particular situation.

7. The instructional context affects culture learning.

The educational circumstances—the school, the curriculum, the intended culture learning outcomes, the materials, the pedagogy, the teachers—all exert great influence on the nature of the culture learning. A second language context, learning culture in the culture, is significantly different from a foreign language context, learning culture from a distance. The degree of direct engagement in the culture—its products, practices, communities, or persons—also makes a difference.

8. The teacher–student relationship affects culture learning.

Because this process takes place in the language-and-culture classroom, the teacher plays a critical role. The nature of the working relationship that the teacher establishes with learners by structuring the cultural experience and guiding learners through the stages of the experiential learning cycle is crucial. To a great extent, this relates to the way that teachers decide to present both culture and culture learning in their classrooms. Damen (1987) proposes, for example, that language teachers can present themselves as "mediators," whose role is to help students make transitions from one culture to the other.

To reiterate, the classroom culture learning model is essentially a procedure for processing the encounters with difference that inevitably arise in language classes.

11.1 *LEARNING CULTURE: TIME LINE*

1. *Make a time line that lists your personal history of language-and-culture learning, beginning with your culture of orientation and including other cultures/languages you have encountered since then, up to the present. List dates, names, places, and durations of experiences. Be as comprehensive as you can. Try to put it on one page if you can. For example:*

2. Draw circles around those experiences that you consider significant in your learning. For each of these circled experiences, write a brief paragraph that describes what made the experience significant. Describe no more than five experiences.

3. Analyze these experiences using the models described in Appendix B. Which help explain your culture learning experiences?

11.2 *TEACHING CULTURE: LEARNERS' TIME LINES*

Have your students map their own culture learning experiences following the above procedures.

To summarize, the process of culture learning is a developmental one that can lead to different outcomes, depending on the abilities and intentions of the learner, the context in which the learning occurs, and the attitudes of the host culture toward the learner. At the core are learners' encounters with differences. Guided by the teacher and the experiential learning cycle, the learner reacts and responds to these differences through a process of comparison, contrast, and ultimately a transition away from culture one toward and into culture two.

In the following pages, Yasuko Ohmi, a Japanese EFL teacher, describes in detail her language-and-culture learning experiences. She tells her story of learning English and her encounters with culture in the United States and elsewhere.

As you read through Yasuko Ohmi's account, map her experiences on a time line. Note the points of stress that she experiences and how she develops responses. Notice her use of culture learning theories.

Yasuko Ohmi

There is no doubt that English learning and crosscultural experiences have been the closest to what I felt were my life needs and goals. What interests me is to find out what has kept me motivated to pursue these needs and goals. In other words, what are my penetrating, hidden, and true reasons for them? What is the meaning of English learning in terms of my goals at the innermost level?

What I intend to do in this section is to objectively reflect on my English learning and crosscultural experiences and critically analyze my motivations. This, I believe, will give me the clues to a better comprehension of my final objectives for learning English.

Until I entered the university, I felt that school was like a prison for me. In the Japanese educational system, entrance examinations for either public or private high schools and colleges/universities are the most stressful obstacles for both teachers and students. What is tested in the examinations generally requires a tremendous amount of memorization. Test scores are the ultimate criteria for evaluating students. For the first three years before passing the exam for high school, and for the next three years prior to the exam for university, I was always threatened by the test scores, and I felt incredible pressure. However, I could not avoid this "examination hell," and I entered a university because I believed that this was the only choice left to me in my little social world, including home and school.

In this unpleasant early period of my schooling, English gave me a different perspective on life, more than any other subject matter, by opening up a world of exciting musicality and otherworldliness. Although I had had very little contact with native English speakers in person until I entered the university and moved to a bigger city, I felt very much attracted to discover the differences in another language. In particular, the musicality of English, its different rhythm, intonation, and fluency, took me into a completely different world, which only people who know those codes can appreciate. This was an extremely exciting and liberating experience for me. In retrospect, it is significant to see that I began finding a way to discover another world through English, and to thereby escape my unpleasant, uncomfortable, and small world.

In Japan, English is introduced as the only foreign language at school, when students move up to the seventh grade, and it is a required subject. Two years before I entered the university, I began questioning what learning was and what I should be doing with English, although I did not find any appropriate places or circumstances to bring up these questions at that time. However, I strongly believed that the language should be communicative, and that the number of words one remembered was not the top priority.

Another thing that I thought important was to be able to pronounce like native speakers, even though the importance of native-like pronunciation was not emphasized very much at school. In Japan's school structure since World War II, "native English speaker" has always meant "white American English speaker." As I practiced pronunciation and fluency out loud all for myself on English programs from TV or radio, I always wondered how the image of myself speaking English was different from what I imagined for myself, and what other Japanese people and native speakers of English actually saw. This special interest and my phonetic skills were going to make me ask important questions about language learning later in my life.

Once I passed the entrance examination for the university, which was the last and most stressful examination in my life, I was greatly relieved. After I recovered from the exhaustion of "examination hell," I realized that I had lost the goal for learning in general, and that I was confused. When my friends began finding professional jobs a few years later, I thought that I should be getting myself to use my English skills. However, I was still unclear about what to do with English. A translator, an interpreter, or using English in one of many kinds of business companies—all of these jobs did not seem to fit my true interests.

Numbers of questions emerged for me: What has English learning been for me? What aspects of English did I want to learn? Why English? What do I want to do with English? These questions, which I grappled with at that point in my life, became the important reason on my own pathway to find a direction for a better and deeper learning, a path I have followed until this day. During that time, I always wished that schools and classrooms could have been the place for everyone to discuss and think about these questions. A teaching job was appealing to me. I was very concerned, however, about the strong pressure of the entrance examination at the public school. Also I was not confident enough because my crosscultural experiences were limited, and not sufficient for teaching English.

After graduating from the university, I worked as an administrative secretary at a private English school for about a year. I observed many native speakers of English who taught there. During this period, I realized that every native speaker of English was not necessarily able to teach the language effectively. Sometimes a nonnative speaker of English like me can see more about what specific points in the language need to be explained and how, because I had had the same kinds of problems the students were struggling with. This realization was the reason why I decided to teach English for the first time in my life. Thus I got a teaching position at another English school, which had much less pressure about the examinations and where I was freer to do what I wanted in the classroom.

When I began teaching, not only was my linguistic English knowledge very limited, so was my sociocultural knowledge. I studied many available textbooks published in America or in Britain. The teaching job made me study about the language and cultural differences more carefully. I learned many lessons from the students' errors. I also asked American friends to help answer grammatical questions and explain differences of nuances in similar vocabulary words. Discussing cultural differences also made me think about my life values. All of this was the most satisfying and effective learning experience that I had had up until then. In fact, I tried to take in Western ways of thinking and to integrate them into my whole being.

At the same time, I was feeling more and more suppressed by Japanese society. The social pressure on me at that age was to get married and adjust my career plans to my future husband's, all of which did not interest me. Because I was feeling uncomfortable with my life problems, I also heard all kinds of difficult life problems from my students, young and old. I found that many people, whether young or old, men or women, were having difficulties with their own lives and yet they could not find any place other than my English class to talk about these critical problems. Since many of my classes were private and carried out in English, which was foreign both to the student and to me as the teacher, we had an opportunity to express ourselves more freely and on a more equal footing regardless of the age differences.

This experience made me feel bewildered with life in general. My students talked about their important life questions with me in class. However, I had no place to talk about my own true feelings and questions about life in Japan. Outside the classes I felt unwelcome, disoriented, and uncomfortable in my own country. This made me decide to leave Japan to give myself time and space to discover more about myself. Also, these negative feelings toward my native country made me more motivated to assimilate myself to Western ways because they seemed more accepting and understanding of me.

Thus I finally got the first chance to leave my country. It was a Japanese teaching intern position on a voluntary basis for a school year at a public high school in Wisconsin. Even though everything I did in the United States was a new experience, actually, it seemed to go well, very smoothly and naturally. At least the people around me observed it that way. One major reason for this was that my pronunciation was much closer to that of many Americans than that of many Japanese speakers of English. The other reason was that I knew basic social reactions and responses from information and skills through textbook readings, simulation practices, and role-plays with my students from my teaching situations. Also, I had already taken in some Western values as part of my own value system even before I came to the United States, although I was not clearly aware of it at the time.

This situation felt unbalanced to me and sometimes caused me to have contradicting emotional feelings, such as satisfaction and frustration, confidence and worry, excitement and exhaustion. I analyzed later that this was due to a big gap between my image of myself and others' image of me, and also between my expectations of myself and their expectations of me. This experience gave me an awareness that knowing from direct, concrete experience was quite different from knowing through intellectual information. I believe that experience helps people gain more real, powerful, and deeper understanding of themselves.

Another awareness that helped me in deciding the direction of my English learning was my realization of sociocultural differences between the United States and Japan. The stereotyped images that Americans in general have about Japan, and those of Japanese about the United States, largely reflected socioeconomic, socio-political, and historical backgrounds in the two countries. I was quite shocked about how little Americans in general knew about Japan, aside from its economic prosperity. This also made me real-ize how much I had been influenced by various sociocultural fac-tors, many of them outside my personal control. It was very disap-pointing for me to realize that I also knew very little about my own culture and had not even attempted to know in the past. Once again, I questioned my motivation and the meaning of English learning. My English skills were helpful in keeping me from feeling disoriented in my native culture, and this was significant for me. I had not realized, however, that I had been somewhat indifferent to my own culture and language. I had simply been looking for a way out of the frustrations I had experienced in Japan and a way into the wonders I saw in English. I had not realized that my own cul-ture was such an integral part of my identity.

This awareness was very significant for me because it made me think about myself as a social being, about who I am, in a broader and deeper sense. However, this question was too big and difficult for me at that time. Instead, I felt even more confused than when I left Japan a year earlier.

A year of living experience in the United States left a great impact on me but also left unresolved questions, both cognitively and affectively. Even before I left Japan for the United States, I had already discarded some part of my own social identity. The ques-tion "Who am I?" in regard to Japan's social structure had no importance to me at all. I had no specific desire to play an expected social role in Japan, although I missed Japan, particularly the ele-ments of "Japaneseness" in terms of language and familiar cultural dynamics. Despite some reservations, I had to return to Japan. My conflicting feelings on my identity, however, put me in a very diffi-cult situation when it came to adjusting to my own country again. Besides that, what made me feel even more insecure was that I began questioning and doubting myself and my own set of values.

I realized that my value system was developed from my individual historical experience over time. However, it was also a symbolic entity that conveyed meaning to my existence resulting from human social interactions that I had had in my life so far. When I attempted to analyze the meaning of my value system I had to admit that I had not only ignored but also even devalued my self identity by learning from and imitating the West. This realization made me lose confidence in my understanding of who I was. I reasoned that the 13 years of time and energy I had spent in English learning had led me in the wrong direction. At that time, I did not think that I belonged either to Japan or to the United States—or, for that matter, to anywhere else in the world. I felt lost and helpless. I lost the motivation to continue learning English. As a result, after my return to Japan from Wisconsin, I refused to have any interaction with an English language world for a few years.

After this prolonged period of time, I received an invitation to participate in an Asian conference for social concerns, held in the Philippines. This became a pivotal occasion to reevaluate myself as an English teacher. There were about 50 participants from over 15 Asian countries, none of whose native language was English. I clearly realized the importance of English as an international language during this conference. This experience helped me become aware of myself as a person born in Japan, in the modern postwar era, whose behaviors and values had become greatly westernized, with a fluent, white American English accent. Even so, I felt I was not able to grasp a native speaker's innate sense of the depth and impact of certain words and phrases in English because I had not been exposed to the cultural background of English as much as the people who grew up with that language. On the other hand, I had experienced firsthand the difficulties of learning a foreign language and culture. As a stranger to that language, I did have a uniquely objective perspective on English. Becoming an English teacher made great sense to me after this conference. I also felt a deeper sense of responsibility to help nonnative speakers of English become more articulate in expressing their own values in crosscultural situations.

Following this experience, I decided to enroll in a Master's program in TESOL (MAT) in the United States. In my studies there, I encountered a theory of second language acquisition that helped me to a deeper understanding of my questions on identity.

The acculturation hypothesis for second language learning that I learned in the MAT program was very helpful for understanding my identity more comprehensively. "Acculturation" is defined as follows:

> A process in which changes in the language, culture, and system of values of a group happen through interaction with another group with a different language, culture, and system of values (*Longman Dictionary of Language Teaching and Applied Linguistics*)

The significance of this finding for me was that I gained an ability to accept my "betweenness of identity," as I named it. "Betweenness of identity," as I define it, is a psychological state of mind that is distinct from that of a typical, traditional standard in native language and culture and second language and culture characteristics or customs. This state of mind, which is recognized in one's language, cultural behaviors, and/or system of values, is a result of the whole recreation process of a person's own identity after taking different characteristics from the second language or culture into the person's original identity, arranging and integrating them so that the whole self identity can stand coherently. Therefore, it exists somewhere in between native language/culture and second language/culture. However, this is considered not as an incomplete or inferior identity, either to native language/culture, or second language/culture, but as another, originally created, independent one.

Before I defined this concept, I thought I had to choose one or the other in order to feel a sense of belonging to a specific social group. This put a lot of pressure on me and resulted in my being pushed aside from both cultures. In other words, I marginalized myself culturally. I felt uncomfortable and painfully lonely, since my state of mind was not strictly Japanese any more, in a traditional pattern, and yet I did not desire to be an American either. The acculturation hypothesis helped me realize the importance of understanding and accepting who I am, as I am.

As I began to regard the "betweenness" as one of the key concepts of my identity, I also began to recognize the application of this concept to other people's different situations. Some are in between other cultures; some are in between genders. The commonality of betweenness created a sense of connectedness among people. For me, this has also provided heartfelt support and encouragement to me, which I truly appreciated. Before I knew it, I found that I had become a little less confused, a little less lonely, and a little more secure.

I found that the betweenness includes a good deal of vagueness, confusion, inner and outer conflict, and frustration, and that it is a highly individualized and intangible process. What was helpful to me from the MAT experience was to have been able to label this phenomenon as betweenness, and to have received understanding support from friends and faculty members.

I see that my English language learning process has played a most essential role in my search for the innermost self. Learning English has created a great deal of opportunity for crosscultural experiences, which have helped me reflect, test, and transform my values, beliefs, and helped my state of mind.

11.4 *LEARNING CULTURE: APPLYING MODELS OF CULTURE LEARNING*

Review the time line you constructed for Yasuko Ohmi in Investigation 11.3. Identify critical experiences or incidents and circle them. Share your results with those of a colleague. Discuss the following questions:

- What strikes you as most significant in her account?
- Which of the models in Appendix B best characterize her learning experiences?
- How does her experience compare with your own?

Culture learning can follow different paths and accompanying processes. As language-and-culture teachers, our most useful strategy is to concentrate on knowing oneself. When we encourage learners to give voice to their experiences, we can help them make sense of them. Existing models of culture learning can provide learners with useful points of comparison. As Yasuko Ohmi recounts, the framework of acculturation spurred her to invent an interpretation of her experience, "betweenness." This allowed her to break through a dilemma and come to terms with her learning.

All learners have a story of their own, equally compelling, waiting to be heard.

Suggested Readings

I find that biographies and autobiographies of language-and-culture learners are excellent resources for insights into the process of culture learning. There are many such books. One of my favorites by Eva Hoffman is *Lost in Translation: A Life in a New Language,* a compelling story of a young woman who emigrates to Canada from Poland, and how she gradually adjusts to language, culture, and identity, eventually making her living as a writer in her second language, English. I also like *French Lessons: A Memoir,* where Alice Kaplan tells her story of learning French, French culture and literature, leading her to a position as a college professor of French. Her path was quite different from mine. *Distant Mirrors: America as a Foreign Culture* (DeVita and Armstrong, 1998) is a compilation of accounts of cultural anthropologists from other countries who describe cultural differences they encountered in the United States and analyze the reasons. These accounts show the impact of approaching culture learning as a conscious process.

12

TEACHING CULTURE

*I stood an the edge of the courtyard next to the bus with the other
French teachers and group leaders, watching the end of our day trip
to the lycée near Honfleur unfold. All 30 American students were
there, scattered about, engaged in conversations with three times as
many French students from the lycée that overlooked the courtyard.
Groups of French and American teenagers were standing, sitting on
benches, or cross-legged on the flagstones, leaning toward one
another, gesturing, laughing, and obviously talking. I turned to the
other teachers and smiled, thinking to myself, "It's working."*

The bus driver blew the horn. Students looked up and saw us motioning to
get on the bus. It was time to say good-bye. And, of course, the French
teenagers said good-bye in their way: They kissed the Americans on both
cheeks—*la bise.* I watched the Americans at first recoil slightly, or hesitate, or
perform the gesture awkwardly. Gradually, as they said good-bye to more and
more French boys and girls, they gained confidence, coordination, and in a few
cases even initiated the kissing themselves.

The day before in class we had rehearsed exactly this act of greetings and
leavetakings in anticipation of the visit to the *lycée.* We had asked the young
Americans to practice *la bise* with each other through role-plays. The reactions
came fast and furious. Almost all of them refused to do it, a few even rejecting
the whole notion. "I'll just shake hands," one announced, his arms folded across
his chest. Even though we discussed their reactions and explained this custom,
many students were still not convinced. Now, as they climbed on the bus, one
of the boys smiled and said to me, "They really do kiss each other!" His smile
broadened, and he added, "I did it!"

It was a privilege to observe our language students in action in the culture,
applying what they had not quite learned, pulled by the force of relationships,
by real people in a real situation. This is the ultimate goal of teaching culture,
when learners move from the classroom culture learning model out the door
into the other way of life.

There are many techniques and materials for teaching culture in language
classrooms. If you opened the book directly to this chapter looking for a collection of such techniques, you will probably be disappointed. I do describe a
few, but other books will give you many more. Instead, what I offer in this chapter is an approach to teaching culture, an overall strategy for addressing culture
with language learners. If you have arrived at this chapter by reading the preceding ones, you know that this approach involves merging the content of
culture—products, practices, perspectives, communities, persons—with the

process of culture learning through the experiential learning cycle, and the cultural knowings, in what I call the cultural experience.

I begin with a summary of the guidelines I propose for teaching culture, followed by a detailed summary of the cultural knowings framework, then offer suggestions for working with the distinct teacher roles, and end with a review of the cultural experience.

GUIDELINES FOR TEACHING CULTURE

1. Teaching culture consists of guiding learners through the cultural experience to develop cultural knowings.

2. Organizing the cultural experience involves joining cultural content and the learning process through the four stages of the experiential learning cycle.

3. The cultural content learners examine derives from an analysis of products, practices, and perspectives of the culture, which are set within certain communities and uniquely manifested in persons of that culture.

4. As learners move through each of the stages of the experiential learning cycle they develop cultural behaviors (knowing how), acquire cultural information (knowing about), discover cultural explanations (knowing why), articulate personal responses (knowing oneself), and, by repeatedly employing this process, build skills as culture learners (personal competence).

5. To engage in each of these stages, learners acquire the language-and-culture of participation, description, interpretation, and response.

6. The teacher needs to identify culture learning outcomes. Outcomes vary greatly depending on the educational context, the curriculum, the learners, and teachers, and they can range from culture-specific understanding in a foreign language context to assimilation into the culture in a second language context.

7. Every learner goes through the culture learning process in a unique way. Because of these individual variations, one of the primary tasks for the teacher is to help learners express and respond to their cultural learning experiences.

8. The experiential cycle, by organizing the learning process into four distinct stages, delineates language-and-culture content, activities, and outcomes. Each stage—participation, description, interpretation, response—deals with a different aspect of culture and culture learning.

9. For each stage of the cycle, the teacher needs to select and structure particular content areas, learning activities, and accompanying learning outcomes. In each stage, learners are thus engaged in distinct tasks.

10. In teaching each stage, the teacher must play different roles. These roles stem from different teaching strategies and call for different outlooks or attitudes on the teacher's part. Teachers need to consciously

interact differently with learners when teaching knowing how, knowing about, knowing why, and knowing oneself. The working relationship the teacher establishes with the learners through these roles is crucial.

11. Teachers need to be versatile. They need to be able to present or elicit cultural information, coach and model cultural behaviors, guide and conduct cultural research and analysis. They also need to be able to enter learners' worlds by listening, empathizing, and sharing their own experiences as culture learners so as to help learners step out of their worlds into another language, another culture.

12. Teachers need to be learners of culture. They need to go through the cultural experience that they propose for learners in their language classes. Such experiences will help teachers learn the culture of the learners and may also help lead teachers to new areas in their own culture learning.

As is evident, the approach to teaching culture I summarize in these 12 guidelines is based on culture learning. Put simply, the nature of the learning determines the teaching.

FROM LEARNING TO TEACHING

Joyce and Weil (1986) in *Models of Teaching* describe several approaches to teaching that are based on specific kinds of learning organized into four broad categories: information processing, personal, social, and behavioral. In very general terms, they classify these teaching strategies in terms of helping students "acquire information, ideas, skills, values, ways of thinking, and means of expressing themselves…also teaching them how to learn" (p. 1). Although none of the approaches relates specifically to culture learning as a whole, many of them are applicable. More specifically, Damen (1987) describes culture teaching in terms of culture learning. Based on her definitions of culture learning (derived principally from ethnography), she proposes five teacher roles: counselor, participant observer, resident pragmatic anthropologist, mediator, and fellow learner (p. 327).

My approach is similar. By examining the nature of the learning interactions—content, activities, outcomes, language functions—for each of the cultural knowings, I have identified specific teaching roles that lend themselves to the particular learning at hand.

CULTURAL KNOWINGS AND TEACHER ROLES

The chart below outlines the key roles for each of the cultural knowings, along with accompanying features of language-and-culture content, activities, and outcomes.

Table 12.1: **Cultural Knowings and Teacher Roles**

	Content	Language Function	Activities	Outcomes	Teacher Role
Knowing How	cultural practices	participating	developing skills	cultural behaviors	model coach
Knowing About	cultural information	describing	gathering information	cultural knowledge	source resource arbiter elicitor
Knowing Why	cultural perspectives	interpreting	discovering explanations	cultural understanding	guide co-researcher
Knowing Oneself	self	responding	reflection	self-awareness personal competence	listener witness co-learner

The nature of the learning interactions is the critical factor. Jaimie Scanlon used the cultural knowings framework to supplement the cultural content in the ESOL textbook at their university in Japan. In particular, they focused on the nature of these interactions as a way to help them identify cultural content, activities, and outcomes for a unit on greetings and introductions.

> Here is an outline of the curriculum supplement I prepared, along with the thinking that led to it.

Teachers' Voices

Jaimie Scanlon

Table 12.2: **Greetings and Introductions as Cultural Knowings**

Knowing About	Knowing How	Knowing Why	Knowing Oneself
Students learn:	Students experience:	Students explore:	Student reflect upon:
• that different types of handshakes exist. • that some handshakes are appropriate and some are inappropriate. • that eye contact is important in North American introductions. • the appropriate time for a handshake in an introduction. • reasons why small talk is important. • appropriate and inappropriate small-talk questions. • ways to respond to inappropriate personal questions.	• shaking hands in a variety of ways. • the contrast between a "comfortable" and an "uncomfortable" handshake. • making a natural, appropriate self-introduction in English. • initiating a conversation in English and using small talk to get to know a stranger. • North American style small-talk interaction. • asking and responding to appropriate and inappropriate questions.	• reasons why some topics may be considered polite or impolite by North Americans or Japanese. • values behind the handshake and the bow.	• how the bow is used in different situations. • their feelings and attitudes toward doing a North American style greeting. • similarities and differences between Japanese and North American small talk • their own reactions toward using a North American communication style. • their own cultural values regarding taboo topics. • personal views regarding what topics are OK to discuss

(Hansford, Sandkamp, and Scanlon, 2001)

For my greetings and introductions unit, I wanted to include a cultural component to add dimension to the language. I brainstormed what those could be, e.g., handshakes, appropriate or inappropriate small-talk topics, factors relating to age, gender, and so forth. I used the framework even in this process, looking at the four knowings and trying to brainstorm around these categories.

This resulted in my coming up with a much more extensive list of possible areas to cover in the unit than if I had relied solely on what was in the course textbook or off the top of my head. This was especially the case with knowing why and knowing oneself. Adding objectives into those areas was something I thought was extremely valuable for my students and for really helping to reach them on a deeper personal level.

Following the brainstorming process, I set about designing activities to reach the objectives I had made. For this, my two colleagues and I decided that we needed to define the learning interaction for each knowing. We finally decided that it referred to the way that students interact with the class material, i.e., knowing about—reading or listening about facts and getting information; knowing how—physically doing something in a way that differs from their own culture's way of doing it; knowing why—discussing or writing questions or guesses they may have about another culture's values or characteristics; knowing oneself—discussing or writing comparisons between the target culture's features and their own culture and discussing or writing about their reactions to particular features of another culture.

Once we determined these, it became easier to design concrete in-class activities to reach the objectives. For example, when the goal was for students to learn about handshakes, I came up with one activity in each applicable knowing category related to handshakes. They did a reading activity about handshakes, practiced different types of handshakes, contrasted Japanese bowing and Western handshakes, and wrote about their reactions to shaking hands during the in-class activity.

Investigations

12.1 *TEACHING CULTURE: CULTURAL KNOWINGS*

Choose a unit or chapter from your language curriculum. Use the four columns to brainstorm content, activities, and outcomes for each of the cultural knowings. Afterwards, compare your process with the way that Jaimie Scanlon went about it.

Once content, activities, and outcomes are established, we move into the classroom to teach culture, that is, to guide learners through the cultural experience, focusing on each of the cultural knowings.

THE CULTURAL EXPERIENCE

As explained above, the four cultural knowings correspond to the four stages of the experiential cycle. When presented in the form of key questions, each stage has a particular focus, as the diagram below indicates. These questions not only focus the learning for learners at each stage, they also focus the teacher's roles and responsibilities. By holding to the questions at each phase and consciously playing the accompanying roles, teachers can guide learners through the cultural experience.

Table 12.3: Focus Questions for the Cultural Experience

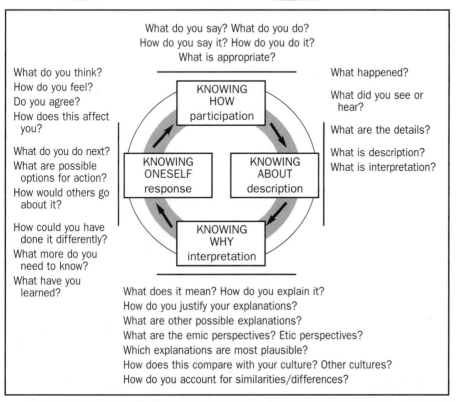

The sequence can begin with participation by putting the students directly into an experience of some sort, then following it with the other stages. Another common starting point is to begin before the experience with response, where students are asked to anticipate what they are about to encounter, using techniques of advance organizers or schema-activation (Carrell and Eisterhold, 1983), or preparation for experience (Jerald and Clark, 1989). Once the participation takes place, however, I recommend following the sequence of description, interpretation, and response.

In the following pages I present each of the cultural knowings through a table, followed by a discussion of teacher roles. The tables provide a summary of the content, activities and outcomes, as well as teacher roles. With the exception of the teacher roles, these topics have been addressed in previous chapters.

In presenting them separately, I acknowledge that we can work on each knowing by itself. This does not necessarily mean devoting an entire lesson to a particular knowing, although this is possible. The key is that teachers should be aware of which knowing they are working on and, as a result, which teaching roles they are enacting. This awareness helps maintain focus and purpose, especially when learners change the subject or when we are tempted to move on ourselves. Patience and persistence tend to pay off, in my experience. However, because learning tends to be a nonlinear process, where learners make nearly simultaneous connections when they are engaged in learning culture, holding too tightly to the pursuit of each knowing can sometimes derail learners. As with most teaching, it is a question of balance.

Table 12.4: **Knowing How Summary**

Content

Cultural behaviors consist of the skills required to engage effectively and appropriately in the practices of the culture: operations, acts, and scenarios.

- *Language*

    Mastery of the linguistic forms (phonology, lexicon, syntax)

- *Language-and-culture*

    Ability to select and use linguistic forms and nonverbal behaviors that are appropriate for a given social situation, or in a particular community through acts, operations, or scenarios

- *Culture*

    Ability to manipulate the products of the culture in an appropriate manner

Learning Outcomes	**Learning Activities**

The primary learning outcome is that learners demonstrate performance of the cultural behaviors, or competence. Competence includes these dimensions:
 	
- learners' ability to perform the behaviors effectively, or accurately
- learners' ability to select the appropriate forms of behavior
	Cultural behaviors can be presented and practiced through many forms:
	
	- *Operations*
	    Use of tools, artifacts, or other products of the culture
	- *Rituals*
	    Brief exchanges enacted in the classroom that reflect the everyday tasks of teaching and learning, done in the manner of the target culture
	- *Dialogues*
	    Scripted exchanges between two or more speakers
	- *Role-plays*
	    Structured, unscripted social situations in which learners carry out specific communicative tasks through specific roles

Learning Activities, *continued*

- *Performances*
    Participation in song, dance, sports, and games of the culture

- *Drama*
    Enactments of scripted scenarios (plays) with specific characters, actions, settings, props, etc.

- *Simulations*
    Creation of a simulated social scenario in the classroom where learners carry out certain scenarios in specific settings (e.g., a bank, a restaurant, customs, a meal)

- *Field Experiences*
    Excursions into the culture in which learners carry out specific tasks, followed by discussion and analysis in the classroom

Teacher Roles

The teacher plays two key roles in helping learners acquire cultural behaviors.

- *Model*
    The teacher demonstrates the cultural behaviors.
        "Watch me do it."

- *Coach*
    As learners perform the cultural behaviors the teacher shows/tells them how to do it.
        "Do it this way."

Knowing how is all about action: talking, doing, moving—even dancing, singing, playing music, eating, or otherwise expressing oneself in the manner of the people of the culture. With such an emphasis, role-playing becomes a central learning strategy. Learners need to act differently in the new language-and-culture, very much like actors on stage. They need to try out the range of expression available to them before ultimately deciding on how they want to present themselves in the new language.

As **model** and **coach**, the teacher shows learners what to do and how to do it. Modeling is rather straightforward, and consists of showing students the words or actions. Teachers can either perform the behaviors themselves or show learners other models, using audio- or videotapes or other outside sources. Coaching is somewhat different, and involves indicating to learners what to do as they are involved in the actions. As with other kinds of coaching, this also involves offering encouragement, support, and guidance.

Knowing how requires a good deal of practice. Acquiring skills or behaviors—verbal and nonverbal—is a trial-and-error process. Learners generally need numerous opportunities in order to master the linguistic, paralinguistic, and extralinguistic forms that make up cultural practices. Coordinating verbal and nonverbal language in one's own speech and in interaction with others is no small task. Not only do learners need to practice specific behaviors, they also need practice in choosing appropriate behaviors, according to the requirements of the social circumstances.

Modeling, however, entails much more than demonstrating gestures or pronunciation. It also means portraying oneself as a speaker of the language-and-culture. This relates to teachers' perceptions of themselves in relationship to the language-and-culture. As we have seen, this is a matter of identity. I believe it applies to both native and nonnative teachers. At the very least, learners are in the process of becoming bilingual, and teachers need to keep this in mind. A number of the teachers' voices sections in this book have addressed this kind of modeling, including those of Yasuko Ohmi, Joe Barrett, Minhee Kang, and Ani Hawkinson.

More than the other knowings, knowing how is a whole-person experience. Learners engage with actions, thoughts, and feelings. They cannot learn to participate in the culture by taking an intellectual approach, by learning about it; they have to do it. Participating in the culture, either directly or indirectly, can be at once exciting and intimidating. This experience often brings out feelings that need to be aired and addressed if learners are to develop the cultural behaviors in question. And in this respect, I believe that the teacher also has to create or model a safe classroom atmosphere for learners to risk these new behaviors.

12.2 *Teaching Culture: Knowing How*

Choose a short dialogue that features both verbal and nonverbal language. Present this to students and have them practice the interactions. Play the role of model and coach. Afterwards, ask students to comment on the process you were using as a teacher. What do these teaching roles demand of you?

Table 12.5: **Knowing About Summary**

Content
Cultural information includes several topic areas:

- *The target culture*
  Information about the products, practices, perspectives, communities, and persons of the culture(s) of the language

- *The learner's culture(s)*
  Information about the products, practices, perspectives, communities, and persons of the culture(s) that the learners bring to the classroom

- *Concepts of culture*
  Information about the nature of culture—definitions and theories, along with the terminology

- *Culture learning*
  Information about the nature of learning culture—concepts of enculturation, acculturation, adaptation, identity development, and strategies for managing encounters with cultural differences

- *Personal experiences*
  Information about teacher's and learners' direct (or indirect) experiences in the target culture or other cultures, and in culture and language learning

Learning Outcomes

The primary learning outcome is that learners demonstrate comprehension of the information presented:

- learners' ability to recall or restate the information presented
- learners' ability to separate "fact" (the information presented) from their interpretation or evaluation of that information
- learners' ability to recognize the nature of the information presented— as "fact" or opinion

Learning Activities

Cultural behaviors can be presented and practiced through many forms:

- *Authentic material*
  Products of the culture including documents, artifacts, or other cultural texts (e.g., books, newspapers, film, video, music, photographs, etc.)
- *Pedagogical material*
  Learning materials prepared for language and culture learners (e.g., textbooks, videos, films, sociological or anthropological studies, etc.)
- *Experiences*
  Direct participation in the culture (e.g., travel, field trips, home-stays) or participation in classroom cultural experiences (simulations, role-plays, demonstrations, etc.)
- *Personal accounts*
  Learners' and teacher's true stories about experiences in the target culture or in other cultures, or about culture learning experiences

Teacher Roles

The teacher plays four key roles in helping learners acquire cultural information.

- *Source*
  The teacher provides the cultural information.
  "This is what I know. This is what I have experienced."
- *Resource*
  The teacher shows students where to find the cultural information.
  "Read this. Look at this. Talk to this person. Write to this person."
- *Arbiter*
  The teacher evaluates learners' comprehension of the cultural information.
  "What did you read? What did you see? What did you hear? What happened? Is it there (in the text) or is it your opinion? Is this information fact or opinion?"
- *Elicitor*
  The teacher asks students about the cultural information.
  "Tell me what you know about this. What more would you like to know?"

Acquiring cultural information, knowing about, is the foundation of culture learning. Without a solid, well-rounded knowledge of the culture, learners' ability to develop cultural explanations will be limited or superficial. Information, as I see it, is not just about the culture under study, but also includes other topic areas essential for language-and-culture learning, such as the learners' culture(s), general concepts of culture, the culture learning process itself, and personal experiences. In fact, any aspect of culture can be presented and processed as information.

As **source**, the teacher role is to acquire information and present this to learners. As we have seen, acquiring all information about all the culture(s) of the language we teach is an impossible task, but we do have a responsibility to "know about," nonetheless. We need to be realistic, however. I believe that providing structures or systems for organizing knowledge (as in the cultural pentad) is a useful strategy. As **resource**, teachers serve as a conduit of information, showing learners where to go to find out what they need to know, and allowing learners to be a source of information for others in the class, including teachers. This is where the role of **elicitor** applies, asking students to share what they know. Together, these three roles ease the unreasonable pressure that teachers can place upon themselves to be experts in cultural knowledge.

As **arbiter**, the crucial role for teachers is to recognize content as information—as facts or data. This may sound obvious, but I have found that the distinction between fact and opinion frequently needs to be clarified for learners. Also, certain kinds of cultural information are more within the realm of fact or truth ("The capital of France is Paris."), whereas others fall more within the realm of interpretation or opinion ("Many French people have a special interest in food and its preparation."). The risk in presenting opinions and interpretations as facts is presenting cultural stereotypes or faulty generalizations as truths. In addition, learners need to focus on the information that is there (in the text), not on what is not there. Learners always bring their own interpretations and opinions of this information, and as arbiters, teachers need to point out the difference.

Another essential aspect of the arbiter role is to distinguish knowing about from knowing why. Simply providing students with information about cultural perspectives does not mean that students understand the significance of these perspectives through their own inquiry or hypothesizing. For this reason, it is critical to separate inference from fact when asking students to work with cultural information. Inference is the beginning of interpretation, an entirely appropriate strategy for the knowing why phase.

It can be difficult to hold learners to just the facts of a cultural phenomenon. In my experience, especially in the early phases, learners often resist this kind of emphasis and rush to interpret or declare their personal reactions. In time, however, this becomes part of the discipline of cultural inquiry. Learners sharpen their powers of observation. They see and hear more. They recognize when their own cultural frame of reference comes into play to influence their interpretation.

Information about the target culture(s) is essential. At the same time, because the cultural experience joins cultural information with culture learning, knowing about includes both content and process. Language teachers also need to know about how culture is learned. Such knowledge, when offered to learners, helps them understand what they are experiencing. Recall Yasuko Ohmi's story of culture learning in Chapter 11 which shows how she used information about the cultural adaptation process to come to terms with her own culture learning.

Knowing about the culture learning process is an effective antidote to many language teachers' chronic malady of not knowing enough about the culture they teach. Language teachers cannot know all about the culture they teach, especially if they are non-native speakers; there is simply too much to know about. Moreover, cultural information is constantly evolving, whereas the process that learners go through is much more predictable. Cultural information may change, but the process of acquiring that information remains relatively constant. Adding knowledge of the culture learning process can provide language teachers with a more balanced view of what they know.

To this end, teachers' awareness of their own cultural knowing is essential. In my work with language teachers, I have noticed that they tend to overlook the importance of their own learning experiences as a tool for teaching culture. These experiences can bring life to cultural information. Language teachers need to consciously take stock of what they know about the culture (and other cultures) and how they learned this.

There are various ways to articulate what one knows, but I believe that personal narratives, stories, and anecdotes are very effective. Language teachers can "story" their own language-and-culture learning experiences. The key to storying one's experience lies in making sense of it, namely by describing, interpreting, and responding to the experience. After all, this is what good personal stories are all about. They have characters, setting, action, plot, suspense, climax; they illustrate a theme; and they reveal something about the person. In the language classroom, the stories make a cultural point, linking cultural meanings and personal significance. Such stories become, in a manner of speaking, a body of knowledge that a language teacher, in the role of **source**, can provide to learners.

12.3 *TEACHING CULTURE: KNOWING ABOUT*

1. *Show students a picture or photograph that represents a social scene from the culture, preferably with lots of detail. Ask them one question: "What do you see?" As they answer this question, hold them to their observations and point out to them their interpretations. Stay with this exercise as long as you can. Consciously play the role of elicitor and arbiter. Afterwards, ask students to comment on the process you were using as a teacher. What do these teaching roles demand of you?*

2. *Following this activity, tell students a brief personal anecdote about your own experiences with some aspect of this social scene. Prepare your narrative beforehand by storying your experience as described above. Tell your story, playing the role of source. Afterwards, ask your students for their reactions to your telling of the story. What do you notice about this teaching role?*

Table 12.6: Knowing Why Summary

Content

Cultural interpretations include:

- *Emic perspectives*
    Perceptions, values, beliefs, and attitudes that the members of the culture use to explain themselves and their worldview

- *Etic perspectives*
    Perceptions, values, beliefs, and attitudes from other cultures or from culture-general concepts that the learners use to interpret the target culture

- *Comparisons*
    Explicit juxtaposition of emic and etic perspectives to gain insight into the similarities and differences between (and among) cultures

Learning Outcomes

The primary learning outcome is that learners demonstrate the ability to make cultural explanations. Explanations are of three types

- understandings of the culture on its own terms
- understandings of the culture using outside frameworks
- comparisons of the target culture to other cultures

Learning Activities

Cultural interpretations can be presented and practiced through many forms:

- *Cultural analyses*
    Structured inquiry into any cultural phenomenon where teachers ask students to explain the cultural meanings of the phenomenon. This inquiry can be in response to cultural information in texts (printed, spoken, visual) or cultural experiences (direct or simulated).

- *Research projects*
    Classroom-based or school-based research where learners gather information on cultural topics

- *Field experiences*
    Field-based research where learners enter the culture to gather information (observations, interviews, documents) to use in finding cultural explanations for particular topics

Knowing why is perhaps the most intellectually demanding of the knowings. Learners have to make sense out of the new cultural phenomenon. To do this, they bring their own worldview to the task, and their natural tendency is to explain what they see from their own etic perspective—as outsiders. To make accurate cultural explanations, they need the insider's view, the emic perspective. In effect, learners have to take on another worldview, to see from the viewpoint of the other. Learners need to consciously go back and forth from etic to emic, using comparison and contrast with their own culture as the primary learning strategy.

As **guide**, the teacher's role is to ask questions and generally not to give answers. The questions are designed to help learners go from the concrete to the abstract, from the cultural information they have acquired to the underlying cultural perspectives. This involves asking learners to hypothesize, to infer, to explain, to generalize, to justify, and to do other analytical tasks. As a guide, the teacher role is to note patterns, consistencies, inconsistencies, or to point out areas for further inquiry. I have found that the major task in this role is to resist the urge to answer one's own questions and give the impression that there is an answer. In many instances, there may indeed be one "right answer," but just as frequently, there are many. To develop skills in knowing why, learners need to seek out multiple perspectives.

As guide, the teacher works both inductively and deductively. The teacher can present learners with a cultural topic they know little about and ask them to use the information they do have to generate possible cultural explanations. To work well, the inductive strategy requires adequate information. It is a critical strategy and learners need to practice devising hypotheses based on their observations. However, if learners can go no further, it helps to employ a deductive strategy. In this mode, the teacher provides learners with a valid cultural explanation and then asks learners to search for evidence that supports this explanation. This strategy is necessary simply because we are all limited in our ability to induce cultural explanations. We need to consult cultural studies and other sources and apply the etic or emic perspectives they offer.

Cultural explanations need to be grounded in cultural information. Part of the inquiry process is eliciting or making explicit the connections between learners' explanations—hypotheses, assumptions, generalizations—and their sources for these views. Developing valid generalizations about a culture is a challenging task, especially for cultures with many communities. Learners need to be able to make generalizations that are reasonably valid and to avoid overgeneralizing or stereotyping.

As **co-researcher**, at the appropriate time—usually after learners have developed their own explanations—sharing one's own explanations may be helpful to learners. It follows that teachers need to do their own work on knowing why, as amateur cultural anthropologists or ethnographers.

12.4 *TEACHING CULTURE: KNOWING WHY*

Continue with the description of the social scene in the picture where the focus was on knowing about (see p. 147). Now ask students to interpret the cultural meanings in this social scene. (Before you begin, make sure that you have studied this picture and done your own interpretation of the cultural perspectives.) Play the roles of guide and co-researcher. Afterwards, ask students to comment on the process you were using as a teacher. What do these teaching roles demand of you?

Table 12.7: **Knowing Oneself Summary**

Content

The content of knowing oneself is the individual learner's worldview and personal competence.

- *Reactions*
    Thoughts, feelings, beliefs, and attitudes that emerge in reaction to the phenomena and experience of the target culture or culture learning. These are frequently expressed through feelings, "gut reactions," or other immediate reactions done without reflection or stopping to think.

- *Responses*
    Reflections on one's reactions, on the choices one faces in entering or adapting to the culture. This is a thoughtful, purposeful examination that requires stopping to think about one's reactions and analyzing them, and selecting strategies for subsequent culture learning.

- *Explorations*
    Examination and expression of one's worldview apart from reactions or responses to the target culture. Such explorations involve clarification of one's own values, beliefs, attitudes, and practices outside a specific cultural context.

Learning Outcomes	Learning Activities
The primary learning outcome is learners' expressions of self-awareness: <ul><li>awareness of one's own culture</li><li>awareness of oneself as a cultural being</li><li>awareness of one's own feelings, perceptions, beliefs, values, and attitudes</li><li>awareness of the consequences of one's actions</li><li>awareness of culture learning strategies and of oneself as a culture learner</li></ul>	Self-awareness activities consist of opportunities for self-expression through: <ul><li>*Reflection* Structured opportunities for learners to contemplate questions or topics as these relate to learners' lives and worldviews</li><li>*Focused talking* Structured conversations and discussions with others on these topics or questions</li><li>*Focused writing* Opportunities to reflect and write on these topics and questions</li></ul>

Teacher Roles

The teacher plays three key roles in helping learners acquire self-awareness.

- *Listener*
    The teacher listens to what the learner says.
        "Tell me how you feel about it. What do you think about this?"
- *Witness*
    The teacher states perceptions of learner words or behavior.
        "This is what I think you are saying/doing."
- *Co-learner*
    The teacher engages in the cultural exploration alongside learners, offering alternative explanations, information, and responses.
        "In my experience, I have felt this way about it."
        "This is how I resolved it."
        "These are the questions I'm still asking."

With knowing oneself, the subject matter is no longer the culture, it is the learner. Learners react to their encounters with the culture through their cultural conditioning. With reflection and distance, they respond. And all the while, they are in a process of exploring themselves in relation to another way of life. Knowing oneself is the most critical stage in culture learning, for it is the learner who ultimately must decide whether or not, or how, to respond to the culture. The more awareness learners bring to these decisions, the more informed their next steps.

In the role of **listener**, the teacher shifts the focus to entering learners' worlds and finding out as much about them as needed. Although very motivating, culture learning can also be extremely threatening to learners, especially when they are faced with making changes to their accepted ways of doing and being. In order to hear learners, the teacher needs to establish an atmosphere that allows them to feel secure, to express what they think and feel, and to articulate strategies for continued culture learning. In my experience, listening in this way is a willed act of empathy, a conscious decision to suspend one's own worldview, to accept—for the moment—whatever the learner has to say. Restatements, paraphrasing, and other forms of active listening are essential strategies.

Self-awareness is not always easily put into words. However, in order to monitor knowing oneself, the teacher needs to rely on learners' spoken and written language. More important, learners need to hear themselves name their thoughts, feelings, and questions. By putting this into words, they gain distance from themselves, which can lead to self-awareness. Learners will rightly determine the degree of personal information they are willing to share. Therefore, the teacher needs to be sensitive to learners' privacy. In some instances, learners may not realize what their personal boundaries are, and they may go too far by saying too much, which calls for teacher discretion.

Learning another language and culture often brings to the surface issues related to identity and acceptance. Teachers need to recognize that all language learners are embarked on a process of becoming multilingual, and this is a distinct realm of identity development. Adapting or integrating into another culture through another language calls for changes in attitudes and behaviors. Learners need to articulate the choices they face and recognize the reasons for their decisions. To focus on personal competence, teachers need to explore with learners the strategies they are using as culture learners. This involves learners' awareness of their learning goals and selecting relevant learning strategies.

As **witness**, the teacher role is simply to state what he or she sees in the learner's words. This is not just paraphrasing or active listening but is rather a form of interpreting what the learner is expressing. What makes it witnessing is that the teacher is not seeking any outcomes on the learner's part but is simply making statements.

As **co-learner**, teachers can play an important role by sharing their own processes of culture learning. As there are many paths to culture learning, it helps learners to make sense of their own by hearing others' stories.

12.5 *Teaching Culture: Knowing Oneself*

Following the interpretation of the social scene in the picture (see p. 147), focus on knowing oneself by asking students to explain the significance to them personally. (Make sure you have identified your own response beforehand.) Afterwards, ask students to comment on the process you were using as a teacher. What do the roles of listener, witness, and co-learner demand of you?

Thus, each cultural knowing concentrates on a particular kind of culture learning with accompanying teacher roles. The knowings can be addressed separately or they can be organized and sequenced through the cultural experience using the focus questions listed in Table 12.7.

Ani Hawkinson describes how she organizes and conducts a language-and-culture lesson in Swahili for adults, using the experiential learning cycle. (She uses versions of Kolb's terms for each stage.)

Ani Hawkinson

> On the first day of class this summer, I worked with the idea of greeting elders and demonstrating respect through the choice of greeting. I did this experientially.

I wrote a greeting for elders or teachers, *shikamoo*, on the blackboard, plus a response that a younger person would make to someone greeting them using a common (non-elder or teacher) greeting, specifically *sijambo*, which is the response for *hujambo*. I didn't tell students what anything meant or how to use it. I used no English whatsoever, since I wanted to simulate an actual experience of interacting as one would in the context I was working with—a more formal interaction between a teacher and student.

I simply entered the room, pointed to the first greeting, stood, and waited. Eventually someone said *shikamo*. I gestured to them that they needed to come up close to me, face me directly, and shake my hand as they said the greeting. Once they did this, I responded, with the appropriate response, *marahaba*.

I then greeted the students with an appropriate greeting, in this case *hujambo*. When they tried to respond with the response that I used, I pointed to the one on the board. Eventually they figured out that they needed to say *sijambo*.

I then invited other students to try to greet me and guided them with gestures to read the board and to interact with me as I would expect a student or younger person in a more formal context would do.

This was the end of the **experience** phase of the lesson.

For **reflection**, still using no English, I pointed to the words on the board, and wrote blanks, one following *shikamoo* and the other preceding *sijambo*. I then gestured for them to fill in the blanks with the appropriate words. We then pronounced the four words to make sure everyone had them. I also pointed to each sequence and tried to see if students could identify whom to use them with. So, for example, I would hobble around acting old and then point to the board and query (with my face) about which one to use. Then I chose two students and had one kneel (to indicate being shorter, younger, a child) and then gestured for them to use the correct greetings to one another.

For **generalization**, once I felt that everyone understood the significance of what they had seen in the experience, that is, one greeting for an elder, the other for a younger person, I proceeded to let them practice, with half the class on their knees being young, and half being old. I let them choose—using gestures, which by this time they were more comfortable with—whether they wanted to be old or young. Invariably the older students figured out that they could be the elder, and the younger ones accepted the younger role. Then I had them reverse roles. They moved around the room, practicing the greetings with one another. Kneeling and acting young or old tended to invite an element of play into what might otherwise have been a routine repetition exercise, and moving around the room choosing one's own partners allowed for some independence.

Also, through this exercise, I was providing them with the experience of greeting everyone individually, something which was important in my African family, at least, and in most settings I was in. You don't just come into a group and sit down, unless of course it is a Western-type setting. But this was not, of course, what I was teaching at the time. At this point, the experience was not explicit, so I didn't expect everyone to get it. But by the second or third day, after I have refused to begin the class until everyone had taken the time to greet their peers, they have learned the importance of greetings, and how they are more in-depth, less perfunctory than in U.S. culture.

Experimentation occurred when I stepped back and let them create what they wanted with the little language that they had. Someone would invariably try the elder greeting with another elder, and look to me to see if it worked. Or they would try it between two 'children' to see if that worked. If the greeting was appropriate, I would simply watch; if not, I would shake my head. So, over the course of experimenting on their own, they worked out which greetings could be used with which combinations of people.

At the end of class, there was time to talk about the whole lesson in English. They could verify that they had understood correct usage of the different greetings and could explore in discussion the significance of the differences that they noticed between what they were used to and what we did. This included thinking about how relationships between people might be different based on the apparent differences in how greetings were done. Some things I confirmed. For others, I told them to keep watching to see if their hypotheses bore fruit in future classes.

I wanted them to look behind the behaviors to what motivated them, not to accept things at face value and then move on. To cultivate this, I had to leave some of their questions unanswered, to value the asking of the question rather than the finding of an answer. There aren't always single answers for different cultural patterns anyway. Instead, there are usually different behaviors possible in one setting, as well as different reasons for one behavior. For students to begin to seek to understand what underlies the things that they see, that is, the behaviors, the process of active inquiry has to be encouraged, right from the beginning.

12.6 *TEACHING CULTURE: THE CULTURAL EXPERIENCE*

Analyze the way that Ani Hawkinson organized and conducted her lesson. How did she interpret each of the stages of the experiential learning cycle? How does her approach contrast with your own?

The cultural experience and the experiential learning cycle are acquired strategies. Learning styles and learning itself do not naturally occur in the form of four stages and four cultural knowings. Consequently, learners need practice with this approach to culture learning, just as they do with any learning strategy. The ultimate outcome, in my experience, is not only acquisition of language-

and-culture, but also self-awareness and personal competence—a capacity to enter other ways of life with purpose, confidence, and empathy.

Suggested Readings

In the chapter "Ways and Means" of *Culture Learning: The Fifth Dimension in the Language Classroom*, Louise Damen (1987) provides an excellent summary of many classic techniques for teaching culture, including critical incidents, cultural assimilators, culture capsules, and others. Tomalin and Stempleski (1993), in their book *Cultural Awareness*, provide a concise, comprehensive list of techniques and activities that focus on developing cultural awareness and promoting cross-cultural interaction in the language classroom. In *Intercultural Learning in the Classroom: Crossing Borders*, Helmut Fennes and Karen Hapgood (1997) have written an excellent book of accessible theories and many practical activities for fostering culture learning in classrooms in Europe. While not specifically addressed to language teachers, all the activities can be adapted to language classrooms. Kohls and Knight (1994) have compiled a number of excellent techniques for developing intercultural awareness, and in the appendices of their book, they have a useful list of resources for culture-general learning activities, including simulations and videos. Another valuable source for culture teaching materials and resources is the publisher Intercultural Press (www. interculturalpress.com).

Appendix A

ETIC CULTURAL PERCEPTIONS

These perceptions assume that all peoples, or humankind, share certain realities as part of the human condition. They further assume that all cultures have a point of view on these realities. Cultures perceive these realities differently; therefore, the perceptions appear on a continuum.

I have synthesized the following etic perceptions from a variety of sources (Peace Corps, 1997; Samovar and Porter, 1997; Lustig and Koester, 1999; Storti, 1999; Ting-Toomey, 1999), all of whom cite Kluckhohn and Strodtbeck, and have added others from other sources. Language teachers can use the self-rating scale to assess their own cultural perceptions as well as those of their students. Linking perceptions to practices is an effective clarification strategy.

1. Perceptions of Humankind (Kluckhohn and Strodtbeck)

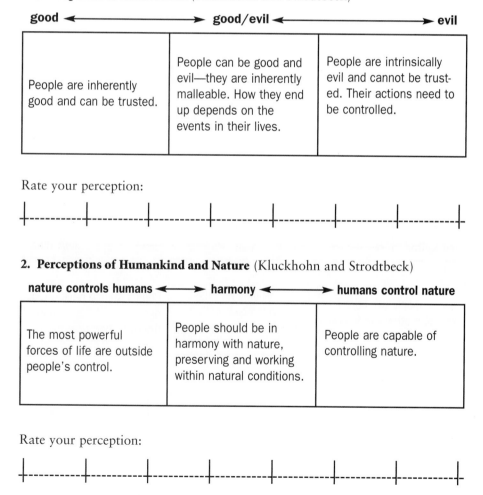

good ◄————————► good/evil ◄————————► evil

People are inherently good and can be trusted.	People can be good and evil—they are inherently malleable. How they end up depends on the events in their lives.	People are intrinsically evil and cannot be trusted. Their actions need to be controlled.

Rate your perception:

2. Perceptions of Humankind and Nature (Kluckhohn and Strodtbeck)

nature controls humans ◄————► harmony ◄————► humans control nature

The most powerful forces of life are outside people's control.	People should be in harmony with nature, preserving and working within natural conditions.	People are capable of controlling nature.

Rate your perception:

3. Perceptions of Activity (Kluckhohn and Strodtbeck)

being ◄─────────► being-in-becoming ◄─────────► doing

Spontaneous activity; the current activity is the one that matters most.	Meditation, contemplation, inner and spiritual development are most important.	Accomplishments are measurable by external standards. Action is essential.

Rate your perception:

├╌╌╌╌╌┼╌╌╌╌╌┼╌╌╌╌╌┼╌╌╌╌╌┼╌╌╌╌╌┼╌╌╌╌╌┼╌╌╌╌╌┤

4. Perceptions of Time (Kluckhohn and Strodtbeck)

past ◄─────────► present ◄─────────► future

The past—history and tradition—is seen as important.	The present moment has the most significance. What is real exists in the here and now.	The future is emphasized and is expected to be better than the present.

Rate your perception:

├╌╌╌╌╌┼╌╌╌╌╌┼╌╌╌╌╌┼╌╌╌╌╌┼╌╌╌╌╌┼╌╌╌╌╌┼╌╌╌╌╌┤

5. Perceptions of Social Relationships (Kluckhohn and Strodtbeck)

authoritarian ◄─────────► group ◄─────────► individual

Some people are born to lead and others to follow.	Group affiliations take precedence over individual goals.	People should have equal rights and complete control over their destiny.

Rate your perception:

├╌╌╌╌╌┼╌╌╌╌╌┼╌╌╌╌╌┼╌╌╌╌╌┼╌╌╌╌╌┼╌╌╌╌╌┼╌╌╌╌╌┤

6. Perceptions of Obligations (Peace Corps, 1997; Storti, 1999; Ting-Toomey, 1999)

universalism ◄————————————————————► **particularism**

Universalists see principles/rules/laws as applicable to all persons in all social circumstances, regardless of one's relationship to other persons, be they family, friends, or other associates. No one is seen as excepted from principles/rules.	Particularists see principles/rules/laws as relative, dependent upon specific social circumstances and the specific persons involved. One's family, friends, and other in-group members are seen as excepted from principles/rules.

Rate your perception:

|————————|————————|————————|————————|————————|————————|————————|

7. Perceptions of Inequity (Power distance: Hofstede)

low power distance ◄————————————————————► **high power distance**

People see inequalities in power and status as largely artificial; it is not natural, though it may be convenient, that some people have power over others. Those with power tend to deemphasize it, to minimize the differences between themselves and others.	People accept that inequalities in power are natural and existential. In the same way, they accept that some people are smarter than others. Those with power tend to emphasize it, to hold it close and not delegate or share it, and to distinguish themselves as much as possible from those who do not have power.

Rate your perception:

|————————|————————|————————|————————|————————|————————|————————|

8. Perceptions of Uncertainty (Uncertainty Avoidance: Hofstede)

low uncertainty avoidance ◄─────────────► high uncertainty avoidance

People do not feel threatened or anxious about uncertainty in life and do not have a need to limit or control it. They seek to legislate fewer areas of human interaction and tolerate differences better. They feel boxed in by too much structure or too many systems. They are curious rather than frightened by the unknown and are not uncomfortable leaving things to chance.	People feel especially anxious about the uncertainty in life and try to limit and control it as much as possible. They have more laws, regulations, policies, and procedures and a greater emphasis on obeying them. They also have a strong tendency toward conformity, hence predictability. They take comfort in structure, systems, and expertise— anything that can neutralize the unexpected.

Rate your perception:

9. Perceptions of Self and Others (Individualism/Collectivism: Hofstede)

individualism ◄─────────────► collectivism

The individual identifies primarily with self, with the needs of the individual being satisfied before those of the group. Looking after and taking care of oneself, being self-sufficient, guarantees the well-being of the group. Independence and self-reliance are greatly stressed and valued. In general, people tend to distance themselves psychologically and emotionally from one another. They may choose to join groups but group membership is not essential to identity or success. Urban settings.	One's identity is in large part a function of one's membership and role in a group, e.g., the family or work team. The survival and success of the group ensures the well-being of the individual, so that by considering the needs and feelings of others, one protects oneself. Harmony and interdependence of group members are stressed and valued. Group members are relatively close psychologically and emotionally, but distant toward non-group members. Rural settings.

Rate your perception:

Appendix B

MODELS OF CULTURE LEARNING

Hanvey: Levels of Cross-Cultural Awareness

Hanvey, Robert. "Cross-Cultural Awareness." In *Toward Internationalism: Readings in Cross-Cultural Communication*, eds. Elise C. Smith and Louise F. Luce. Rowley, MA: Newbury House, 1979, 46–56.

Hanvey's model of culture learning interprets this process as one of learners' increasing awareness, culminating in their subjective understanding of the culture from the perspectives of its members. This model is often cited in language teaching (Damen, 1987; Galloway, 1992; Mantle-Bromley, 1992; Omaggio-Hadley, 1993) as a guide to inclusion of culture in the foreign language classroom.

	I	II	III	IV
Level of Cross-Cultural Awareness	Awareness of superficial or very visible cultural traits: stereotypes	Awareness of significant and subtle cultural traits that contrast markedly with one's own	Awareness of significant and subtle cultural traits that contrast markedly with one's own	Awareness of how another culture feels from the standpoint of the insider
Mode	Tourism, textbooks, *National Geographic*	Culture conflict situations	Intellectual analysis	Cultural immersion: living the culture
Interpretation	Unbelievable, exotic, bizarre	Unbelievable, frustrating, irrational	Believable, cognitively	Believable because of subjective familiarity

In this model, learners shift their attitudes toward the culture, progressing from "unbelievable" to "believable," each with two distinct feelings attached. For Hanvey, the subjective nature of this awareness is essential. It represents a "felt" understanding, resulting from learners' extended living and working in the culture. In fact, Hanvey based much of his model on his analysis of Peace Corps volunteers' three-year experiences in the Philippines.

To achieve Level IV is no easy accomplishment, even for Peace Corps volunteers, but it is possible. Hanvey elaborates:

> ...it is not easy to attain cross-cultural understanding of the kind that puts you into the head of a person from an utterly different culture. Contact alone will not do it. Even sustained contact will not do it. There must be a readiness to respect and accept, and a capacity to participate. The participation must be reinforced by rewards that matter to the participant. And the participation must be sustained over long periods of time. Finally, one may assume that some plasticity in the individual, the ability to learn and change, is crucial. (1979, p. 51)

The "participation" that he describes consists of actions that are of interest to the learner and that bring social approval from members of the culture. Much of the culture learning process depends on the attitudes and intentions of the learner—a "readiness to respect and accept, and a capacity to participate." Beyond suggesting these prerequisite states of mind and heart, Hanvey does not describe what learners need to do to move from one stage to the next, nor does he stress the importance of language in this process, although this is certainly implied in "direct participation."

Nonetheless, the important point in this model is the fusion of behaviors, cognition, and affect. Direct participation, awareness, and feelings are parts of a whole, guided by the intentions of the learner. Culture learning is thus a holistic experience for learners, but one that fits the norms and expectations of the culture. Also important is the distinction between cognitive and affective believability—that there is a difference between intellectually understanding the difference and feeling that understanding, which can only come from direct participation in the culture.

Hoopes: The Intercultural Learning Process

Hoopes, David S. "Intercultural Communication Concepts and the Psychology of Intercultural Experience." In *Multicultural Education: A Cross Cultural Training Approach*, ed. Margaret Pusch. 9–39. Yarmouth, ME: Intercultural Press, 1979, 9–39.

Hoopes describes the intercultural learning process as a continuum, with ethnocentrism on one end and a range of cultural adjustment options on the other end. The process features shifts in understanding and attitudes toward the other culture, and adds the importance of behaviors as learners approach the decision about the four options for adjustment.

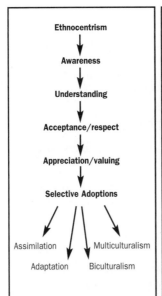

Ethnocentrism The relatively blatant assertion of personal and cultural superiority, accompanied by a denigration of other cultures and other ways

Awareness The awareness of other cultures as something other than the enemy

Understanding Recognition that culture is a complex process that can be understood in terms more rational than one's response to "them"

Acceptance/respect Recognition and acceptance of the validity of the cultural differences one encounters without comparison or judgment against one's own

Appreciation/valuing Putting into perspective the strengths and weaknesses of a culture and investing in appreciating and valuing specific aspects

Assimilation Adoption of the second culture, language, and behaviors as a primary and rejection of one's primary culture

Adaptation Adapting one's mode of behavior to feel comfortable and function effectively within it but not absorbing or incorporating the new behaviors; role playing

Biculturalism Development of a dual cultural personality

Multiculturalism Development of one's ability in the process of crosscultural learning, communication, and human relations—applied to any intercultural situation

Hoopes proposes that the ultimate outcome of culture learning is in fact four selective options—assimilation, adaptation, biculturalism, or multiculturalism. These four possible outcomes reflect the goals and circumstances of individual learners. There is a pragmatic bent to these options in that learners can adjust to cultures enough to get along, informed by an empathetic understanding of the culture, but not necessarily achieve or even desire further integration. This captures the ambivalence or values clash that can occur in cultural learning and reinforces the need to take into account the learner's intentions as well as the receptivity of the host culture.

Hoopes acknowledges culture shock, even though it is not a particular point along his continuum. He describes four different kinds of reactions to culture shock: fight (perceiving those of the other culture as competitors), flight (retreating from the other culture into home-culture enclaves), going native (acculturating rapidly, aping the other culture, and rejecting one's home culture identity), and adaptation (as suggested in his model). The first three options are essentially defensive responses, each a form of ethnocentrism.

Brown: Stages of Acculturation
Brown, H.D. *Principles of Language Learning and Teaching*, 3rd ed., Englewood Cliffs, NJ: Prentice-Hall, Inc., 1994.

Brown's model is based on acculturation, "the process of becoming adapted to another culture," and in particularly on the role that language learning plays in this process. In his model, the stages of acculturation are based on the culture shock experience and the process of recovering from it to either assimilate or adapt to the new culture. Brown is particularly interested in the role that cultural adjustment plays in mastering the language.

Stages of Acculturation

I Excitement/ Euphoria	II Culture shock	III Gradual recovery Culture stress	IV Near or full recovery
The individual feels excited by the newness of the surroundings.	Individuals feel the intrusion of more and more cultural differences into their own images of self and security.	Some problems of acculturation are solved while other problems continue for some time. *Anomie*: a feeling of homelessness	Either assimilation or adaptation, acceptance of the new culture and self-confidence in the "new person" that has developed in this culture

The third stage is a turning point for learners, which Brown calls the critical period. At this point, the learner is experiencing anomie, a feeling of homelessness, not having fully assimilated or adjusted to the new culture, but just beginning to master the language. Learners may find that they can bypass additional language study and simply get along with the language ability that they have, complete with fossilized errors. They never achieve mastery in the language because they don't need to. The key to whether they choose to master the language or not lies with learners' perceptions of the new culture.

Specifically, Brown applies the social distance hypothesis (Schumann, 1976) to propose that learners' acculturation process is a factor of their perception of their own culture in relation to the new culture. The reverse holds true as well, that is, the perception that members of the new culture have of the learners' culture affects the learner. In other words, the perceived relationship between the two cultures affects language and culture learning. The more socially distant the two cultures, the more challenging language learning becomes. By the same token, the socially closer the two cultures, the more conducive to language learning circumstances become. In simple terms, it's easier to learn the language of cultures that are similar to our own, and more challenging to learn the languages of those that are very different from our own.

Brown portrays this process as an intensely psychological experience. The ultimate outcome is not only assimilation or adaptation, but also fluency in the target language, along with the development of a new identity in the language/culture. Brown doesn't make much of a distinction between assimilation and adaptation, although the consequences would seem significant if the learner becomes a "new person" in the language.

Bennett: Intercultural Sensitivity
Bennett, Milton J. "Towards Ethnorelativism: A Developmental Approach to Training for Intercultural Sensitivity." In *Education for the Intercultural Experience*, ed. R. Michael Paige. Yarmouth, ME: Intercultural Press, Inc., 1993, 21–71.

Milton Bennett has proposed a model of culture learning that stresses the development of intercultural sensitivity, a process that entails learners' movement from ethnocentrism to ethnorelativity, or from seeing one's own culture as the center of the universe to seeing that there are many views of the universe. It is a developmental model with six sequential stages, each with two substages, which are equated with "stages of personal growth" (p. 22). Although his model incorporates cultural understanding, acquisition of behaviors, and identity, and addresses adaptation, the primary focus is on transformation of learners' thinking and attitudes, or as he puts it, "the learner's subjective experience of cultural difference" (ibid.).

Developmental Model of Intercultural Sensitivity
Responding to Difference

Denial	Defense	Minimization	Acceptance	Adaptation	Integration
isolation separation	denigration superiority	physical universalism transcendent universalism	respect for behavioral difference respect for value difference	empathy pluralism	contextual evaluation constructive marginality

Ethnocentric Stages   **Ethnorelative Stages**

Each of these stages is represented by a particular learner attitude or outlook toward cultural differences, as the diagram illustrates. At the end of the third stage, Bennett says that learners need to make a "paradigmatic shift" in order to move from ethnocentrism to the beginning stages of ethnorelativity.

Bennett bases his model on cognitive and moral developmental theory, in particular that of Perry. He suggests that learners go through a sequence of thinking, feeling, and doing as they move from ethnocentrism to ethnorelativity:

> It is also useful to consider intercultural development as it moves through cognitive, affective, and behavioral dimensions. The separation of these dimensions is not always clear for each stage, nor should it be, since development is multidimensional. Nevertheless, a tentative sequence can be suggested. Initial development is cognitive—the generation of relevant categories for cultural difference. The reaction to this development is affective—a feeling of threat to the stability of one's worldview. The developmental treatment for a threat response is behavioral—joint activity toward a common goal—and the response to this treatment is cognitive—consolidation of differences into universal categories. Subsequent appreciation of cultural difference is affective and is combined with increased cognitive knowledge of differences. This change is followed by behavioral applications involving the building of intercultural communication skills. Finally, all three dimensions are integrated in the operation of "constructive marginality" (p. 26).

At the heart of this model is learners' perception of and response to difference. The overall outcome goes beyond adaptation to a specific culture and involves learners' development of an ethnorelative outlook on cultures and self. Learners come to see and accept themselves as not belonging exclusively to any one culture or combination of cultures but as being on the margins of all cultures—a "constructive marginal" identity. Such persons are able to evaluate cultural behaviors, events, or perceptions in a relativistic manner, saying, in effect, "it depends on the culture."

Bennett does not include language proficiency or communicative competence as an integral component of his model, although he does acknowledge its importance in the ethnorelative stages.

Bennett emphasizes that learners' attitudes at any particular stage must be addressed by teachers or trainers with appropriate teaching materials or strategies. Learners in the ethnocentric stages, for example, will not respond well to techniques designed for those in the ethnorelative stages. In fact, some of these techniques may have the opposite effect, causing learners to strengthen their ethnocentric views.

Kim: Stress-Adaptation-Growth Dynamic

Kim, Young Yun. *Communication and Cross-Cultural Adaptation*. New York: Multilingual Matters, 1988.

Kim proposes a model for culture learning that is based on learners' repeated encounters with cultural differences. These encounters produce "cultural stress" in learners. Learners react to this stress by temporarily retreating into their own cultural worlds but then respond by using this stress as an impetus to adapt to the target culture. This process is repeated again and again, and in a spiral fashion, learners increase adaptation and achieve personal growth as a result. Personal growth, in Kim's view, consists of "increased functional fitness" (p. 68) and "psychological health" (p. 69) vis-à-vis the host environment.

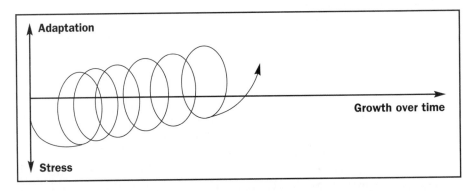

This model features a constant back-and-forth between the learner's culture and the target culture, a process that Kim calls acculturation—learning new ways of thinking, acting, feeling, and deculturation—"unlearning" previously acquired cultural habits that don't apply. The speed or efficiency of adaptation depends on a number of factors.

First and foremost is the learner's ability to communicate, which lies "at the heart of cross-cultural adaptation as the essential mechanism that connects strangers and the host society." Language, in a word, is essential. A second key factor is the target culture environment: the host culture's receptivity to the learner, the degree of conformity the host culture expects of strangers, and the degree of solidarity or strength of the stranger's ethnic group within the host culture. Another factor is the "predisposition" of learners, their preparedness and willingness to adapt, along with their ethnicity and personality.

Adaptation, therefore, depends not only on the learner but also on the receptivity of the host culture to the learner.

This model, perhaps more than any other, stresses the interaction between the learner's culture and the host culture. This back-and-forth hinges on encounters with cultural differences, which Kim maintains is an ongoing, inevitable process. The stress these encounters provoke motivates learners to adapt. In many ways, this spiraling dynamic assumes that learners will not face all cultural differences in one single incident but rather in repeated instances over time.

Paige: Intensity Factors in Intercultural Learning

Paige, R. Michael. "On the Nature of Intercultural Experiences and Intercultural Education." In *Education for the Intercultural Experience*, ed. R. Michael Paige. Yarmouth, ME: Intercultural Press, 1993, 1–20.

Paige does not map the culture learning process with a beginning and end point but instead examines the psychological dimensions of the experience. He presumes that culture learning is "psychologically intense" and that "the process of adapting to a new culture requires learners to be emotionally resilient in responding to the challenges and frustrations of cultural immersion" (p. 1). Learners need to know how to "manage their emotional responses" (ibid.). He lists ten intensity factors and offers hypotheses about what makes for a high degree of psychological intensity.

Intensity Factor	Conditions that contribute to the degree of psychological intensity
Cultural Differences	1. The greater the degree of cultural difference between the sojourner's own and the target culture
	2. The more negatively the sojourner evaluates the cultural difference
Ethnocentrism	3. The more ethnocentric the sojourner
	4. The more ethnocentric behavior the host culture exhibits
	5. The more racist, sexist, and in other ways prejudiced the host culture
Language	6. The less language ability the sojourner possesses
	7. The more essential language ability is to functioning in the target culture
Cultural Immersion	8. The more the sojourner is immersed in the target culture
Cultural Isolation	9. The less access sojourners have to their own culture group
Prior Intercultural Experience	10. The less the amount of prior, in-depth intercultural experience
Expectations	11. The more unrealistic the sojourner's expectations of the host culture
Visibility and Invisibility	12. Being physically different from members of the host culture and feeling highly visible to them
	13. Feeling invisible to members of the host culture because they do not know or cannot accept important aspects of the sojourner's identity
Status	14. Sojourners who do not feel they are getting the respect they deserve or, conversely, who feel they are receiving undeserved recognition
Power and Control	15. The less power and control one possesses in the intercultural situation

Adapted from Paige (1993)

These intensity factors show how individual learners can vary in their responses to cultural differences. Significantly, these factors depend not only on the learner but also on the nature of the culture, in particular how people of that culture might perceive the learner. Culture learning is thus a cooperative venture, not a solitary expedition. Some cultures may not welcome outsiders or may limit the degree of outsiders' involvement in the culture. Although certain culture learners may seek to assimilate or integrate fully into such a culture, its members may simply not allow this.

The range of intensity factors also points to the variety of experiences that individual learners might have. Paige, by stressing factors over stages of culture learning, puts the emphasis on variation, the fact that many learning processes are possible. These various possibilities reinforce the uniqueness of the culture learning process and the need for language teachers to acknowledge this in learners in their classrooms. Paige also acknowledges the role of language as a critical factor in cultural adaptation, but notably, it is simply one among many factors.

Gochenour and Janeway: Cross-Cultural Interaction

Gochenour, Theodore, and Anne Janeway. "Seven Steps in Cross-Cultural Interaction." In *Beyond Experience*, eds. Donald Batchelder and Elizabeth G. Warner. 2nd ed., Yarmouth, ME: Intercultural Press, 1993, 1–10.

Gochenour and Janeway emphasize the process of establishing oneself in the culture and developing relationships with members of the host culture. In fact, the stages in their model read like a series of tasks that learners consciously set for themselves as opposed to a series of circumstances they encounter or reactions they have to cultural experiences. The overall goal is "to develop an appreciative, non-exploitative relationship with people of another culture… as a means of building a closer human community" (p. 2).

Essential Survival Elements			*Bridge*	*Consciously Choosing to Change*		
I	II	III	IV	V	VI	VII
Establish contact and essential communication.	Establish bona fides and be accepted.	Observe what is going on and sort out meanings.	Establish a role within the role definitions of the host society.	Develop conscious knowledge of oneself—as center, as cultural being, as one taking responsibility.	Conscious development of needed attributes and skills—mental, emotional, physical	Conscious establishment of self-sustaining and meaningful relationships within the host culture

The first four stages lead to the ability to function effectively and appropriately within the culture, while the latter three stages derive from a conscious decision to change oneself. This decision leads to increased awareness of oneself as a transcendent cultural being and to deepened relationships with people in the host culture.

The fourth stage, the "bridge," is a critical juncture, where most culture learners choose to stop and not continue.

Just as we are accepted or not on someone else's cultural terms, we can establish a role for ourselves only within the conceptual categories assigned to us by the host culture, not by our own. ...In effect, we are assigned a role to play within that culture. ...Grouping stage IV with the first three, we have a picture of a good many people who can spend time abroad without being touched deeply and without changing any established value or belief. Such persons might be very knowledgeable about their host culture, speak the language well, and be engaged in productive activities. ...An opinion, once formed, feels "too right" to challenge or change. The locals continue to seem alien and outlandish in their beliefs, even if we learn a few rules to deal with them. ...For many, this describes all the cross-cultural interaction which is desirable or required. The question is whether the process need stop here or whether there may be somewhere further to go (p. 5).

Again, this model is distinct from the others in that it proposes a set of strategies and tasks that learners can undertake to transform themselves and establish meaningful relationships with members of the host culture. Culture learning thus becomes a conscious, purposeful process with the learner in charge. Also, the learner needs to develop self-awareness and consciously invoke the attitudes required to change.

References

Adams, B. 1990. *Viewpoint understanding through photo elicitation.* Master's thesis. Brattleboro, VT: School for International Training.

Adler, P. 1982. Beyond cultural identity: Reflections on cultural and multicultural man. In L. Samovar and R. Porter (eds.), *Intercultural communication: A reader* (4th ed.). Belmont, CA: Wadsworth. 410–426.

Agar, M. 1994. *Language shock: Understanding the culture of conversation.* New York: William Morrow and Company.

Ani, M. 1994. *Yurugu: An African-centered critique of European cultural thought and behavior.* Trenton, NJ: Africa World Press.

Archer, C. 1986. Culture bump and beyond. In J. M. Valdes (ed.), *Culture bound: Bridging the gap in language teaching.* New York: Cambridge University Press. 170–178.

Atkinson, D. 1999. TESOL and culture. *TESOL Quarterly* 33 (4): 625–654.

Auerbach, E. R. 1992. *Making meaning, making change: Participatory curriculum development for adult ESL literacy.* Washington, DC: Center for Applied Linguistics.

Auerbach, E. R., and N. Wallerstein. 1987. *ESL for action: Problem posing at work.* Reading, MA: Addison-Wesley.

Banks, J. 1991. *Teaching strategies for ethnic studies.* Needham Heights, MA: Allyn and Bacon, 57–96.

Banks, J. A., and C. A. M. Banks, (eds.). 1997. *Multicultural education: Issues and perspectives* (3rd ed.). Needham Heights, MA: Allyn and Bacon.

Batchelder, B. 1993. Preparation for cross-cultural experience. In T. Gochenour (ed.), *Beyond experience: An experiential approach to cross-cultural education* (2nd ed.). Yarmouth, ME: Intercultural Press. 59–72.

Bennett, J. 1993. Cultural marginality: Identity issues in intercultural training. In R. M. Paige (ed.), *Education for the intercultural experience.* Yarmouth, ME: Intercultural Press, 109–136.

Bennett, M. 1993. Towards ethnorelativism: A developmental approach to training for intercultural sensitivity. In R. M. Paige (ed.), *Education for the intercultural experience.* Yarmouth, ME: Intercultural Press, 21–71.

Bloom, B. S., M. D. Engelhart, E. J. Furst, W. Hill, and D. R. Krathwohl. 1956. *Taxonomy of educational objectives: The classification of educational goals. Handbook I, Cognitive domain.* New York: David McKay.

Brake, T., D. M. Walker, and T. Walker. 1995. *Doing business internationally: The guide to cross-cultural success.* New York: McGraw-Hill.

Brislin, R. W., K. Cushner, C. Cherrie, and M. Yong. 1986. *Intercultural interactions: A practical guide.* Newbury Park, CA: Sage.

Brown, D. E. 1991. *Human universals.* New York: McGraw-Hill.

Brown, H. D. 1994. *Principles of language learning and teaching* (3rd ed.). Englewood Cliffs, NJ: Prentice-Hall.

Byram, M. 1989. *Cultural studies in foreign language education.* Philadelphia: Multilingual Matters.

Byram, M. 1997. *Teaching and assessing intercultural communicative competence.* London: Multilingual Matters.

Byram, M., and M. Fleming (eds.). 1998. *Language learning in intercultural perspective: Approaches through drama and ethnography.* New York: Cambridge University Press.

Byram, M., C. Morgan, et al. 1994. *Teaching-and-learning language-and-culture.* Philadelphia: Multilingual Matters.

Canale, M., and M. Swain. 1980. Theoretical bases of communicative approaches to second language teaching and testing. *Applied Linguistics* 1: 1–47.

Carrell, P. M., and J. C. Eisterhold. 1983. Schema theory and ESL reading pedagogy. *TESOL Quarterly* 17: 553–573.

Chaika, E. 1994. *Language: The social mirror* (3rd ed.). Boston: Heinle & Heinle.

Clark, R. C. 1980. *Language teaching techniques.* Brattleboro, VT: Pro Lingua Associates.

Cohen, A. D. 1990. *Language learning.* New York: Newbury House.

Crawford-Lange, L. M., and D. L. Lange. 1987. Integrating language and culture: How to do it. *Theory into Practice* 26(4): 258–266.

Damen, L. 1987. *Culture learning: The fifth dimension in the language classroom.* Reading, MA: Addison-Wesley.

Darrow, K. and B. Palmquist (eds.). 1987. *Trans-cultural study guide.* Stanford, CA: Volunteers in Asia.

DeVita, P.R. and J.D. Armstrong. 1998. *Distant Mirrors—America as a foreign culture* (2nd ed.). Belmont, CA: Wadsworth.

Dodd, C. H. 1998. *Dynamics of intercultural communication* (5th ed.). Boston: McGraw-Hill.

Fantini, A. E. 1995. At the heart of things: CISV's educational purpose. In *Interspectives: A journal on transcultural and educational perspectives.* Vol. 13. Newcastle, England: CISV International.

Fantini, A. E. (ed.). 1997. *New ways in teaching culture.* Alexandria, VA: Teachers of English to Speakers of Other Languages, Inc.

Fantini, A. E. 2001. "Designing quality intercultural programmes: A framework and process," in *Interspectives: A journal on transcultural education.* Vol. 18 2000/2001: 100–105.

Fennes, H. and K. Hapgood. 1997. *Intercultural learning in the classroom: Crossing borders.* London: Cassell.

Fowler, S. M., and M. G. Mumford (eds.). 1995. *Intercultural sourcebook: Cross-cultural training methods.* Vol. 1. Yarmouth, ME: Intercultural Press.

Fowler, S. M., and M. G. Mumford (eds.). 1999. *Intercultural sourcebook: Cross-cultural training methods.* Vol. 2. Yarmouth, ME: Intercultural Press.

Freire, P. 1973. *Education for critical consciousness.* New York: Seabury.

Galloway, V. B. 1997. Toward a cultural reading of authentic texts. In P. R. Heusinkveld (ed.) *Pathways to culture.* Yarmouth, ME: Intercultural Press, 255–302.

Gaston, J. 1984. *Cultural awareness teaching techniques.* Brattleboro, VT: Pro Lingua Associates.

Gee, J. 1990. *Social linguistics and literacies: Ideology in discourses.* New York: Falmer Press.

Geertz, C. 1973. *The interpretation of cultures.* New York: Basic Books.

Giroux, H. A. 1988. *Teachers as intellectuals: Toward a critical pedagogy of learning.* South Hadley, MA: Bergin and Garvey.

Gochenour, T. (ed.). 1993. *Beyond experience: An experiential approach to cross-cultural education* (2nd ed.). Yarmouth, ME: Intercultural Press.

Gochenour, T., and A. Janeway. 1977. Seven steps in cross-cultural interaction. In D. Batchelder and E. G. Warner (eds.), *Beyond experience.* Yarmouth, ME: Intercultural Press, 1–10.

Grosjean, F. 1982. *Life with two languages.* Cambridge, MA: Harvard University Press.

Guiora, A. Z., R. C. Brannon and C. Y. Dull. 1972. Empathy and second language learning. *Language Learning* 24: 287–297.

Hall, E. T. 1959. *The silent language.* Greenwich, CT: Fawcett.

Hall, E. T. 1966. *The hidden dimension.* Garden City, NY: Anchor.

Hall, E. T. 1977. *Beyond culture.* Garden City, NY: Anchor.

Hall, E. T. 1983. *The dance of life: The other dimension of time.* Garden City, NY: Anchor.

Hall, E. T. and M. R. Hall. 1990. *Understanding cultural differences: Germans, French and Americans.* Yarmouth, ME: Intercultural Press.

Halverson, R. J. 1985. Culture and vocabulary acquisition: A proposal. *Foreign Language Annals,* 18(4): 327–32.

Hansford, V., M. Sandkamp and J. Scanlon. 2001. A model for teaching and learning culture. Center for English Language Education. *Journal* 9: 19–37.

Hanvey, R. 1979. Cross-Cultural Awareness. In E. C. Smith and L. F. Luce (eds.), *Toward internationalism: Readings in cross-cultural communication.* Rowley, MA: Newbury House. 46–56.

Hess, J. D. 1994. *The whole world guide to culture learning.* Yarmouth, ME: Intercultural Press.

Heusinkveld, P. R. (ed.). 1997. *Pathways to culture.* Yarmouth, ME: Intercultural Press.

Hoffman, E. 1989. *Lost in translation: A life in a new language.* New York: Penguin Books.

Hofstede, G. 1984. *Culture's consequences: International differences in work-related values.* Beverly Hills, CA: Sage.

Hoopes, D. S. 1979. Intercultural communication concepts and the psychology of intercultural experience. In M. Pusch (ed.), *Multicultural education: A cross-cultural training approach.* Yarmouth, ME: Intercultural Press, 9–39.

Jerald, M., and R. C. Clark. 1989. *Experiential language learning techniques* (2nd ed.). Brattleboro, VT: Pro Lingua Associates.

Joyce, B., and M. Weil. 1986. *Models of teaching* (3rd ed.). Englewood Cliffs, NJ: Prentice-Hall.

Kaplan, A. 1994. *French lessons–A memoir*. Chicago: University of Chicago Press.

Keesing, R. M. 1974. Theories of culture. In Siegel, B., Beals, A., and Tyler, S. (eds.) , *Annual review of anthropology*, Vol. 3: 73–97.

Kim, Y. Y. 1997. Intercultural personhood: An integration of eastern and western perspectives. In L. A. Samovar and R. E. Porter (eds.), *Intercultural communication: A reader* (8th ed.). Belmont, CA: Wadsworth, 434–447.

Kim, Y. Y. 1998. Cross-cultural adaptation: An integrative theory. In J. Martin, T. Nakayama, and L. Flores (eds.), *Readings in cultural contexts*. Mountain View, CA: Mayfield Publishing Company, 295–303.

Klopf, D. W. 1998. *Intercultural encounters* (4th ed.). Englewood, CO: Morton Publishing Company.

Kluckholn, F. R., and F. L. Strodtbeck. 1960. *Variations in value orientations*. Evanston, IL: Row, Peterson.

Kohls, L. R., and J. M. Knight. 1994. *Developing intercultural awareness: A cross-cultural training handbook* (2nd ed.). Yarmouth, ME: Intercultural Press.

Kolb, D. A. 1984. *Experiential learning: Experience as the source of learning and development*. Englewood Cliffs, NJ: Prentice-Hall.

Kramsch, C. 1989. *New directions in the teaching of language and culture*. NFLC Occasional Papers. National Foreign Language Center at The Johns Hopkins University: Washington, D. C.

Kramsch, C. 1993. *Context and culture in language teaching*. New York: Oxford University Press.

Lado, R. 1997. *How to compare two cultures*. In P. Heusinkveld, (ed.), *Pathways to culture*. Yarmouth, ME: Intercultural Press.

Larsen-Freeman, D. 1987. From unity to diversity: Twenty-five years of language teaching methodology. *The English Teaching Forum* 25 (4): 2–10.

Lustig, M. W., and J. Koester. 1999. *Intercultural competence: Interpersonal communication across cultures* (3rd ed.). New York: Addison-Wesley Longman.

Mantle-Bromley, C. 1992. Preparing students for meaningful culture learning. *Foreign Language Annals* 25(2): 117–127.

McCaffrey, J. A. 1993. Independent effectiveness and unintended outcomes of cross-cultural orientation and training. In R. M. Paige (ed.), *Education for the intercultural experience*. Yarmouth, ME: Intercultural Press, 219–240.

Menzel, P. 1994. *Material world: A global family portrait*. San Francisco: Sierra Club Books.

Moran, P. R. 2001. *Lexicarry: Pictures for Learning Languages*. Brattleboro, VT: Pro Lingua Associates.

Nemetz-Robinson, G. L. 1988. *Crosscultural understanding*. New York: Prentice-Hall.

Nostrand, H. L. 1978. The "emergent model" applied to contemporary France. *Contemporary French Civilization* 2 (2): 277–294.

National Standards in Foreign Language Education Project. 1999. *Standards for foreign language learning in the 21st century*. Yonkers, NY: National Standards in Foreign Language Education Project.

O'Malley, J.M. and A.V. Chamot. 1990. *Learning strategies in second language acquisition*. New York: Cambridge University Press.

Ohmi, Y. 1996. *Second language education for nurturing self-identity*. Master's thesis. Brattleboro, VT: School for International Training.

Omaggio, A. C. 1993. *Teaching language in context: Proficiency-oriented instruction* (2nd ed.). Boston: Heinle & Heinle.

Orwig, C. 1999. *Common purposes of functions of language*. Dallas, TX: Summer Institute of Linguistics.

Oxford, R. 1994. Teaching culture in the language classroom—Toward a new philosophy in J. Atlatis (ed.), *Educational linguistics, crosscultural communication, and global interdependence*. Georgetown University Roundtable on Languages and Linguistics. Washington, DC: Georgetown University Press, 26–45.

Oxford, R. 1990. *Language learning strategies: What every teacher should know*. New York: Newbury House.

Paige, R. M., H. Jorstad, L. Siaya, F. Klein, and J. Colby. 2000. *Culture learning in language education: A review of the literature*. St. Paul, MN: Center for Advanced Research on Language Acquisition, The University of Minnesota.

Paige, R. M. (ed.). 1993a. *Education for the intercultural experience*. Yarmouth, ME: Intercultural Press.

Paige, R. M. 1993b. On the nature of intercultural experiences and intercultural education. In R. M. Paige (ed.), *Education for the intercultural experience*. Yarmouth, ME: Intercultural Press, 1–20.

Paige, R. M., 1993c. Trainer competencies for international and intercultural programs. In R. M. Paige (ed.), *Education for the intercultural experience*. Yarmouth, ME: Intercultural Press, 169–199.

Palmer, G. B. 1996. *Toward a theory of cultural linguistics*. Austin, TX: University of Texas Press.

Peace Corps. 1998. *Culture matters: The Peace Corps cross-cultural workbook*. Washington, DC: Peace Corps Information Collection and Exchange.

Pusch, M. D. (ed.). 1979. *Multicultural education: A cross-cultural training approach*. Yarmouth, ME: Intercultural Press.

Samovar, L. A., R. E. Porter, and L. A. Stefani. 1998. *Communication between cultures* (3rd ed.). Belmont, CA: Wadsworth.

Savignon, S. J. 1983. *Communicative competence: Theory and classroom practice*. Reading, MA: Addison-Wesley.

Saville-Troike, M. 1982. *The ethnography of communication: An introduction*. Baltimore: University Park Press.

Schumann, J. H. 1976. Social distance as a factor in second language learning. *Language Learning* 26, 135–143.

Seelye, H. N. 1994. *Teaching culture: Strategies for intercultural communication* (3rd ed.). Lincolnwood, IL: National Textbook Co.

Singer, M. R. 1987. *Intercultural communication: A perceptual approach*. Englewood Cliffs, NJ: Prentice-Hall.

Sparrow, Lise. 1993. Examining cultural identity. In T. Gochenour (ed.), *Beyond experience: An experiential approach to cross-cultural education* (2nd ed.). Yarmouth, ME: Intercultural Press, 155–168.

Spradley, J. P. 1979. *Ethnographic interviewing*. New York: Harcourt Brace Jovanovich.

Spradley, J. P. 1980. *Participant observation*. Chicago: Holt, Rinehart and Winston.

Steele, R., and A. Suozzo. 1994. *Teaching French culture: Theory and practice.* Lincolnwood, IL: National Textbook Co.

Stern, H. H. 1983. *Fundamental concepts of language teaching.* New York: Oxford University Press.

Stevick, E. W. 1986. *Images and options in the language classroom.* New York: Cambridge University Press.

Stewart, E. C., and M. J. Bennett. 1991. *American cultural patterns: A cross-cultural perspective.* Yarmouth, ME: Intercultural Press.

Stewart, E. C., and J. Ohtake. 1999. Culture heroes in intercultural training. In S. M. Fowler and M. G. Mumford (eds.), *Intercultural sourcebook: Cross-cultural training methods.* Vol. 2. Yarmouth, ME: Intercultural Press, 241–260.

Storti, C. 1999. *Figuring foreigners out: A practical guide.* Yarmouth, ME: Intercultural Press.

Tannen, D. 1986. *That's not what I meant! How conversational style makes or breaks relationships.* New York: Ballantine Books.

Ting-Toomey, S. 1995. Managing intercultural conflicts effectively. In L. A. Samovar and R. E. Porter (eds.), *Intercultural communication: A reader* (7th ed.). Belmont, CA: Wadsworth, 360–362.

Ting-Toomey, S. 1999. *Communicating across cultures.* New York: Guilford Press.

Tomalin, B., and S. Stempleski. 1993. *Cultural awareness.* New York: Oxford University Press.

Van Ek, J. A., and L. G. Alexander. 1975. *Threshold level English.* Oxford: Pergamon Press.

Wallerstein, N. 1983. *Language and culture in conflict.* Reading, MA: Addison-Wesley.

Weaver, G. R. 1993. Understanding and coping with cross-cultural stress. In R. M. Paige (ed.), *Education for the intercultural experience.* Yarmouth, ME: Intercultural Press, 137–168.

Wen, W. 1998. *"If you can read this..." a sociolinguistic study of bumper stickers.* Master's thesis. Brattleboro, VT: School for International Training.

Wendt, J. 1984. D.I.E.: A way to improve communication. *Communication Education* 33: 397–401.

Wilkins, D.A. 1976. National Syllabuses. New York: Oxford University Press.

Wylie, L., and J.-F. Brière. 1995. *Les Français* (2nd ed.). Englewood Cliffs, NJ: Prentice Hall.

Donald Freeman, Series Editor

HEINLE & HEINLE
™
THOMSON LEARNING

"...The **TeacherSource** series offers you a point of view on second/foreign language teaching... As a reader you will find that each book has its own personality; it is not anonymous. It comes as a story, not as a directive, and is meant to create a relationship with you rather that assume your attention."

—*Donald Freeman, Series Editor*

EXPLORING SECOND LANGUAGE READING
Issues and Strategies

Neil J. Anderson
Brigham Young University
Text (240 pp): 0-8384-6685-0

Exploring Second Language Reading: Issues and Strategies is a comprehensive exploration of ESL reading. This text provides an overview of the key issues and practical strategies for teaching reading effectively.

LEARNING ABOUT LANGUAGE ASSESSMENT
Dilemmas, Decisions, and Directions

Kathleen Bailey
Monterey Institute of International Studies
Text (258 pp): 0-8384-6688-5

This text provides a practical analysis of language assessment theory and accessible explanations of the statistics involved.

TEACHING ESL K-12
Views from the Classroom

Helene Becker
Else Hamayan
Text (160 pp): 0-8384-7901-4

Teaching ESL K-12: Views from the Classroom addresses how to prepare English language learners to successfully enter the structures and demands of mainstream classrooms, curricula, and schools. The authors artfully blend insightful classroom and school-based experience with frameworks of research and policy.

PURSUING PROFESSIONAL DEVELOPMENT
Self as Source

Kathleen M. Bailey
Andrew Curtis
David Nunan
Text (160 pp): 0-8384-1130-4

Intended for individual study or teacher-preparation programs, this text provides an up-to-date overview of key ideas and a comprehensive guide to the techniques and procedures of teacher self-development.

TEACHING SECOND-LANGUAGE WRITING
Interacting with Text

Cherry Campbell
Sonoma State University
Text (112 pp): 0-8384-7892-1

Based on the philosophy that writing should be taught in conjunction with social and cultural expectations, this text teaches a variety of writing strategies, such as self-editing and portfolio writing, and provides practical advice on assessing writing and providing constructive feedback to students.

DOING TEACHER RESEARCH
From Inquiry to Understanding

Donald Freeman
School for International Training
Text (272 pp): 0-8384-7900-6

This text focuses on the intersection of teaching and research. By examining how research can fit within and transform the work of teaching, it offers a different perspective to teachers doing research.

DESIGNING LANGUAGE COURSES
A Guide for Teachers

Kathleen Graves
School for International Training
Text (240 pp): 0-8384-7909-X

This clear and comprehensive text provides a practical guide to designing language courses by encouraging teachers to explore ways of evaluating materials and planning and organizing content.

TEACHING BILINGUAL CHILDREN
Beliefs and Behaviors

Suzanne Irujo
Boston University, Emeritus
Text (134 pp): 0-8384-6098-4

Based on a vivid account of Matilde's classroom, this text is a comprehensive exploration of bilingual education theory and practice.

UNDERSTANDING LANGUAGE TEACHING
Reasoning in Action

Karen E. Johnson
Pennsylvania State University
Text (240 pp): 0-8384-6690-7

Teachers are encouraged to reflect on their classroom practice by thinking critically about their own teaching, their colleagues' teaching, and the environments in which they work.

TEACHERS UNDERSTANDING TEACHING
CD-ROM

Karen E. Johnson
Pennsylvania State University

Glenn Johnson
State College Area School District
Dual-Platform CD-ROM (MAC and WIN):
0-8384-4684-1
Site License: 0-8384-6432-7

This cutting-edge CD-ROM supports the breadth of topics in the **TeacherSource** series. Actual footage provides a "virtual seminar" in classroom observation and analysis for both pre-service and in-service teachers.

TEACHING CULTURE
Perspectives in Practice

Patrick Moran
0-8384-6676-1

Teaching Culture: Perspectives in Practice offers multiple viewpoints on the interrelationship between language and culture and how they serve to teach meaning, offer a lens of identity, and provide a mechanism for social participation. Authentic classroom experiences engage the reader and offer teachers invaluable support as they expand their ideas about how language and culture work together.

TEACHING LANGUAGES
From Grammar to Grammaring

Diane Larsen-Freeman
School for International Training
Text (160 pp): 0-8384-6675-3

Viewing grammar as something which is organic and evolving, this text is a refreshing overview of grammar acquisition and language learning. Theoretical frameworks, voices from the classroom, and reflective tasks engage teachers in an interactive debate about language teaching.

LEARNING NEW LANGUAGES
A Guide to Second Language Acquisition

Tom Scovel
Text (160 pp): 0-8384-6677-X

This text explores a wide range of issues that influence how a person learns a second language. By using P.L.A.C.E as an acronym, standing for People, Language, Attention, Cognition, and Emotion, the text offers an accessible way to examine both the practical and theoretical sides of each issue.

WORKING WITH TEACHING METHODS
What's at Stake?

Earl Stevick
Text (197 pp): 0-8384-7891-3

By examining different methods of language teaching, this text models a way for teachers to analyze their own teaching by thinking critically about approaches, techniques, and materials.

Additional Teacher Resource Materials from Heinle & Heinle

TEACHING ENGLISH AS A SECOND OR FOREIGN LANGUAGE
Third Edition

Marianne Celce-Murcia, Editor
Text (560 pp): 0-8384-1992-5

Now in its third edition, this best selling methodology resource gives both experienced and prospective teachers the theoretical background and practical applications they need to succeed. Offering new, personal contributions from more than 40 acknowledged specialists in the field, this text covers methodology, language skills, integrated approaches, learner variables, and teacher skills.

THE GRAMMAR BOOK
An ESL/EFL Teacher's Course
Second Edition

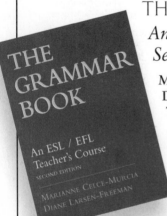

Marianne Celce-Murcia
Diane Larsen-Freeman
Text (800 pp): 0-8384-4725-2

In this highly acclaimed revision, grammatical descriptions and teaching suggestions are organized into sections dealing with Form, Meaning, and Use. *The Grammar Book*, 2/e helps teachers and future teachers grasp the linguistic system and details of English grammar, providing more information on how structures are used at the discourse level.